SOVEREIGNTY AND CONTESTATION

Practices of Pluralism in Canada and the European Union

For centuries, western political thought has addressed the problem of pluralism primarily through the prism of state sovereignty. *Sovereignty and Contestation* explores how contemporary pluralism is shaped by concepts of state sovereignty and how particular practices of pluralism are challenging sovereignty in turn.

The book presents a unique comparison of relations between First Nations and the state in Canada with relations between the union and its member states in the European Union. By placing Indigenous peoples alongside European nations as equal agents in a transnational field of action, the book connects disparate literatures on sub-state and supra-state pluralism.

Using an interdisciplinary and practice-centred approach, Keith Cherry explores how political, legal, and economic practices co-generate unique blends of sovereignty and pluralism in each setting, offering an account of pluralism that significantly expands on traditional political science accounts.

Ultimately, the book identifies two sets of practices that have played key roles facilitating pluralism in both Canada and Europe – interpenetrating institutions and conditional authority claims. Cherry considers the conditions under which these practices are most likely to emerge and to flourish. He concludes that such practices are most successful where all parties can contest the terms and content of their relationships, and where all parties need one another. In doing so, *Sovereignty and Contestation* highlights how contestability and mutual need provide novel criteria through which practices of pluralism can be assessed and developed.

KEITH CHERRY is a postdoctoral researcher at the Centre for Global Studies and the Cedar Trees Institute at the University of Victoria.

Sovereignty and Contestation

Practices of Pluralism in Canada and the European Union

KEITH CHERRY

UNIVERSITY OF TORONTO PRESS
Toronto Buffalo London

ISBN 978-1-4875-5618-1 (cloth)   ISBN 978-1-4875-6143-7 (EPUB)
ISBN 978-1-4875-5837-6 (paper)   ISBN 978-1-4875-5912-0 (PDF)

Library and Archives Canada Cataloguing in Publication

Title: Sovereignty and contestation : practices of pluralism in Canada and
   the European Union / Keith Cherry.
Names: Cherry, Keith, author.
Description: Includes bibliographical references and index.
Identifiers: Canadiana (print) 2024040100X | Canadiana (ebook)
   20240401182 | ISBN 9781487556181 (cloth) | ISBN 9781487558376 (paper) |
   ISBN 9781487561437 (EPUB) | ISBN 9781487559120 (PDF)
Subjects: LCSH: Legal polycentricity – Canada. | LCSH: Legal polycentricity –
   European Union countries. | LCSH: Sovereignty. | CSH: First Nations –
   Government relations.
Classification: LCC K236 .C44 2025 | DDC 340.9 – dc23

Cover design: Heng Wee Tan
Cover image: Frontispiece of *Leviathan* engraved by Abraham Bosse, with
input from Thomas Hobbes, the author; *Du Moulin in Peasant Garb Dancing
at the Opera*, print, Jean Berain (MET,62.676.20)

We wish to acknowledge the land on which the University of Toronto
Press operates. This land is the traditional territory of the Wendat, the
Anishnaabeg, the Haudenosaunee, the Métis, and the Mississaugas of the
Credit First Nation.

University of Toronto Press acknowledges the financial support of the
Government of Canada, the Canada Council for the Arts, and the Ontario
Arts Council, an agency of the Government of Ontario, for its publishing
activities.

Canada Council Conseil des Arts
for the Arts   du Canada

ONTARIO ARTS COUNCIL
CONSEIL DES ARTS DE L'ONTARIO
an Ontario government agency
un organisme du gouvernement de l'Ontario

Funded by the   Financé par le
Government   gouvernement
of Canada   du Canada

Canadä

MIX
Paper | Supporting
responsible forestry
FSC® C016245

Contents

Law(s) and Order(s): Pluralism, Sovereignty, and
the Rule of Law   3

Part 1: Practices of Pluralism in Canada

Part 2: Practices of Pluralism in Europe

Part 3: Practices of Pluralism in Comparative Context

Contents

SOVEREIGNTY AND CONTESTATION

Practices of Pluralism in Canada and the European Union

Law(s) and Order(s): Pluralism, Sovereignty, and the Rule of Law

Introduction

I[1] am at a rally against the Trans-Mountain pipeline. The march has just ended on a small field near the pipeline terminal, but suddenly there is a flurry of activity. People with construction supplies come of out nowhere and everywhere. In a matter of hours, they have built Kwe-kwecnewtxw – a traditional Coast Salish "watch house" to serve as a centre cultural resurgence and a base for resistance to further pipeline construction.[2] As they work, a Tsleil-Waututh woman tells the crowd that her people have never ceded legal authority over their traditional lands. She tells us that the only legitimate laws on this land are Tsleil-Waututh laws. She tells us that the Canadian government has violated those laws and must be stopped. The pipeline companies are criminals. The police and the government are criminals. We are building today, she tells us, so that we can enforce the law and put an end to an illegal pipeline project.[3]

All along the periphery of the crowd, well-armed RCMP officers listen nervously. Only Canadian law is properly law in their minds. The Trans-Mountain pipeline expansion project has been legally approved, they tell us. There is an injunction in place and it is now illegal to protest on Trans-Mountain property, they tell us. Kwekwecnewtxw is built on private property and it lacks the proper permits. It is the protestors and the Tsleil-Waututh who are criminals.

As onlookers, the crowd is confronted with two distinct rule sets, and the relationship between them is not clear. I was new to the west coast and, to be honest, embarrassingly new to thinking about decolonization. Like many Canadians, I found myself struggling to think through what this pluralism means for our political, legal, and economic systems, and for my own ethical, political, and legal responsibilities.

Canadians are used to questions of federalism. The presence of multiple coexisting – even conflicting – legal orders is, in that sense, familiar. But both the federal and provincial governments broadly agree on the limits of the respective jurisdictions and accept a common arbiter, in the Supreme Court, to settle their disputes. Their sovereignties are, in that sense, compatible. Here, there is no clear division of powers and no mutually accepted, over-arching authority to decide the conflict. The claims are, at least potentially, incompatible. This reality raises challenging questions. How do we navigate situations where there are multiple rule-sets at play, multiple sources of authority, and no clear mechanisms for how they should interact? The following book is an exploration of these questions.

Sovereignty and Pluralism

For the last several centuries, western political thought has addressed the problem of pluralism primarily through the prism of state sovereignty.[4] Briefly, we might think of sovereignty as a particular conception of authority.[5] The narrative that underlies sovereignty goes something like this: once upon a time in medieval Europe, there was a plurality of different religious, secular, imperial, and civic actors all making contradictory authority claims.[6] This resulted in frequent conflict – as with the Tsleil-Waututh and the RCMP. As a result, Europe was in a state of constant war and chaos. In order to escape this state of chaos, social actors divided the continent into parcels (states) and empowered a single authority (the sovereign) to rule over each. No matter where one was, they were now subject to only one set of rules. In this way, sovereignty prevents violent struggle between competing authorities.

Hobbes tells a related narrative, perhaps an allegory: once upon a time, humans lived without political society.[7] With no authority to rule over them, each person stole, killed, and pillaged in pursuit of their own interests, making social cooperation impossible. In other words, authority was too diffuse and, as a result, the world was violent and chaotic. In order to secure peace and realize the benefits of organized society, the people created a sovereign capable of making – and enforcing – rules. In other words, they concentrated authority.

Both accounts suggest that peace and order rely on a concentration of authority into one, and only one, body. Dicey therefore lays out two defining features of sovereign authority – a sovereign's authority is total, and it is exclusive.[8] Any actor that contests the total and exclusive authority of the sovereign is a threat, not only to the sovereign, but to the very possibility of social order itself.

Sovereignty and pluralism are therefore at odds – indeed, the entire purpose of sovereignty is to prevent the potential for conflict that pluralism creates. The problem is, state sovereignty has always been more of an aspiration than a reality.[9] In reality, every state grapples with the presence of multiple, overlapping sources of authority. Whether these challenges come from First Nations or international organizations, national minorities or transnational corporations, states the world over *do* navigate the coexistence of multiple competing authorities. In order to maintain a semblance of sovereignty in a pluralist environment, the state must actively eliminate pluralism by continually denying, oppressing, coopting, or absorbing any competing authorities.[10]

Historically, this has been an extraordinarily violent process, deeply tied to global patterns of empire, capital accumulation, and colonization.[11] It has also been deeply tied to what Santos terms epistemicide – the deliberate suppression of First Nations and subaltern world views and their aggressive assimilation into hegemonic ways of thinking and knowing.[12] Thus, Cover describes the sovereign state as "jurispaethic" – its role is to kill alternative sources of law and authority so that only state authority remains.[13]

Under the logic of sovereignty, there is only one possible solution to the conflict between the Tsleil-Waututh and Canadian law – the state must re-establish that its authority is total and exclusive, and so it must deny, suppress, or coopt any authority claimed by the Tsleil-Waututh. To do otherwise – to recognize Tsleil-Waututh authority and engage in negotiation or compromise or dialogue – this would only invite chaos. It would threaten the very foundations of social order itself.

Standing in the presence of the Tsleil-Waututh and the RCMP, this account of the world hardly seems satisfactory. Indeed, it reads as a thinly veiled apology for ongoing colonial dispossession. I find that I am not ready to resign myself to a form of social order that is structurally violent and continually dependent on ongoing oppression. I am not ready to accept the police baton as the only acceptable response to Tsleil-Waututh assertions. I wanted to test sovereignty's claims. Does social order really break down in the absence of concentrated authority? Are there other, less violent ways of dealing with a plurality of authorities? Is there really no room for cooperation and dialogue? In Foucault's words, I wanted "to know how and to what extent it might be possible to think differently"[14] about the problem of pluralism.

Apples to Oranges: Comparing Practices of Pluralism to Challenge Sovereignty

Fortunately, I quickly discovered that I was not alone in my discomfort. Despite the centrality of sovereignty in western thought, critical discourses were proliferating, attaching modifiers like post-sovereignty, shared sovereignty, divided sovereignty, or earned sovereignty.[15] In diverse contexts around the world, the realities of pluralism were challenging sovereign conceptions of authority, even provoking decidedly non-sovereign forms of social order for which western legal thought had no adequate descriptors. In short, there was no need to *imagine* non-sovereign social orders; communities all around the world were actively struggling to *enact* them, here and now.

Drawing on Tully's approach to public philosophy[16] and Santos's concept of a sociology of emergences,[17] I feel that the best way to explore questions of sovereignty and pluralism is not to engage in abstract theorization, but rather to study the actual, extant practices people have already developed on the ground. By carefully theorizing existing practices, by bringing scholarly attention to them, Santos suggests we can help participants to better understand their own institutions, while at the same time helping open the canon of legal and political thought to new ideas. In this way, we enter into a cycle of reciprocal elucidation, learning from and contributing to ongoing social practices in mutually enriching cycles.[18] I therefore set out to investigate sites where pluralism and sovereignty were being contested – to attempt to map the ways in which contemporary practices of pluralism are challenging sovereign conceptions of authority, making it possible to think otherwise about social order.

In addition to helping social actors understand their own practices more critically, I also wanted to help expose people to new ideas, new practices, and new approaches to the questions pluralism raises. I therefore chose a comparative approach to this inquiry. By choosing two wildly different cases where sovereignty is being thrown into question and comparing the practices that arise in each, I hope this inquiry can help participants in both settings to see their struggles in a new light, while also exposing them to new and potentially fruitful ideas.

Of course, there are many sites where sovereignty is being contested and alternatives asserted – from the rise of supranational institutions to the increasing prevalence of sub-state and non-state actors, from the sprawling web of international finance to resurgent Indigenous communities and international coalitions of civil society. I focus on two cases in particular: the relationship between First Nations[19] and the

Canadian state, and the relationship between the European Union and its member states.

I choose these particular cases for three reasons: first, each features at least one actor that does not take the familiar form of a sovereign state[20]; second, in each case, the contest between actors strikes to the very foundation of state sovereignty; and third, each case has seen a wealth of scholarly, political, legal, and civic attention, making them rich sites of reflection about sovereignty and also poignant sites where the introduction of new ideas and analyses may have real, concrete impact on lived political struggles. Both cases therefore represent sites where non-state forms of political authority are operating, where their presence is perceived as a fundamental challenge to the sovereign state, and where this pluralism has birthed rich literatures and practices of contestation.

Last, I choose these two cases because they are fundamentally *different* in a number of interesting ways. First, as smaller entities within a territorially larger state, First Nations communities challenge the state "from below" so to speak, while the supranational EU launches its challenge "from above" the state. Second, relations between First Nations and settler authorities have been forged largely through force and fraud, while the EU has been at least formally consensual. Third, relations between First Nations and settler authorities cross an epistemological and ontological divide, while inter-European relations do not.[21] As a result of these differences, the practices developed in one setting are likely novel to actors in the other.

For all these reasons, the two fields exist in relative isolation from one another. Indeed, relations between First Nations and settler authorities in Canada typically draw comparisons to relations between other Indigenous and settler authorities around the globe. Similarly, the EU is widely considered *sui generis* to such an extent that it is ill-suited to comparative work. When comparisons are drawn, they are typically made to international organizations, on the one hand, or to federal states, on the other.[22] Both literatures are thus to a meaningful extent closed off from one another.[23] I believe there is much to be gained from putting these two highly advanced, but for the most part discrete, literatures on sovereignty into conversation.

Scope of the Inquiry

This book focuses on two relationships, that between First Nations and the Canadian State, and that between the European Union and its member states. It does not present a comprehensive picture of pluralism either in Canada or in Europe. Indeed, I omit a number of closely connected and potentially fruitful sites of inquiry which bear upon the topic of sovereignty in important ways.

In particular, this book does not engage meaningfully with the role of sub-national minorities, Indigenous peoples, Roma peoples, regional authorities, or trans-boundary communities in Europe. This is not to deny that a variety of interesting examples might shed further light on the complex and contested relationship between pluralism and sovereignty. Even my treatment of the relationship between the EU and its member states occurs at a level of generality that doubtless pays insufficient attention to diverse national histories and experiences.

In short, this book cannot purport to offer a comprehensive account of European pluralism. My reasons are twofold. The first is pragmatic – this book is already lengthy. Expanding it to include all the relevant communities would require a sprawling text that would test both the capacity of the author and the patience of the reader. My second reason is simply that the book is not about European pluralism *per se* – it is the *comparison* between the challenges posed by supra-state authorities and those poised by First Nations that lies at the heart of this book's contribution. In order to keep this comparison central to the inquiry, I have chosen to focus on the general relation between the EU and its member states to the exclusion of other potentially informative sites of inquiry. My hope is that this focus will allow for an interesting contribution to the larger discussion of pluralism in Europe without, of course, exhausting the topic.

Similarly, this book does not meaningfully engage with Metis or Inuit relationships to settler authorities in Canada. I am aware that the choice to focus on First Nations performs a regrettable erasure of Inuit and Metis experiences. I certainly do not deny that these experiences carry important teachings and meaningful specificities that could shed additional light on the ways that sovereignty and pluralism are enacted and contested through the colonial encounter. Even my treatment of First Nations is necessarily so broad and general that it runs the risk of flattening diverse experiences and strategies. Nor do I engage with interesting developments at the municipal level.[24] I also acknowledge that the relationship between Canada and First Nations is not neatly separable from other forms of pluralism in Canadian history, especially the interaction of English and French communities and the discourse of multiculturalism. These relationships shape the pluralism that exists between First Nations and the state in intricate and important ways. Once again, my justification for this focus is twofold. First, a comprehensive account of Canadian pluralism would be enough to fill many books. Second and relatedly, my more specific goal is to draw out some of the general conceptual challenges created by the colonial encounter and to compare these to the challenges presented by the growth of supra-state authorities. In order to maintain focus on this goal, I must necessarily leave aside other potentially fruitful foci.

I am also aware that many readers will lack existing expertise in at least one of these contexts and I have tried to write an account that will be accessible to both Canadians and Europeans, and to the general public. Once again, this requires that I focus on the "big picture" and neglect, to a regrettable extent, important specifics in each case.

Simply put, the unusual, "apples-to-oranges" approach of this book aspires to breadth rather than depth. Its contribution is to place two very different cases side by side, not to explore either of those cases exhaustively. My hope is that the unusual approach of this book will offer a novel contribution to a necessarily larger and more diverse effort to understand pluralism, sovereignty, and their contested relationship(s) to one another.

An Interdisciplinary Approach

In order to interrogate sovereignty and explore other possible responses to the presence of pluralism, I conceive of sovereignty not as a legal abstraction, but as a situated political practice.

Following Cover, communities constantly generate plural sources of authority, while the sovereign constantly works to subordinate, absorb, or eliminate them. Sovereignty is therefore a process, rather than a static state. It is an aspirational goal, never complete; indeed, impossible to complete.[25] In this sense, sovereignty is best conceived as a set of sovereigntizing processes that are always defined in relation to counter-processes.

These processes and counter-processes are the stuff of politics, but they cannot be confined by traditional disciplinary boundaries. As Hunt puts it, "social relations are necessarily complex sets of connections between social agents that exhibit a range of potential dimensions. Thus, rather than 'legal relations' and 'economic relations', the claim is that social relations exhibit, among other potential dimensions, legal and economic dimensions."[26] Hunt therefore introduces the concept of an "assemblage" – an intersection of multiple semi-autonomous social processes which do not necessarily constitute a totality or system, but which work together to cocreate social meaning.[27] Thinking of sovereignty in this way, we might say that sovereignty is a type of social relation – a type of authority – which exhibits not only political, but also legal, economic, cultural, and other dimensions, and which therefore requires an interdisciplinary approach.

This book engages with sovereignty and pluralism in its political, legal, and economic dimensions. To be clear, I am a political scientist, not a lawyer nor an economist. My aim is not to contribute to law or economics per se. Rather, I am interested in the forms of authority economic and legal relations help to cocreate. Once again, I aspire to breadth rather than depth. My goal is not to make independent contributions to political, economic, and legal literatures in their own rights, but rather to draw on each of these disciplines in order to better understand sovereigntizing processes and counter-processes.

We might think of this approach as a sort of braiding – a weaving together which draws insights from multiple disciplines without merging them together into a single account or denying their specificity.[28] Rather than producing a single master-narrative, this approach seeks to illuminate the places of overlap and divergence, the points of tension, and even the gaps between strands. Its contribution is not to reveal any one strand in all its richness, but rather to draw out the ways strands relate to one another.

Structure of the Book

In Part 1 of this book, I will devote one chapter each to exploring the political, legal, and economic practices of pluralism in Canada (chapters 1–3).[29] Each chapter will begin with a historical survey, before pulling out some particularly noteworthy practices and discourses for further discussion. Part 1 will conclude with a chapter which attempts to map patterns across the legal, political, and economic fields, braiding them together for a richer understanding of the practices of sovereignty and pluralism they reveal (chapter 4). Similarly, in Part 2, I will explore political, legal, and economic practices of pluralism in Europe (chapters 5–7) and then explore patterns that run through them (chapter 8). In my conclusions, I will compare the practices analysed in Parts 1 and 2 and explore the ways they challenge, and fail to challenge, the logic of sovereignty (chapter 9). Briefly, my argument will unfold as follows.

With respect to Canada (chapters 1–4), I contend that the practices of pluralism that connect settler and First Nations authorities were initially based on the coordination of multiple independent authority claims. A range of practices, including interpenetrating institutions, codecision mechanisms, and conditional authority claims, allowed actors to coordinate these claims without recourse to a sovereign. In this context, no actor exercised anything like total, exclusive authority. As time went on, however, two important shifts occurred. First, as imperial military competition on the continent ended, the fur trade gave way to an agricultural and then industrial economy, and the genocide of First Nations progressed, settler authorities' need for their First Nations partners declined dramatically. Second, and at the same time, pluralistic European empires were transitioning gradually into sovereign states, leading settlers to re-understand their own authority in increasingly total and exclusive terms. Settler authorities worked to render the practice of pluralism consistent with the ideal of sovereignty, working to deny, suppress, or incorporate First Nations polities, legalities, and economies into their settler counterparts. Where elements of pluralism remained, these became increasingly asymmetrical. First Nations have both leveraged agency within settler institutions and continued to enact their own independent political, legal, and economic authority in a prolonged struggle to preserve a degree of pluralism. Those efforts have seen increasing success in recent decades, and long-suppressed practices are beginning to re-emerge. However, these contemporary forms of pluralism remain deeply shaped by sovereign concepts of authority and, as a result, remain constitutively asymmetrical. Contemporary governance is therefore a deeply lopsided form of pluralism that is both shaped by, and at some distance from, traditional concepts of sovereignty. I understand this history as a contested sovereignization process, as settler authorities use their dominant position to impose more total and exclusive forms of authority, and as First Nations work to preserve and restore a system that acknowledges the coexistence of multiple sites of authority, none of which make total or exclusive claims.

In contrast, the European context (chapters 5–8) begins from a place of state sovereignty and gradually moves toward more pluralist conceptions of political community. In the wake of centuries of escalating warfare and civil violence, European leaders adopted a strategy to gradually bind former antagonists together by cultivating shared institutions and mutual interests. Bit by bit, they layered functional agreements on top of each other, gradually transforming a modest coal and steel community into a dense Union. From the beginning, different actors held profoundly different views about where authority does and should lie – Federalists see the EU as sovereign over the states, while inter-governmentalists see the states as sovereign and the EU as a mere tool to serve state interests. Rather than resolving these differences, actors sought pragmatic agreements that allowed both state and Union to exercise authority. Over time, Europe developed a variety of codecision mechanisms, condition-setting practices, and interpenetrating institutions that allow diverse actors to share authority or exercise it jointly without ever resolving their fundamental differences. Progress has been uneven, both in the sense that it proceeds in fits and starts, and in the sense that pluralism remains far more developed in political and legal spheres than it does in the economic sphere. I conclude that Europe is undergoing a de-sovereignization process, as governance comes to rely less on total, exclusive forms of authority, but that this process remains ongoing, contested, incomplete, and deeply shaped by concepts of sovereignty.

In comparing these contrasting historical arcs, I make two broad claims. The first claim is that sovereignty does not, in practice, produce peace, order, and security. In fact, both in Europe and in Canada, those periods which most closely resemble sovereignty have been the most violent and oppressive. In Europe, the era of sovereignty was one of never-ending warfare which declined only when pluralist practices were developed. In Canada, the development of sovereignty closely parallels the ongoing genocide against First Nations. To the extent that pluralism has resurged in recent decades, the situation of First Nations has also begun to improve. In short, the price of sovereignty is deep, and it is paid in blood. The second claim is that pluralism does not, in practice, necessarily lead to chaos or violent competition. In both cases, actors have found ways to coordinate multiple authority claims without recourse to a sovereign. In fact, actors in both settings have developed remarkably similar codecision mechanisms, condition-setting practices and interpenetrating institutions. Whereas traditional federalism provides ways to divide authority, these practices provide ways to share authority. Together, such practices can provide efficacious governance even in the absence of a single, all-powerful authority.

I conclude that sovereignty is not the only, or even the best, available response to the question of pluralism. The narrative of sovereignty tells us that the violence needed to maintain an absolute concentration of power is a regrettable necessity – the only path to social order. The two cases explored here, however, suggest that this narrative is little more than a story the powerful tell in order to justify and expand their own authority. We can reject this story and seek forms of political community that do not rely on the concentration of authority. In particular, we can cultivate the codecision mechanisms, condition-setting practices, and interpenetrating institutions that have proven so effective in such diverse settings. In short, I contend that we need not fear practices that challenge state sovereignty. In fact, we should seek them out. We already have the tools to respond differently to pluralism, if we chose to use them.

PART 1

Practices of Pluralism in Canada

Chapter One

Political Practices

The political dimensions of the relationship between First Nations[1] and settler authorities[2] are complex, contested, and at times downright paradoxical[1] as each party developed multiple distinct, even contradictory, ways of understanding the relationship. Each also found pragmatic reasons to engage the norms of the other, with all the missteps and misunderstandings this entails. Moreover, the encounter itself shaped thought and practice over time, as theory evolved in relation to colonial struggle. Settlers and Indigenous peoples alike navigate this relation in complex, pragmatic, and non-linear ways that vary significantly across time and space, as they respond to local power conditions, cultures, personalities, and incentive structures.

Nevertheless, certain broad trends emerge, allowing scholars to divide the relationship into a number of non-discreet "phases." While imperfect, these phases help us make sense of the encounter.

Broadly speaking, we can identify four successive eras: the peace and friendship treaties of early contact; the supposed "land cession" treaties following the war of 1812; the assimilatory legislation of the postconfederation period; and the modern era of "reconciliation" following the patriation of the Canadian constitution.[2]

---

1 The Indigenous Peoples of Canada include Inuit and Metis populations alongside First Nations. For reasons of scope, however, the following chapters will focus on the latter. See the Introduction, especially the section entitled "Scope of the Inquiry."

2 The term "settler" can encompass a great variety of groups, including European migrants who willfully participated in empire, those who came fleeing persecution of dispossession, those brought to Indigenous lands without their consent via slavery, those who arrived from diverse parts of the world in the centuries following contact, more recent arrivals, and others. The relationship of each of these groups to the settler state, to Indigenous peoples, and to global patterns of colonization and imperialism are distinct. My focus here is not on "settlers" per se, but on the settler state as a sovereignty-claiming entity.

In the early phases, settlers and Indigenous peoples engaged in a nation-to-nation relationship, recognizing one another's autonomy and cocreating ways to share authority. Neither party exercised anything like sovereignty over the other, though European powers did claim something like exclusive authority against one another. As time went on, geopolitical shifts and colonial genocides made the British militarily dominant and settler authorities began to move away from a nation-to-nation relationship, imposing something much closer to a sovereign-to-subject relationship instead. Rather than using treaty to share authority, settlers began viewing treaty as a way to divide authority and, ultimately, as a way for First Nations to cede authority and establish settler authority as exclusive. Eventually, settlers would come to deny First Nations authority almost entirely, re-understanding themselves as possessing exclusive authority with or without an associated treaty. First Nations have persistently contested these shifts and continue to do so today, leveraging their political power to preserve forms of shared and divided authority. In the modern era, settler authorities have responded by working to make the fact of continued pluralism compatible with their own claims to sovereignty, offering forms of recognition which are simultaneously affirmations of settler dominance. Shared, divided, and exclusive conceptions of authority therefore coexist in an uneasy mix, waxing and waning in relative importance and recombining into new constellations as political conditions fluctuate. The result is a sort of deeply asymmetrical pluralism, where authority is not quite total or exclusive enough to be called sovereign in any straightforward fashion, yet remains so one-sided that it is not really multilateral either.

Overall, this story reflects the growing influence of the total and exclusive forms of political authority associated with the sovereign state and a parallel decline in multilateral institutions.[3] We might therefore describe the process as the sovereignization of the relationship between First Nations and settler authorities. This process has been, and continues to be, incredibly violent. It is also incomplete and deeply contested. The following chapter will explore this sovereignization process, briefly tracing its development through four historical phases before exploring some of the most prominent practices and discourses that shape the relationship today.

Four Phases of Political Relations

Before we embark on our first historical survey, a note of caution is appropriate. Because the historical overviews in this chapter and throughout the subsequent two chapters span most of a continent and cover some 500 years, the accounts they present are necessarily quite schematic. In reality, there is a daunting degree of variation across regions, over time, and according to the particular interests, political contexts, and actors involved. Rather than proceeding through strict historical periods, it is more helpful to think of the relationship as involving a number of important patterns and overall trends which play out in different ways and at different times in different regions, subject to local variations.[4] The following chapters therefore move through a series of phases which describe broad patterns that are recognizable in different ways in different contexts. I have indicated very rough time frames as an aid to readers, but these phases did not occur at the same time or even in the same way across Canada.[5] Indeed, the attentive reader will notice that the date ranges for many periods overlap considerably. The phases are not discrete historical periods. They are simply analytical devices designed to help make sense of the shifting relationship, helping us to map, in broad strokes, how different dimensions of sovereignty have been developed and resisted over time.

The "Middle Ground"[6]: Contact and the "Peace-and-Friendship" Treaties (Contact–~1763)[7]

From the very earliest days of the encounter, the authorities of Europe were conflicted regarding the political status of Indigenous peoples. Some felt non-Christian nations had no valid authority claims, others felt First Nations were essentially full international actors on par with European states, while others saw First Nations as enjoying some, but not all, of the rights of statehood.[8]

These strands of thought coexisted in a context defined by cross-cultural geopolitical competition, as First Nations and settler authorities both worked to draw one another into pre-existing geopolitical struggles. European authorities used the colonization process as an extension of their longstanding conflicts in Europe, and First Nations drew Europeans into their own longstanding conflicts with one another,[9] each side using new allies and economic opportunities to seek advantage over old rivals. During this period, it is difficult to speak of the relationship in simple cross-cultural terms, as an encounter between settlers and First Nations. Neither side self-identified as a cultural unit.[10] Rather, cross-cultural blocks were the operative unit of competition, one centred around the French, Huron and Algonquin peoples, and the other centred around the Dutch and later British along with their allies the Haudenosaunee.[11]

In practice, early agreements and treaties, generally known as "peace and friendship" treaties, were primarily concerned with military and economic alliance. Broadly speaking, both settler and First Nations authorities recognized one another's independence, and neither sought to exercise meaningful control over their treaty partners.[12] Peace and friendship treaties were not designed to divide territory into mutually exclusive blocks nor to extend the power of one party over the other, but to facilitate military and economic cooperation. Both parties largely managed their own internal affairs, while also developing practices to share authority in matters of shared concern.

For example, both sides worked to draw the other into their own diplomatic and political structures. Settler officials took part in First Nations ceremonies, engaged in traditional gift exchanges, and took on First Nations names and kin relations.[13] In all these ways, First Nations drew settler officials into their political structures, offering them a voice within their system of kin-based, clan-based, and treaty-based authority structures. Similarly, settler authorities offered First Nations medals, uniforms, and titles within their own political and military institutions, seeking to bring First Nations into the network of settler authority structures as well.[14] This allowed settler and First Nations political systems to interpenetrate in ways that helped the communities to coordinate and manage conflict. Settler and First Nations leaders also took part in treaty councils which drew on both settler and First Nations diplomatic traditions and which provided a forum for joint action.[15] Treaties could also lay out a series of conditions on which cooperation hinged, for instance, many treaties stipulate non-interference with First Nations hunting, fishing, and land use.

Thus, neither side treated its own authority as exclusive, recognizing the claims of the other, and neither side treated its own power as total or absolute, recognizing the need for negotiation. Instead, each party retained a high degree of autonomy, while also cocreating practices of shared authority. Instead of being instruments that transfer sovereignty, treaties were a recognition of a decidedly non-sovereign state of affairs – a political environment characterized by multiple parties, each with non-exclusive, non-total forms of authority. Indeed, both of the major treaty systems of the early contact period – the Covenant chain, or wampum belt treaty system of the Haudenosaunee and the French treaty system – are remarkably similar in their emphasis on shared land and shared authority, as are other early-contact relationships across the continent.[16] For example, the Two Row Wampum, a metonymic device expressing the treaty relationship, features two parallel rows of coloured beads – representing First Nations and settler peoples as a canoe and a ship respectively – bound together by rows of white beads in between them, symbolizing a river. The wampum expresses that each party steers its own vessel, but also that they move down the same river together.[17] As Asch puts it, "[t]he goal of the treaty relationship would not be to share the land by cutting it into 'parts,' but, as the Oxford English Dictionary puts it, to share in the sense of 'to participate in … to perform, enjoy, or suffer in common with others.'"[18]

From the beginning, however, treaties often contained sweeping claims of settler sovereignty or dominance which were either not properly explained to their First Nations signatories or else added without their knowledge.[19] Such provisions were probably intended for a European audience as a means to preclude claims from rival colonial powers, rather than to reflect the actual relationship with First Nations.[20] Thus, claiming "sovereignty" over a First Nation meant simply that it would be improper for another European power to attempt to establish relations with that same people. Indeed, settlers were quick to back away from any claim of dominance or subordination in conversation with First Nations. "Presented with the earlier text of the aborted treaty of 1693, they [Wakaneki leaders] were shocked to hear how English translators had misrepresented their words and how their original offer of mutual friendship had turned into a pledge of submission to the English Crown."[21] Colonial Governors, eager to avoid conflict, reassured them the treaty intended nothing of the sort before it was reconfirmed.[22] The idea of sovereignty was therefore present from the very beginning, but it stood alongside an intercultural relationship based on shared authority – one that was decidedly non-sovereign in practice.

The "Divided Ground"[23]: British Dominance and the Royal Proclamation and Treaties of Land Secession (~1763–~1921)[24]

The fall of New France to the British and their allies marked the beginning of a major shift, leaving only one European power on those parts of Turtle Island later called Canada. Where the British had once needed strong First Nations allies in order to compete with the French, they now increasingly sought dominance over their erstwhile partners. As a result, relations took on a decidedly more antagonistic and intercultural character.[25] Treaty practices followed suit, coming to revolve less and less around shared authority and military-economic cooperation, and more and more around the creation of mutually exclusive territories, the dispossession of Indigenous territory, and the imposition of hierarchy.

For example, the treaty of Paris, which ended French-English competition in the lands later called Canada, is notable in comparison to its predecessors for its focus on firm territorial boundaries and the centralization of formerly overlapping authority structures and legal statuses.[26] Likewise, the Royal Proclamation, which laid out Britain's post-conquest Indian policy, explicitly divides the continent into settler and First Nations zones and required settler authorities to purchase or treat for any new land before occupying it.[27] Informed by these increasingly exclusive conceptions of authority, the Royal Proclamation positions treaty not as a means of sharing land and authority, but rather as a means of dividing it – and, crucially, a means by which land and authority could be transferred from one party to another. Treaty-making practices shifted accordingly, and the treaties of the era – typically called the "numbered treaties" – were understood by settler authorities as something much closer to deeds of sale than documents of alliance.[28] Once a treaty was concluded, First Nations political authority was assumed to have been ceded entirely.

The movement toward exclusive conceptions of authority was not, however, totally coherent. While the Proclamation recognizes zones of First Nations governance, the document also proclaimed those zones to be under British sovereignty. As such, the Proclamation extended certain rules and restrictions even over "Indian lands."[29] Thus authority was exclusive within the settler zone in that it largely excluded competing First Nations institutions, but beyond the settler zone First Nations authority continued to be viewed as non-exclusive of overlapping settler claims.[30] In this sense, the relationship was not only becoming increasingly characterized by divided authority, but also increasingly hierarchical. Where settler sovereignty claims had initially been understood as claims addressed to other colonial powers, rather than to First Nations, they were now re-understood as diminishing First Nations' political rights, creating a political status that was independent but also subordinate.[31]

In all these ways, settlers worked to re-conceptualize treaty-making practices in ways that were compatible with an increasingly exclusive and absolute understanding of their own political authority. Treaty-making practices also became increasingly coercive, with governments leveraging or even inducing disease, starvation, ecological collapse, and social division to secure "consent" for their territorial and political claims.[32]

Indeed, it is notable that the Treaty of Paris was negotiated without any First Nations representatives, despite their prominent role in the war. Similarly, as a Proclamation, Britain's revised Indian policy was unilateral in nature, rather than negotiated. In its wake, British generals waged aggressive wars and sought treaties that explicitly subjugated First Nations to British authority.[33] Some First Nations leveraged the idea of divided authority, claiming something like exclusive authority in their own lands as a means of resisting settler encroachment.[34] Others resisted the shift from shared authority.[35] Pontiac's war, for example, can be understood as a rejection of British sovereignty claims and ended only when Superintendent of Indian Affairs William Johnson convened a series of treaties, including perhaps the largest treaty gathering ever held, affirming a nation-to-nation relationship and even gifting a Two Row wampum to signify the agreement.[36] For many First Nations, and indeed for some settlers, treaty remained a way to share authority, rather than cede it. In this sense, the increasingly unilateral cast of the relationship was partial, contested, and incomplete, as settlers and First Nations alike navigated a shifting constellation of norms in pragmatic ways.[37]

Uneven Ground: The Post-Confederation Treaties and Assimilation (~1850–~1969)[38]

The next major shift in the treaty relationship began when the imperial dominions of British North America confederated into the new Canadian state, largely because this process solidified the transition in responsibility for the relationship with First Nations from imperial military authorities to colonial civil authorities as the British began to see First Nations increasingly as domestic subjects rather than international allies.[39] Imperial authorities, whose business is international relations, had largely come to understand their sovereignty claims as diminishing, but not effacing, First Nations authority. They therefore understood treaty as a means of acquiring land and authority from not-quite-sovereign but still politically independent nations. Civil authorities, whose business is domestic governance, increasingly understood themselves as already in possession of full sovereignty, and thus re-understood treaties not as a means of acquiring authority, but as policy statements through which a sovereign stated its intentions toward its subjects.

Having re-understood treaty in ways consistent with their own claims to exclusive, total authority, settler authorities also began to regulate the relationship more and more through unilateral legislation.[40] In fact, most of Canada's westernmost province was colonized without any treaties at all, as the local government understood itself to have the power to authorize the dispossession of First Nations land unilaterally, through legislation.[41] This shift within the settler tradition was, however, far from frictionless, with several imperial officials reprimanding their colonial counterparts and insisting on older understandings of treaty.[42]

Nevertheless, the general thrust of the period was to re-position First Nations as subjects, rather than distinct political communities, through extensive unilateral legislation. Across the country, extensive efforts were made to enfranchise First Nations as citizens of the colony – and hence, no longer First Nations in a political sense.[43] Colonial officials also began regulating band membership, introducing a regressive set of rules designed to gradually diminish and even eliminate so-called status Indians as a political category.[44] Eventually, these efforts were consolidated into the *Indian Act*. The act established "band councils" as sort of municipal governments operating under the supervision of settler "Indian Agents" and, ultimately, the Minister of Indian Affairs. At the same time, settlers worked to outlaw and suppress traditional First Nations governments and institutions. Settler authorities also established residential "schools" to separate First Nations youth from their families and indoctrinate, assimilate, abuse, and – with startling frequency – kill them. This system was designed to disrupt the intergenerational transmission of cultural knowledge and undercut the foundations of First Nations autonomy. Colonial officials also began regulating the movement of First Nations and confining them to reserves.[45] Efforts were made to encourage individual ownership of reserve lands, again positioning First Nations members as plain citizens and property holders, rather than self-governing political communities. Settler authorities also began unilaterally regulating and curtailing treaty rights.[46] Overall, this legislative framework is characterized by the striking concentration of power in the federal executive.[47] Ministerial discretion, in practice usually delegated to federal bureaucrats, was almost unfettered and typically unchecked by even the colonial legislature, let alone by First Nations.

In all these ways, settler legislation works to position settlers as the bearers of exclusive, total authority. When First Nations insisted on shared authority in accordance with the terms of their treaties, settler authorities replied that treaties were not binding international agreements but rather non-binding policy statements laying out the unilateral intentions of the Crown, and thus could be ignored at will.[48]

First Nations both exercised agency through the new legislative scheme and its associated band councils and also contested the shift toward exclusive, total forms of authority, consistently centring a nation-to-nation vision which continued to emphasize shared, and sometimes divided, forms of authority. In 1876, thirty-three Haudenosaunee Chiefs wrote to the Superintendent of Indian Affairs stating that "we are not subjects but we are allies to the British government" and insisting that they would follow their own leaders and laws, not those of the British.[49] Similarly, when Plains Cree and Metis leaders felt their authority claims were not being taking seriously, they began a series of rebellions designed to force Canada to negotiate bringing Manitoba into the federation as a recognized jurisdiction, thereby reasserting a form of layered multilateralism.[50] On the west coast, the Nisga'a, Gitxsan, and Tsilhqot'in were all using warfare or direct action as means to force settler governments to back away from their unilateral claims, recognize overlapping First Nations authority, and enter into treaties.[51] In 1911, Shuswap, Okanagan, and Couteau chiefs explained the transition to Prime Minister Laurier:

> Some of our Chiefs said, "These people wish to be partners with us in our country. We must, therefore, be the same as brothers to them and live as one family. We will share equally in everything-half and half" ... Gradually as the whites of this country became more and more powerful and we less and less powerful, they little by little changed their policy towards us and commenced to put restrictions on us ... They treat us as subjects without any agreement to that effect and force their laws on us without our consent, and irrespective of whether they are good for us or not. They say they have authority over us ... We demanded that our land question be settled and ask that treaties be made between the government and each of our tribes.[52]

Thus, the accelerating shift from shared to exclusive forms of authority was subject to consistent, widespread, and continual contestation.

Grounds for Recognition: The *Constitution Act 1982* and the Modern Treaty Process (~1969–~Present)

This conception of settler sovereignty as exclusive of First Nations authority reached a symbolic high-water mark and underwent another transformation with the now infamous 1969 White Paper on Indian policy and the subsequent resistance to it. This document proposed eliminating the legal and political status of First Nations entirely, recognizing instead a common, undifferentiated citizenship for all Canadians.[53] In other words, it represented the completion of the sovereignization process – the consolidation of all authority in a single government.[54]

The White Paper, however, catalysed a prolific political response. First Nations opposition not only forced the government to withdraw its proposal, but eventually saw the same government enshrine collective First Nations rights in section 35 of the newly repatriated constitution in 1982.[55] The fact that the same government could pursue both total assimilation and constitutional recognition speaks to the complex ways that exclusive and shared conceptions of authority coexist, and the ways this ambiguity allows actors to respond pragmatically to shifting political circumstances – and political circumstances were certainly shifting. When constitutional negotiations at Meech Lake failed to recognize a right to self-government, Indigenous groups mobilized, helped kill the accord, and then successfully inserted self-government into the subsequent Charlottetown negotiations, though they also failed to achieve ratification.[56] Similarly, direct action in Northern Quebec birthed the first Modern Treaty in 1975,[57] while blockades across British Columbia – including the then largest act of civil disobedience in Canadian history at Clayoquot Sound – helped prompt the BC Treaty Process.[58] Occupations, blockades, and direct actions across the country – famously including armed standoffs at Oka – further resulted in a Royal Commission to study Crown-First Nations relations in 1991.[59] In all these ways, First Nations assertions of persisting political authority forced concessions in settler unilateralism.

These political circumstances meant that the total denial of First Nations authority was no longer a viable political strategy for settler authorities. Instead, settler governments have shifted to an era of "reconciliation" politics, offering to accommodate First Nations political claims, but only in ways that fundamentally presume the sovereignty of the settler state. Forms of divided and shared authority have therefore re-emerged, but in modified forms that position settlers as the dominant parties.[60] For example, the modern treaty process recognizes forms of internal self-government and often establishes comanagement bodies for specific issues. However, even jurisdiction over internal affairs is subject not only to the *Charter of Rights and Freedoms* but often to the paramount or concurrent jurisdiction of provincial and federal governments and the supervision of settler courts.[61] Likewise, comanagement bodies are often advisory in nature, with ultimate decision-making power vesting in a minister of the settler government.[62] In this manner, the politics of reconciliation works to both recognize First Nations' political agency and simultaneously position that authority as subordinate to settler authority, and thus compatible with settler sovereignty.[63] As Coulthard explains, this logic works to shore up the legitimacy of settler sovereignty by offering nations a place within it.[64] Johnny Mack captures the ambivalent nature of such recognition well: "we [as Indigenous peoples] are lured into a liberal field by an offering to recognize our claims, but the recognition turns out to be a domestication in which the claims are transformed to fit with the current structure."[65]

While many First Nations are leveraging these new forms of recognition, most also continue to centre a nation-to-nation relationship emphasizing shared forms of authority. In their Modern Treaty negotiations, for example, Hul'qumi'num Treaty Group emphasized the need for shared authority and cogovernance.[66] Likewise, the Stó:lō have proposed forms of multilevel governance within their territories.[67] In their submission to the National Energy Board, the Tsleil-Waututh insist that the Crown "engage with First Nations as jurisdictions" by committing to "joint decision making and co-management regimes."[68] Similarly, when the Barriere Lake Algonquin sought a resolution to conflicts on their land, they pushed for a trilateral agreement where the jurisdiction of each party is concurrent, contingent on good management, and defined in relation to the laws of the others.[69]

The modern era therefore extends longstanding patterns of contestation – forms of divided and shared authority persist and even resurge, but they are being re-formulated so as to be compatible with an increasingly sovereignized understanding of political authority.

Practices of Note

The political relationship between First Nations and settler authorities has therefore reflected a contested and shifting conceptual basis. In the early stages, settler and First Nations authorities recognized one another's autonomy and developed forms of shared authority. Neither party treated its own authority as total or exclusive. Sovereignty, to the extent that it was present at all, was relevant only between European powers. As time went on, however, settler conceptions of authority became more exclusive and unilateral. At the same time, the fall of New France and the impacts of colonial genocide shifted the balance of power, leaving settler authorities physically dominant. Treaty practices began to focus on dividing, rather than sharing, authority and, crucially, on transferring authority from one party to the other. As time went on, settlers began understanding themselves as already in possession of sovereignty, such that First Nations authority could be denied almost entirely. First Nations resistance ultimately forced concessions, and forms of shared authority are beginning to re-emerge. However, this new pluralism is shaped by sovereignty – it works to both recognize First Nations political agency and simultaneously position that authority as subordinate to settler authority, and thus compatible with settler sovereignty. This sovereignization process, aggressive but always incomplete, continues today even as First Nations continue in multipronged attempts to reassert practices of pluralism. The result is a contested relationship that is both pluralist but also deeply and fundamentally asymmetrical, as the settler drive toward sovereignty works to deform pluralist practice, producing forms of multilateralism that are simultaneously methods of subordination. The following section takes up a few of the primary practices through which the contested assertion of sovereignty is managed today.

Modern Treaties

Modern Treaties can be understood as a response to the legal, political, and economic uncertainty created by persistent First Nations activism and by the settler judiciary's acknowledgment of aboriginal title.[70] In essence, the Treaties provide a mechanism to exchange potentially expansive but ill-defined and largely unrecognized claims to independent political authority for more tightly defined but enforceable rights within the settler polity. Fundamentally, this involves an agreement by the First Nation in question to "cede and surrender" or "release"[71] any and all pre-contact claims for all time. In exchange, the Nation typically receives ownership of a small portion of the land claimed, a cash settlement, various degrees of self-government, and participation in a number of comanagement bodies, particularly relating to wildlife, hunting, fishing, and environmental protection.[72]

There are important variations between modern treaties. Where settler populations are small and land is readily available, modern treaties have been more robust. For example, the establishment of Nunavut has created an Inuit-dominated public government with many of the powers, if not the constitutional status, of a settler province.[73] In urban settings like Tsawwassen, powers are more akin to a municipal government. This spatial variation is consistent with longstanding historical trends. Nevertheless, certain broad patterns can be traced from the first modern treaty in James Bay through the latest Treaties in British Columbia.

Typically, claimed lands are split into a number of categories, usually including a relatively small percentage which the nation receives in something like fee simple,[74] a comparatively much larger portion which becomes Crown land, and other portions which become Crown land subject to certain special rights.[75] Thus, Treaties work to take vast areas of overlapping Crown and Aboriginal title and convert them into Crown zones, First Nations zones, and zones where overlapping rights persist. In so doing, they both participate in and contradict an ongoing process where authority over land is becoming more exclusive – holding out forms of multilateralism, but only at the cost of accepting unilateralism in other areas.

The governance powers accorded to First Nations vary by Treaty.[76] A general rule is that matters considered primarily internal – language or education, for example – are within the Nation's competence, while matters that affect surrounding communities – criminal law or foreign affairs, for example – are federal or provincial jurisdictions.[77] However, First Nations jurisdiction is not typically exclusive, but rather concurrent with federal and provincial jurisdiction. Concurrent powers are managed through paramountcy provisions. As a rough rule, there are few areas where First Nations' laws take precedence; otherwise federal and provincial laws tend to take precedence.[78] In other areas, First Nations can pass laws provided they meet or exceed settler standards in that area. In all cases, First Nations legislation must conform to the Canadian *Charter* and may be appealed before Canadian courts. The federal government also typically retains paramountcy for any matter of "peace, order and good government" or "overriding national importance."[79] Many agreements also include comanagement bodies, though these are typically advisory in nature[80] and limited in scope.[81] Settler governments therefore continue to dominate comanagement processes.

For many signatory Nations, the Treaties constitute skilful efforts to carve as much autonomous space as current political circumstances allow. Modern treaties also retain some important features from earlier, more balanced eras of Indigenous-settler relations, including forms of comanagement, limited overlapping rights, and concurrent authorities. To this extent, modern treaties constitute an exception to exclusive forms of authority inherent in the concept of sovereignty. However, modern treaties also incorporate First Nations into the settler polity, therefore rendering their claims compatible with settler sovereignty. Indeed, Woolford concludes that the primary purpose of modern treaties is not to do justice to First Nations claims, but rather to manufacture legitimacy for settler rule.[82] Modern treaties are therefore both a challenge to and an expression of sovereignization, illustrating how practices of pluralism have simultaneously become methods of subordination.

Consultation, Impact-Benefit Agreements, and Comanagement Agreements

The potential that First Nations claims could disrupt economic development projects has also given rise to practices of consultation, as both private and public bodies seek to avoid contestation by securing First Nations' consent.[83]

Corporate consultations often involve Impact Benefit Agreements (IBAs) through which First Nations offer their consent (and often promise to suppress political opposition)[84] in exchange for guaranteed jobs, a share of project revenues, and limited input on environmental issues or other project details. These deals are primarily about the distribution of financial benefits, rather than the distribution of political authority. Notably, these consultations emphatically do not recognize a First Nations "veto," and refusing to offer consent rarely results in a project being cancelled. Thus, First Nations are empowered to say yes and claim their share of project benefits, but saying no often has little effect beyond sacrificing revenues that, after centuries of dispossession and government-induced poverty, are often sorely needed.[85]

Public bodies have a constitutional duty to consult First Nations where their rights may be affected.[86] This "duty to consult" operates on a spectrum – the more legally established a First Nation's claims are, the higher the standard of consultation. Importantly, consultations rarely require consent – settler government must listen, they must respond in good faith to what they hear, but they are ultimately free to proceed even over First Nations objections.[87] In the very strongest cases – where settler courts have recognized Aboriginal title – consultations may require consent. However, as of writing only one nation in all of Canada has actually received settler recognition of its title, and even then settler governments can infringe on title so long as they can justify the infringement to the satisfaction of their own settler courts.[88]

These consultation practices retain some of the dynamics of earlier periods, with settler authorities seeking coordination with First Nations. However, their contemporary form presumes Crown sovereignty – it is settler courts who will decide how much consultation is required, when that bar has been met, and whether settler governments are justified in overriding First Nations objections, and they will do all of this unilaterally. In this way, First Nations are recognized as polities with their own agency while simultaneously positioned as subjects of a sovereign settler state, whom they may petition for redress.

Comanagement practices, which place resource development under the control of a joint council, are more promising in this regard. Indeed, comanagement is reminiscent of the shared political structures typical of the early encounter. However, most comanagement structures today have a primarily advisory role, leaving ultimate authority with the relevant settler cabinet minister.[89] Moreover, such arrangements are typically geared at the outset toward settler authorities' goals – First Nations input is limited to how, exactly, those goals will be achieved.[90] Thus, comanagement bodies also work to both recognize First Nations authority and simultaneously reaffirm settler sovereignty.

Consultation and comanagement structures therefore represent a limited success in First Nations' push to preserve multilateralism. Like modern treaties, these mechanisms offer much needed financial benefits and limited forms of political control, yet they also participate in and help to legitimize a system where settler authority is understood as sovereign.[91] In this way, consultation and comanagement structures illustrate both the success of, and the ongoing contestation of, sovereignization processes.

The Indian Act

While treaties and negotiations with corporate actors have always been fundamental to the relationship between settler authorities and First Nations, colonial governments have also sought to define the relationship extensively, and unilaterally, through legislation. Indeed, the current legislative framework can trace its roots back to pre-confederation imperial policy.

One of the early milestones in the development of this framework was the *Gradual Civilization Act* of 1857,[92] which allowed people to trade in their status as members of a First Nations polity for the status of a Canadian citizen. Only one First Nations person is known to have been voluntarily enfranchised under this act.[93] The 1869 *Gradual Enfranchisement Act* therefore took matters a step further, allowing for enfranchisement against an individual's will. Eventually, these and other acts would be consolidated into the 1876 *Indian Act*, which remains in place to this day.[94] The *Indian Act* goes well beyond transferring individuals from one political system to another, establishing an elaborate system of colonial interference with tribal government, including regulating movement between reserves,[95] defining band membership,[96] and the industrial-scale indoctrination of First Nations youth.[97] In particular, settler authorities established "band councils," typically comprising members amenable to settler interests, alongside traditional First Nations governments and began interacting with, and channeling funds through, these governments while denying the legitimacy of established First Nations authorities.[98] The recognized authority of these bands was circumscribed tightly and enforcement of their decisions relegated to settler courts and police forces.[99] Moreover, such decision-making power as remained was subject to the approval or veto of the federal cabinet or sometimes even the local Indian agent, in a system Nichols calls "administrative despotism."[100] The *Indian Act* is thus another technique by which settler governments offer recognition, funding, and self-governing authority while simultaneously affirming their own sovereignty over First Nations authorities.

First Nations today use the funds and recognized authority the band council system offers as one way to express their continued political agency. However, many nations have also persisted in their traditional governments, enacting governance beyond the settler state.

The relationship between band council and traditional governments remains hotly contested today.

Enacting Pluralism through Persistence and Resistance

Even as settler authorities work to make First Nations autonomy consistent with settler sovereignty, and even as many Nations leverage the recognition the state offers, First Nations have also consistently persisted in exercising their own agency in ways that exceed and conflict with state structures. By enacting First Nations authority directly, these practices create a degree of pluralism on the ground that defies easy assertions of settler sovereignty. Often, settler authorities are forced to negotiate or offer concessions in response.

Indeed, despite prolonged and violent attempts to assimilate First Nations and destroy their traditional governance structures, many nations have found creative ways to keep their independent political systems intact. For example, when the potlatch system of governance and its associated gifting and dancing practices were criminalized, many Nations defied the ban outright, while others began holding ceremonies on Christmas to mask their intent or disguised feast halls as food banks, and others separated dancing and gift-giving phases of the ceremony in order to evade colonial laws.[101] Today, potlach-based systems remain active and underwrite some of some Canada's most active sites of anti-colonial struggle, including the Wet'suwet'en struggle against the Coastal Gas Link pipeline.[102] Faced with an imposed band council system, the Mohawk, one of the nations of the Haudenosaunee confederacy, simply locked the doors to their council chambers, preventing elected councillors from entering and sparking a long series of court cases and political contests that persist to this day.[103] Haudenosaunee warriors have since played crucial roles in resistance struggles at Oka,[104] Caledonia,[105] and Landback Lane.[106] When settler authorities tried to depose a traditional Algonquin government that threatened local extractive interests and replace it with a more compliant elected band council, the Algonquin of Barrier Lake (ABL) occupied band offices and schools, initiated a series of court battles, and eventually elected their traditional leaders to newly imposed band council posts.[107] Here, too, traditional governance helped incubate a series of blockades and occupations, as ABL enacted its authority to contest Crown sovereignty on the ground.

By persisting in their own forms of political organization, First Nations put the lie to settler authorities' pretensions of unilateralism and reassert a pluralistic political landscape.

Often, settler authorities have been forced to negotiate. For example, when Kwakwaka'wakw concerns about open-net fish farms failed to garner a provincial response, hereditary chiefs initiated a series of occupations which ultimately saw the BC Premier visit their Big House, hear their concerns, and enter into negotiations.[108] Likewise, when Ontario issued development permits for tracts of land claimed by the Mohawk nation of the Haudenosaunee confederacy, ignoring centuries of requests for direct negotiations, traditional leaders led a series of blockades, occupations, and court cases until the province agreed to trilateral negotiations with the federal government.[109] When settler authorities ignored Kitchenuhmaykoosib Inninuwug (KI) requests for negotiations and issued mining permits, they too launched a series of blockades, once again triggering court cases, until courts ordered negotiations.[110]

By asserting the persistence of their own political authorities, First Nations contest settler sovereignty, frequently forcing settler authorities to accept a degree of multilateral engagement. This mutually reinforcing blend of resistance and persistence has been a recurring and important practice in the relationship between settler and First Nations authorities, playing a role in major developments like the Royal Proclamation, the constitutionalization of First Nations rights, the development of the modern treaty process, and the adoption of UNDRIP.

Contemporary Political Discourse: Resurgence and Reconciliation

As we have seen, the political practices that structure the relationship between settler and First Nations authorities are dynamic and deeply contested, with different conceptions of authority waxing and waning over time and in response to shifting political circumstances. These practices once suggested something like a nation-to-nation relationship where neither party expected the exclusive, total control associated with sovereignty. However, settlers have gradually worked to impose something closer to a sovereign-to-subject relationship instead, enacting more exclusive and total forms of authority, first dividing it and then monopolizing it as their relative power grew. First Nations have consistently contested this shift, emphasizing shared authority and nation-to-nation equality. In the modern era, this contestation has resulted in a system that recognizes First Nations political claims, but only in ways that affirm settler sovereignty. Contemporary political discourse can be understood as two different – though not necessarily contradictory – orientations to this political opportunity structure.[111]

The first approach, typically called "reconciliation," involves Nations leveraging the sorts of recognition that settler authorities are willing to extend in order to improve their conditions, build their capacity, and assert their agency. At the same time, their growing role within the settler system puts Nations in a better position to push for even more expansive forms of accommodation. Thus, each concession facilitates the next. In essence, this approach seeks to transform the settler state from within, building on limited, even problematic forms of recognition to gradually foster pluralism without necessarily contesting state sovereignty outright. By subjecting state sovereignty to internal divisions, comanagement structures, consultations, and other practices, we might eventually reach a place that bears little resemblance to sovereignty at all. This approach has long historical precedent, finding resonance in the ways that First Nations have used settler institutions, conceptions of divided authority, and even *Indian Act* governance as ways to express their political agency.

The second approach, "resurgence"[112] is critical of participating in the forms of recognition the settler state offers on at least three grounds. First, participation works to legitimize the deep asymmetry between First Nations and settler authorities by creating the illusion of First Nations consent. Second, participation can create dependency on, and even psychological attachment to, the settler state. Finally, by embroiling First Nations leaders in settler institutions based on settler logics including sovereignty, participation can alienate First Nations from their own institutions, ontologies, and conceptions of authority.[113] Thus, participation in reconciliation risks reinforcing colonialism at both the material and the conceptual levels.

Instead of seeking accommodation from the state, resurgence scholars advocate "turning away" from the state, revitalizing traditional First Nations institutions and practices, then enacting First Nations autonomy directly, outside of and even against state institutions.[114] As Simpson puts it, resurgence is primarily inward-looking, focusing on "the flourishing of the Indigenous inside" rather than trying to "transform the colonial outside."[115] By building independent political capacity, this approach seeks to reduce the settler state to one player in a more pluralist environment, thereby re-creating a nation-to-nation context on the ground and putting First Nations once again in a position to negotiate the terms of their relationship on a basis of equality.[116] This approach, too, has deep historical roots in the ways that First Nations have continually exercised agency outside of and against settler structures, making use of direct action, non-cooperation, and even war to enact independence on the ground.

These approaches are not, and have not historically been, mutually exclusive – indeed, many nations employ both strategies at the same time. The Wet'suwet'en, for example, have led both ground-breaking Aboriginal rights cases and inter-governmental negotiations alongside blockades and direct action campaigns.[117] The L'nu have fought for their treaty rights to fish in court and at the negotiating table, and have also launched a fishing fleet under their own inherent authority, in contravention of settler law.[118] Indeed, Borrows contends that many of the limited forms of recognition that reconciliation offers are themselves a result of contestation that exceeded state institutions.[119] Likewise, the increased agency and improved material conditions that come along with reconciliation can facilitate political activity beyond state structures. While the two approaches can certainly conflict, they can reinforce one another as well.

Contemporary discourse therefore reflects the odd mixture of autonomy and asymmetry that characterizes the political relationship between settler and First Nations authorities. Both approaches, in their own ways, continue to contest the ongoing transition from nation-to-nation types of relations to subject-to-sovereign types of relations. Both, in their own ways, also work to contest the very idea of sovereignty itself, centring forms of shared authority instead. Like historical contestation, contemporary struggles therefore include not only the distribution of authority between the parties, but also the nature of authority itself.

Case Study: The Kunst'aa Guu – Kunst'aayah Reconciliation Protocol

The Kunst'aa Guu – Kunst'aayah Reconciliation Protocol holds these tensions in a usefully illustrative manner. Like most First Nations in the province of British Columbia, the Haida have never signed any treaties with settler authorities. In the 1970s, the colonial government was logging the Haida homeland aggressively, sparking intense and prolonged resistance.[120] The Haida moved to negotiate, but logging continued. A series of important court battles, blockades, and direct actions ensued, leading to plans to make much of the islands a national park. The Haida relented their pressure, and negotiations stalled. Once again, the Haida erected blockades and initiated legal challenges. After important public relations and legal victories, the Haida signed an agreement establishing a park. Advocacy continued. Years later, British Columbia and the Haida nation signed a Protocol Agreement establishing shared control of resource extraction on Haida Gwaii.[121] Under the agreement, the southern half of Haida Gwaii was set aside as a conservation area, while logging activities on the northern half were put under the control of a joint council with equal numbers of settler and Haida representatives.[122] Remarkably, the agreement's preamble features the following passages, in parallel columns, which are worth reproducing in their entirety:

WHEREAS: A. The Parties hold differing views with regard to sovereignty, title, ownership and jurisdiction over Haida Gwaii, as set out below.

The Haida Nation asserts that: Haida Gwaii is Haida lands, including the waters and resources, subject to the rights, sovereignty, ownership, jurisdiction and collective title of the Haida Nation who will manage Haida Gwaii in accordance with its laws, policies, customs and traditions.	British Columbia asserts that: Haida Gwaii is Crown land, subject to certain private rights or interests, and subject to the sovereignty of her Majesty the Queen and the legislative jurisdiction of the Parliament of Canada and the Legislature of the Province of British Columbia

Notwithstanding and without prejudice to the aforesaid divergence of viewpoints, the Parties seek a more productive relationship and hereby choose a more respectful approach to coexistence by way of land and natural resource management on Haida Gwaii through shared decision-making and ultimately, a Reconciliation Agreement.

Under this Protocol, the Parties will operate under their respective authorities.[123]

As these statements attest, the Haida and the Crown continue to hold conflicting views regarding sovereignty over Haida Gwaii and, as a consequence, regarding the nature of the agreement itself. It is, in this sense, an agreement to disagree about the relative status of their claims.[124] Nevertheless, each party accepts that some of its decision-making powers will now be exercised in concert with its partner through codecision practices. These practices do not exhaust the agency of either partner.

The Haida thus continue to express political agency both within and beyond Canadian institutions, employing a mixture of reconciliatory and resurgent practices to resist a sovereign-to-subject relationship, creating something closer to a nation-to-nation relationship in its stead. However, settler authorities also continue to exercise unilateral authority according to their own legal norms. Because of the *de facto* power imbalance between settler and Haida authorities, their respective capacity for unilateralism is deeply asymmetrical. Shared and exclusive conceptions of authority therefore intermix in complex ways, facilitating pragmatic responses to specific political circumstances.

In all these ways the Haida agreement holds within it many of the central tensions of political relations between settler and First Nations authorities. Where settler governments seek to exercise unilateral control, First Nations resistance has forced a partial return to practices of pluralism. The resulting relationship is not quite one of sovereign-to-subject, but it is not quite nation-to-nation either, representing instead a deeply asymmetrical form of pluralism.

Conclusions

The political relationship between First Nations and the settler state has therefore reflected a contested and shifting conceptual basis. In the early phases, settler and First Nations authorities engaged in nation-to-nation relations, recognizing one another's autonomy and working to cocreate mechanisms of coordination. As time went on, however, settler authorities' conceptions of authority became increasingly unilateral, even as demographic and military shifts reduced settler need for their former partners. As a result, settler authorities began imposing increasingly sovereign-subject relations instead.

First Nations have continually resisted this shift, and their efforts have preserved a degree of multilateralism. In response, settler governments have begun offering limited forms of recognition, trying to account for First Nations agency in a way that is compatible with a unilateral and exclusive understanding of their own political authority. The current political relationship is therefore deeply asymmetrical, and yet still defies any understanding of the settler state as properly sovereign.

Chapter Two

Legal Practices

This chapter explores the legal dimensions of the relationship between First Nations and settler authorities, exploring how legal practices have shifted over time and how these shifting practices are challenging and being shaped by the logic of sovereignty. Once again, regional and spatial variations in the relationship are considerable, making the following overview necessarily schematic. Nevertheless, certain broad, recurring patterns are discernable.

In the earliest phases of encounter, each party seemed to recognize the other as an independent source of legality[1] and to expect negotiation on shared concerns. Flexible, ad hoc, and interpenetrating legal procedures allowed both sides to contest outcomes and offer accommodations on an ongoing basis. As time went on, however, settler authorities began to reimagine First Nations legalities as autonomous components of a broader imperial legality, much like the colonies themselves. Gradually, this conception gave way to a view of First Nations law as internal to the local colonial legality and, finally, internal to the settler constitution. With each phase, settler authorities understood First Nations law as increasingly internal to their own legality, thereby denying it an independent status of its own. By attempting to make First Nations' laws fit within their own institutional frameworks, settler authorities empowered themselves to determine if, when, and how First Nations law would apply. In this way, the process of internalization makes the presence of multiple legal systems compatible with the larger project of settler sovereignty.

Mills describes this process as "constitutional capture" – a process by which Indigenous law is brought within, and therefore subjected to the control of, the settler constitutional order.[2] First Nations, however, have consistently worked to assert the independent status of their laws and legal institutions, and to insist on a negotiated relationship between legalities. We might think of this as "constitutional refusal."[3] Together, these trends have produced a contemporary jurisprudence which limits settler sovereignty without recognizing First Nations sovereignty. This odd blend of unilateralism and pluralism allows settler authorities to make practical concessions in the face of First Nations advocacy without compromising either their self-conception of sovereignty or their lived reality of physical dominance.

The following chapter will explore these processes of capture and refusal, tracing their development through four historical phases before exploring some of the most important ways they are expressed today.

Four Phases of Legal Relation

In mapping the legal relationship and its changing connection to concepts of sovereignty, it can be useful to tease apart several distinct aspects of sovereignty. Webber lists four:[4] Sovereignty 1 describes total and exclusive authority. This is the sense in which I have generally used sovereignty in this book. Sovereignty 2 means having the attributes of a state in international law, Sovereignty 4 consists of having the standardized, rationalized institutional structure associated with the modern state, while Sovereignty 3 simply means that the sovereign actor constitutes an independent site of legal authority which is not derivative of any other source of authority. As we will see, various aspects of sovereignty have been ascribed and denied to First Nations at various times, and this has helped construct settler authority as sovereign as well.

The Early Period: Justice of the Peace/Common Law(s) (Contact—~1763)[5]

The earliest days of contact and colonization reflect an ad hoc state of legal affairs. Legal relationships between specific First Nations and settler polities varied widely as each community incorporated the other into its own legal processes. Eventually, this gave rise to hybrid or shared legal practices as well. These processes reflected local balances of power, and the mechanics of the arrangement could vary considerably. By and large, however, whatever arrangements prevailed were established by and regulated through negotiation. Thus, we might say that each party considered the other to be, at the least, an independent party to be negotiated with.

Consider criminal jurisdiction, for example. In the French-occupied zone, it appears that First Nations and settler authorities alike generally agreed that *inter se*[6] offences would be dealt with by each community internally.[7] Intercommunal offences were sometimes resolved using First Nations diplomacy, when settler authorities so consented, and sometimes using settler courts, when First Nations so consented. In this way, each party drew the other into its own legal processes. Ad hoc, shared institutions were also common. For example, many cases involved hybrids of various sorts – semi-trials where French court procedures were imperfectly followed, First Nations councils acted as juries;[8] and, notably, the sentencing phase was almost always absent, with redress left to local chiefs.[9] These ad hoc forms of justice were often lopsided, following local power imbalances, economic and social structures, and national dispositions. Nevertheless, they show that both the French and their First Nations interlocutors recognized the other's legality and engaged in forms of codecision which drew on both legal systems.

British practice was perhaps more structured, though no less variable. Broadly speaking, English colonies distinguished between First Nations who lived in English settlements, those who lived independently but in areas surrounded by English settlements, and those who lived beyond the pale of English settlements entirely.[10] It seems that those who lived with the English were, almost from the outset, subjected to English law in local courts. Likewise, British subjects living in First Nations communities were typically subject to First Nations law, at least where the offence concerned the First Nations community.[11] First Nations living as groups within the asserted borders of English colonies were perceived as self-governing but subordinate.[12] Similarly, British forts in Indian country were typically self-governing, subject to the broader treaty relationship. Those nations beyond British settlement were totally independent *inter se*, and intercommunal matters were the subject of negotiation.[13] The particular mix of jurisdiction prevailing in any particular place was "usually achieved through diplomatic negotiations of various kinds."[14]

Throughout all this variation, it appears both parties typically recognized the other as having an independent claim to legal authority. The borders of these claims were adjusted primarily through negotiation and treaty, though these always coexist with actual and implicit coercion in complex ways.[15] Read together, these arrangements suggest an image of legal authority which roughly parallels Webber's concept of "sovereignty 3."[16] Here, being sovereign means being recognized as an independent, non-derivative site of legal authority. It does not, however, carry the broader connotation of total or exclusive authority. That is, settler and First Nations legalities alike were recognized as independent legal authorities, but neither enjoyed nor expected unilateral control.

The Middle Period: Lazy Suzerainty (~1763–~1860)[17]

The first half of the nineteenth century was a time of transition for the relationship between settler and First Nations legalities. With France vanquished and an end to the British war with America, First Nations lost much of their military importance. With the fur trade in decline and agricultural and industrial growth taking seed, First Nations were losing economic leverage. Perhaps most importantly, settlement, disease, war, and dispossession drove shifting demographics, which tilted the balance of power decidedly in favour of the British.

These trends are reflected in the legal relationship. Whereas negotiations between parties had once expressed a wide variety of relationships, the practices of settler authorities began to solidify around a view of First Nations as subordinate but autonomous components of the British Empire – a sort of intra-imperial status not unlike that enjoyed by protectorates, or by the colonies themselves. Thus, when conflicts arose between settler and First Nations legalities, the parties often sought mediation by the imperial government, just as two colonies would do. In the place of direct negotiations of the previous era, parties now increasingly turned to the imperial government as an overarching authority capable of arbitrating between them.[18]

For example, *Keutrokwen's Case* was heard before the Secretary of the Indian Department (an imperial official at this time), the departmental agent for the reserve, and four "Principal Chiefs" – suggesting the structure of an intra-imperial special inquiry, or in any case certainly not following the format of regular municipal court.[19] With respect to jurisdiction, the chiefs concluded that "in conformity with the Custom of their Nation all Complaints relating to property in their Village should be settled amongst the Indians themselves." Indian Department officials apparently concurred that the Nation constituted an independent legality, at least for internal matters. However, *Chief Bernabé's Case* involved a charge that the chief had been disloyal and ought to be removed. The chief was not so removed, but it seems clear that the imperial authorities contemplated that they were empowered to remove chiefs because these chiefs constituted subordinate agents of the Empire.[20] Thus, settler authorities considered the Nations in question to have separate legalities autonomous from the colonial legal system but subject to broader imperial authority. This represents a first step in the process of constitutional capture. While interpenetrating institutions and forms of codecision persisted, they were increasingly reimagined as internal to the imperial legality, and this increasingly put settlers – or at least Europeans – in a position to control legal outcomes.

Many First Nations denied that operating under imperial jurisdiction diminished their status and engaged in processes of "constitutional refusal," working to maintain forms of relation that exceeded the constitutional parameters settler authorities sought to impose. In 1727, for example, a spokesperson for the Wabanaki recounted such an interaction:

> he again said to me – but do you not recognize the king of England as king over all his states? To which I answered – yes I recognize him as king of all his lands; but I rejoined, do no hence infer that I acknowledge thy king as my king, and king of my lands. Herein lies my distinction – my Indian distinction. God hath willed that I have no King, and that I be master of my lands in common. He again asked me – do you not admit that I am at least master of the lands I have purchased? I answered him thereupon, that I admit nothing, and that I knew not what he had reference to.[21]

To use Webber's language, the Wabanaki were refusing to recognize Sovereignty 1 in favour of Sovereignty 3, thereby implying a continued need for negotiation. Likewise, the Mohawk have consistently asserted that they were allies, not subjects of the Crown, appealing to direct diplomacy or international law even as they made use of intra-imperial fora.[22]

Settler authorities responded to these assertions, affirming forms of First Nations autonomy and continuing forms of codecision. For example, colonial and imperial law continued to recognize First Nations autonomy over *inter se* offences on First Nations lands.[23] Again, this suggests that settler authorities saw First Nations legalities as autonomous. However, the assertion of settler jurisdiction over intercommunal offences, even when they occurred on First Nations lands, shows that First Nations legalities were seen as a part of, and therefore subordinate to, a larger imperial legality.[24]

The Middle Period therefore saw at least two important shifts. First, intercommunal matters shifted from direct negotiations between the parties to mediation by imperial officials. In this way, codecision was gradually approaching settler unilateralism. Second, First Nations jurisdiction was more consistently circumscribed, both territorially and personally, while settler authorities' jurisdiction became more expansive. In both these ways, the legal relationship was becoming more lopsided.

The Late Period: A Cold Reception (~1860–~1960)[25]

As the balance of power continued to shift, and as responsibility for "Indian policy" shifted from imperial authorities to local colonial authorities, patterns of incorporation grew more unidirectional and more lopsided. Rather than incorporating First Nations legalities into the imperial order as subordinate but autonomous polities, settler authorities began treating First Nations legal traditions as sources of 'customary law' which could be recognized at common law. This had two important consequences. First, settler judges, using the framework of customary law, felt empowered to determine unilaterally if and how First Nations law would be recognized and implemented. Second, because First Nations had been re-understood as domestic subjects rather than citizens of a distinct polity[26], judges began to assume that First Nations could be subjected to settler authority unilaterally through colonial legislation or jurisprudence, rather than bilaterally through treaty or trilaterally through imperial commission.

Jackson v. Wilkes illustrates the tenor of the period well. The case turned on whether the Haldimand deed, granting land to the Haudenosaunee, had been properly authorized.[27] In the alternative, however, Chief Justice Robinson entertained the argument that the grant was also deficient for lack of grantee, given that the Haudenosaunee were neither a corporation nor an individual and hence did not enjoy legal personhood. In essence, Robinson was reasoning that the Haudenosaunee were nothing more than a collection of British subjects. Ultimately, Robinson concluded that the deed itself rendered the Nation a "constructive corporation."[28] In so doing, he recognized a sort of collective status for First Nations at law, but one that was created by, and subject to, colonial law.

In the *Indian Annuities Case*, the court reasoned that because First Nations were British subjects the Robinson Treaties were a mere "promise and agreement, which was nothing more than a personal obligation by its governor," not a legal agreement between peoples.[29,30] International forums reflected a similar logic. In *Cayuga Indians*, an international tribunal held that "[a] tribe is not a legal unit of international law," ruling that so far as an Indian Tribe exists as a legal unit, it is by virtue of the domestic law of the sovereign within whose territory the tribe resides.[31]

The implications of this domestication were profound. Because First Nations were seen as subjects, any special status was purely a creation of colonial law, and as such, colonial legislatures were free to regulate, change, or ignore it as they saw fit, unilaterally. As the court in *Commanda* put it, "it does not matter whether Indians have any rights flowing from [a] … treaty or not. [They] … may be taken away by the … [l]egislature without any compensation."[32] Settler governments began regulating protected treaty rights unilaterally, taking up First Nations lands unilaterally and working to assimilate First Nations aggressively. In fact, First Nations legal institutions that existed outside of settler courts were the object of criminalization, as potlatches, sundances, and other independent legal institutions were outlawed.[33]

In place of the direct negotiations of the early period or the imperial mediation of the middle period, the late period is defined by colonial unilateralism.

Many First Nations worked to resist this shift toward unilateralism. In *Sero v. Gault*, for example, a Six Nations woman argued that the Indian department had no jurisdiction on reserve because the Six Nations were "an independent people".[34] When Sero lost the case, she took her cause to the League of Nations. Indeed, recourse to international mechanisms was common when domestic courts failed to produce results.[35] In other instances, First Nations simply enacted their own legal authority outside,[36] alongside,[37] through,[38] and even in contravention of[39] settler institutions. In all these ways, First Nations continued to assert independent legalities that could not be regulated unilaterlally but only through negotiation.[40] Settler governments were often forced to respond, offering executive clemency,[41] for example, or negotiating treaty adhesions long after treaties were deemed legally unnecessary.[42]

The Modern Period: Rights and Wrongs (~1970–~2020)[43]

In the modern era, the internalization of First Nations legalities by settler legalities has taken on new forms with the inclusion of Aboriginal rights within Section 35 of the settler constitution in 1982. On the basis of this shift, settler courts developed an Aboriginal rights jurisprudence, which is in some ways a retreat from unfettered sovereignty and which has to that degree improved the legal position of First Nations. However, the constitutionalization of Aboriginal rights also continues the broader trend of positioning First Nations law as internal to settler legality and adjudicated by settler institutions. In this way, the modern era continues to position settler authorities as the final decision-makers of the system, even as those decisions are subjected to new constraints.

S35 recognizes and affirms both treaty rights, based in agreements with settler authorities, and "Aboriginal" rights, based on the First Nations' pre-existing legal authority. The recognition of treaty rights represents a partial retreat from the previous era, where treaties were not really considered law at all. Under s35, treaties are indeed law – but they are domestic law, binding not because First Nations have international status, but rather because the "honour of the Crown" requires the government to keep promises made to its subjects.[44] As instruments of domestic constitutional law, treaties can be used to limit settler governments, but they are also interpreted, applied, and enforced unilaterally by settler courts. Thus, the recognition of treaty as law is both a limit on settler action and an affirmation of settler sovereignty.

Aboriginal rights flow from an acknowledgment that First Nations did indeed possess independent authority and that this authority survived the imposition of settler law.[45] If an Indigenous nation or individual can demonstrate that it enjoyed certain legal privileges before contact, and if it can show that this privilege was integral to their distinctive culture[46] and never extinguished by settler law, then settler courts will express those privileges as modern rights and will strike down any settler legislation that violates those rights.[47] Once again, the pre-existing authority of First Nations is recognized, but at the same time transformed into something defined, interpreted, and enforced by settler courts.

Moreover, both Aboriginal and treaty rights can be violated by the settler government if the government can "justify" the infringement to the satisfaction of a settler court.[48] Notably, this system ensures that governing authority remains entirely with the settler state. Settler courts will determine whether an Aboriginal right exists, what its content is, whether it has been violated, whether that violation can be justified, and what remedy, if any, is appropriate – all unilaterally, without any negotiation with, or input from, First Nations authorities, except in their capacity as plaintiffs or witnesses in a settler court. As the court has repeatedly made clear: "aboriginal societies exist within, and are a part of, a broader social, political and economic community, over which the Crown is sovereign."[49]

Thus, the modern era introduces important limits on the sovereignty of settler governments, who are no longer free to ignore their treaties with First Nations or deny First Nations' inherent rights. However, these limits are defined, enforced, and waived unilaterally by settler courts. In this sense, they represent a sort of auto-limitation, allowing settlers to make concessions to First Nations in practice without compromising their self-understanding as sovereign authorities. In the place of pluralism, s35 creates a sort of restrained unilateralism. Indeed, settler courts are quite explicit that their goal is to respond to the fact of pluralism and make it compatible with settler sovereignty. The entire purpose of s35 is to "reconcile" the fact that Indigenous nations were already exercising authority when the Crown arrived with the assertion of Crown sovereignty.[50]

First Nations have made use of the openings that the constitutionalization of Aboriginal rights have created, and to that end have often phrased their claims in the court's language. However, many First

Nations have also consistently forwarded a view of their legalities as constituting independent jurisdictions, whose relation to Canadian jurisdiction must be negotiated. In *R. v. Fournier*, for example, defendants appealed to the Royal Proclamation to insist that neither settler courts nor legislatures had valid jurisdiction on Algonquin lands until a treaty was reached.[51] *R. v. Francis*, *R. v. Chief*, and *R. v. Yellowhorn* all made similar claims.[52] In a 1982 submission to the United Nations Commission on Human Rights, the Grand Council of the Mi'kmaq Nation characterized itself as an independent colony of Great Britain, analogous in jurisdiction to Canada or Australia.[53] Similarly, the Barriere Lake Algonquin and the Haudenosaunee have been to the United Nations repeatedly to assert the international status of their treaties and their equality with Quebec and Canada, as heirs to the English and French Crowns.[54] Thus, First Nations continue to make use of settler law without necessarily acting within the settler legality, using settler institutions to trouble the narrative of constitutional capture. In so doing, they reassert Sovereignty 3 (existence as an independent legal authority) to contest the Crown's assertions of Sovereignty 1 and re-centre the need for negotiation.

Practices of Note

As we have seen, the relationship between First Nations and settler legalities has been ambiguous, shifting, and contested. From the beginning, settler authorities oscillated between treating First Nations as something like international allies, something like intra-imperial polities, and something like domestic subjects. The particular blend of practices is not doctrinally coherent, but rather reflects shifting power relations as settler authorities sought practices that more closely approximated sovereignty, pursuing strategies of constitutional capture in proportion to their growing dominance. First Nations have made use of each of these statuses when it suited their interests, and also contested the broader trend toward constitutional capture by enacting their own legality beyond and against settler law in reciprocal acts of constitutional refusal. As Beaulieu puts it, the multiplicity of legal understandings became "a useful collection from which they [all sides] might draw selectively in crafting colonial legal systems." Such practice "does not allow for the identification of a coherent and logical system ... Rather it highlights the detours, improvisations, and tinkering done."[55] In the following section, I explore some of the most persistent and influential patterns, showing how current practice is both challenging and challenged by concepts of sovereignty.

Status, Hierarchy, and Equality

In reviewing the literature and writing this chapter, the most prominent and consistent problem that emerged was this: settlers want to sort First Nations into categories, either that of a foreign nation or an imperial protectorate or domestic citizens. For settler authorities, categorizing First Nations is extremely important because status is tied to jurisdiction. Thus, determining whether First Nations are akin to a country or a province or a municipality determines what powers First Nations can claim. This in turn determines the extent and scope of settler authority. Categorizing First Nations according to a hierarchy of political units has therefore been an important practice of colonization, with each categorization working not only to affirm some level of First Nations autonomy, but also to carve out an inverse sphere of settler unilateralism.

However, First Nations practice often does not map well onto any particular category. Indeed, many First Nations seem to traverse settler political categories constantly and without linear directionality. Some First Nations (the Mohawk, for example) have consistently asserted something close to international status. Others have been clear that they seek a place *within* Canada. However, since the beginning, and still today, many First Nations interact with multiple levels of settler governance – from the UN and the Queen to the local courthouse – all at once and seemingly without contradiction. Thus, the Haudenosaunee could insist on their freedom to maintain independent diplomatic relations one day, and ask settler courts to resolve an internal dispute the next.[56] A century later, the Indian Brotherhood could appeal to London and then negotiate with provincial Premiers.[57] If we ask what "status" these interactions imply using settler categories, the answer appears schizophrenic.[58] Indeed, it is tempting to attribute the oscillation to mere pragmatism. Perhaps this is sometimes the case. Yet if one sets aside settler categories and turns toward First Nations political concepts, a more coherent explanation comes into view.

According to a recent court submission, the Anishinaabe, for example, organize themselves at the family, clan, village, national, and confederacy levels, and each of these levels engages with the other horizontally.[59] A continent away, Stó:lō self-descriptions are remarkably similar, describing different levels of government which are not hierarchically arranged, but rather interact as equals.[60] Where settler authorities see different levels of social organization as nested within a hierarchy, this is not necessarily true in many First Nations communities. Thus, where settler authorities seek to slot First Nations into a hierarchically arranged set of statuses, First Nations often seem to frustrate these attempts and transgress the boundaries of settler categories, not because the Nations are inconsistent, but because their political agency is informed by their own political structures and world views. In this sense, the practice of engaging multiple levels of settler authority as equals can be read as a practice of refusal, whereby First Nations insist on their own political and legal ontologies.

Both the ascribing and the refusal of differentiated hierarchical statuses have therefore been important practices through which the overall relationship is contested.

Doctrinal Gaps

Another striking pattern that emerges from the attempted absorption of First Nations legalities by settler legalities has been, ironically, a lack of clarity about that very process. From the beginning, at every stage since, and still today, settler legal doctrine does not provide a coherent explanation of how exactly settler jurisdiction was obtained, nor how First Nations jurisdiction was displaced.

For example, where did settler sovereignty come from? Conquest provides one possible explanation, but courts have recognized that this is historically inaccurate.[61] First Nations were not conquered. The racist doctrine of *terra nullius*, which claims that Indigenous peoples were simply too savage to have ever had sovereignty, offers another answer. Thankfully, courts have rejected this as well.[62] Treaty provides another possible answer.[63] Yet the Crown claims sovereignty even where no treaties exist.[64] As a result, the courts are not able to articulate any clear foundation for settler authority.[65]

In practice, settler authorities have employed all these arguments pragmatically, as suited their fluctuating interests. In negotiations between the French and British, for example, France, whose theory of sovereignty did not generally rely on treaty making, came to insist that they could not cede sovereignty to the British because they had never acquired it through treaty. The British, whose own approach to sovereignty claims did generally rely on treaty, argued that the French had sovereignty whether they had treated for it or not.[66] Thus, each took positions that suited their interest, even though these positions contradicted their own long-standing practices.

Even today, the court continues to presume Crown sovereignty without requiring any conceptual or historic support for those claims.[67] The courts themselves seem aware of this confused state of affairs, and have lately begun attaching modifiers like "assumed" or "*de facto*" onto their descriptions of Crown sovereignty, but without clearly explaining what these are meant to signal.[68] Constitutional scholar Kent McNeil describes the jurisprudence on the subject as "confused and embarrassed," concluding that the origin of Crown sovereignty is an "unresolved constitutional conundrum."[69] A recent BC Supreme Court ruling, having reviewed the relevant jurisprudence, was blunter, concluding that Crown sovereignty "is simply a legal fiction to justify the de facto seizure and control of the land and resources formerly owned by the original inhabitants of what is now Canada."[70] Likewise, Walters, Harring, and Foster all contend that there was never a clear doctrinal foundation for extending settler criminal jurisdiction over *inter se* offences – judges simply began asserting it, without offering explanations.[71]

In many cases, courts have gone beyond mere inconsistency to outright ahistoricism. In *Ramsay*, Robinson claimed First Nations had "never" been exempt from criminal law – when of course they had – citing a report which stated that Indians had "always" been subject to British justice – when of course they hadn't.[72] In *Syliboy*, the court claimed that treaties had "never" been recognized as binding, when of course they had.[73] And even today, *Sparrow*, which has become a major authority on the subject, simply states that there was "never any doubt" that title and sovereignty vested in the Crown, when even a cursory glance at the historical record shows that there was nothing but doubt.[74] By claiming a false historical pedigree, courts have been able to dodge the question of how things had come to be so – they had always been so, so there is nothing to explain.

This doctrinal ambiguity has been an important practice of constitutional capture. However, ambiguity has also proven an important reservoir of resources for constitutional refusal. First Nations can contest settler authority on unceded land, for example, precisely because settler law has no coherent reply at the ready. First Nations can ask for imperial tribunals because it is not doctrinally clear why they should no longer be entitled to them, and Aboriginal title can be reasserted after centuries of dormancy because settler law never developed a clear account of why it was being ignored. In all these ways, doctrinal confusion has been an important means of asserting unilateralism and also a rich resource for reasserting negotiation and codecision.

Discretionary Exceptions/De Jure Unilateralism, De Facto Accommodation

Another important practice which has persisted from the earliest days of contact until the present is the pragmatic pairing of universal rules and discretionary exceptions. For settler authorities, the formal recognition of their unilateral decision-making power has always been more important than the particular decision reached. Conversely, First Nations often sought forms of power which centred on the ability to force relational, contextual negotiations.[75] As a result, settler authorities often insisted on their unilateral authority while simultaneously using that unilateral discretion to offer informally negotiated accommodations. This allowed settler authorities to maintain the self-image of sovereignty while also engaging in pragmatic negotiations. In this sense, discretionary exceptions work as a method of constitutional capture and a tool of constitutional refusal at the same time.

Consider the following episode between the French and their allies.[76] The French insisted that French criminal procedure apply to an intercommunal crime, but this was only made possible by assuring that the defendant would be pardoned and released. Similarly, as settler authorities attempted to shift intercommunal crimes definitively into municipal courts in the 1800s, they frequently gave First Nations offenders remarkably short sentences – two years for murder in Nova Scotia, for example.[77] Two statutes from 1802 and 1821 are often cited to ground jurisdiction over unceded First Nations lands, but in practice cases were only brought against settlers.[78] There was a well-recognized but always informal exception for First Nations. In British Columbia, judges developed a pattern of imposing regular sentences but requesting their commutation by the executive, often in response to petitions from First Nations leaders and with an eye to avoiding the repercussions of overplaying their hand.[79] Today, Gladue reports serve a similar role, allowing judges to reach verdicts in the normal way while providing a means to give lighter or more culturally appropriate sentences to First Nations offenders.[80] In all these ways, discretionary exceptions work to accommodate First Nations power and recognize the continuation of a multilateral, negotiated relationship without compromising the sovereign pretensions of settler law.[81]

This practice has spatial and temporal dimensions. Because exceptions are often discretionary, rather than binding, their prevalence tends to fade away as the control of settler authorities solidifies. In the early 1800s, First Nations were almost never tried for anything short of murder or rape, but over time this exception was gradually withdrawn.[82] In the early days of colonization on the prairies, arrest numbers were low and the NWMP rarely acted without the explicit sanction of First Nations leaders.[83] Fifty years later, when the demographic balance had shifted, arrests had skyrocketed and First Nations leaders themselves were frequently arrested.[84] The same logic animates spatial variations.

For example, the NWMP were exercising a light hand on the prairies even as more settled areas in Ontario saw intrusive policing.[85] Fidler was pardoned for a crime that occurred in remote Saskatchewan at a time when members of First Nations in the cities enjoyed no such clemency.[86]

In all these ways, discretion allows settler authorities to assert sovereignty while at the same time engaging in forms of informal interpenetration and codecision, making it an important tool of constitutional capture and a mechanism of constitutional refusal at the same time.

International Law Appeals and Exclusions

Another key contest has been over which legal forums First Nations have access to. Over time, settler authorities have worked to foreclose international forums, forcing First Nations into the domestic settler system as their only recourse. In this sense, the closure of international law has been crucial to the perceived domestication of First Nations legalities. Conversely, repeated appeals to international law, both settler and inter-national Indigenous law, have been an important practice in troubling this internalization and re-centring the independent status of First Nations' laws.

The first key practice for settler authorities has been defining international agents in increasingly exclusive and territorial terms. The proposition that there can be only one international actor on a given territory has been an important tool. Since First Nations fall within the borders claimed by settler polities, and since these settler polities are recognized as international agents, First Nations can only be subjects of some kind. In *Mohegan*, for example, the tribunal found that because the Mohegan fell within the territorial limits of British claims, they were properly subject to the imperial rather than international legal system.[87] Likewise, an international commission in 1926 found that the Cayuga, who straddled the British-American border, fell within the boundaries of sovereigns and, as a result, their relations with settler states were a matter for domestic, not international, law.[88] As western international law took on a more developed institutional form, the League of Nations and its successor the United Nations both systematically excluded First Nations as participating units. In Webber's terms, Sovereignty 2 – international recognition – was relied upon to ground Sovereignty 1 – final decision-making authority.

Nevertheless, First Nations have fought for fuller membership in the international community. The Haudenosaunee sought recognition of their full international sovereignty at the League of Nations, and the

Mi'kmaq (or L'nu) asserted their status as a separate state and equal member of the British commonwealth to the UNHCR.[89] In both cases, settler authorities appealed to the indivisibility of sovereignty and to their own territorial claims to reposition the issue as a question of domestic law. For example, in response to the Mi'kmaq, Canada argued that self-determination "cannot affect the national unity and territorial integrity of Canada" and thus that treaties "are merely considered to be nothing more than contracts between a sovereign and a group of its subjects."[90] The Mi'kmaq responded that only consent could make them subjects of another legal order – in effect repositioning themselves as international agents.[91]

Colonial authorities have also exploited the ambiguity in their shifting conceptions of First Nations' status, extending recognition in partial and selective ways.[92] The Royal Proclamation, for example, recognizes First Nations as sovereign enough to transfer sovereignty to a settler state, but not sovereign enough to exercise full membership in the international community themselves. Similarly, First Nations were seen as sovereign enough to be justly conquered if they violated treaties with settler states, but not so sovereign that settlers were obligated to honour those treaties themselves.[93] Macklem contends that this ambiguity produced a pattern – settlers saw Indigenous peoples as either fundamentally different from or totally interchangeable with European powers, or something in between, depending on which image suited settler needs at the moment.[94] As a result, First Nations were afforded all of the obligations and none of the prerogatives of international agency. This "logic of exclusion-inclusion"[95] granted legal recognition to First Nations, but it was "a recognition that afforded native subjects the right only to dispossess of themselves" and, one might add, to legitimize settler sovereignty.[96]

Alongside pressing for full international recognition, First Nations have also made pragmatic use of such recognition as does exist, leveraging opportunities at the intra-imperial level. For example, in 1906 the Nisga'a sent a delegation to London.[97] When First Nations were shut out of constitutional discussions in 1982, numerous delegations again appealed to London.[98] When "Idle No More" protests broke out in 2013, movement figurehead Theresa Spence demanded negotiations with the governor general, not the prime minister.[99] In each case, the choice of imperial forums was in part a strategic reassertion of legal independence.

Appeals to international forums to resolve complaints against the government without challenging settler sovereignty directly are also common. For example, Lovelace won an important victory at the

UN – embarrassing, although not legally forcing, the government of Canada into action.[100] More recently, First Nations undertook the momentous task of drafting a declaration of their rights through the UN. Although the rights expressed therein are international, they depend on the domestic state for voluntary self-enforcement, and indeed explicitly affirm the inviolable territorial integrity of settler states, thereby perpetuating the domestic status of First Nations at international law.[101] Nevertheless, the very existence of the UN Declaration shows that Indigenous peoples have found continued ways to participate in the international system.

First Nations have also made use of their own inter-national forms of diplomacy to assert their independence. As the power of settler authorities grew, powerful confederacies like the Wabanaki or Blackfoot began to form or solidify as a counterweight.[102] The Haudenosaunee continued to jealously guard their right to maintain independent relations with other First Nations groups into the 1800s.[103] And even today, more than 150 nations from across Turtle Island have signed a treaty alliance against the expansion of fossil fuel production from tar sands.[104] These moves can also be understood, at least in part, as assertions of international agency.

In sum, by working to define international law so as to exclude or selectively recognize First Nations, settler authorities attempt to position their own courts as the default site of legal contestation, allowing them to domesticate, subordinate, and control the legal relationship unilaterally. By troubling this exclusion and asserting independent international agency, First Nations problematize settler sovereignty and the use of settler-controlled forums to regulate intercommunal affairs, re-centring the need for nation-to-nation negotiation.

Contemporary Legal Discourse: Inside or Out?

As we have seen, the legal dimensions of the relationship between settler and First Nations authorities has undergone important changes over time. The early period was characterized by mutual need between parties, and so involved shared institutions which recognized both parties as independent sources of legal authority. Ad hoc, shared legal processes provided a means for both parties to contest and revise their relationship over time. As time went on, however, settler conceptions of legal authority became more and more hierarchical and exclusive. As shifting balances of power made settler authorities physically dominant, settler authorities sought practices that more closely resembled sovereign unilateralism. In short, settler authorities engaged in strategies of constitutional capture designed to re-present First Nations law as internal to the settler legality. First Nations engaged in acts of constitutional refusal by continuing to enact their independent legalities, thereby centring the need for negotiation. Together, these trends have produced an uneasy mix of sovereignty and pluralism, as contemporary jurisprudence limits settler authority without recognizing First Nations authority. Like historical practice, contemporary discourses around First Nations law can be understood in reference to these ongoing strategies of constitutional capture and refusal.

One important discourse surrounding the relationship between First Nations and settler legalities comes from the settler courts. As we have seen, the courts' position is that certain rights and titles,[105] which pre-existed settler sovereignty, were never legally extinguished.[106] As a result, the courts are prepared to recognize these rights and titles at common law. This recognition takes the form of an act of translation – the court identifies a pre-existing legal entitlement and then attempts to find or fashion an equivalent right[107] which can then be enforced, and infringed, by settler courts.[108] Conceptually, then, the Aboriginal rights paradigm works to recognize unextinguished First Nations law, but not unextinguished First Nations legalities. Rather, the courts' doctrines work to bring First Nations law into the settler legality, re-expressing First Nations legal concepts through settler institutions and world views.[109] Materially, this paradigm works to make settler courts the arbiters of First Nations law. Settler judges decide if a right has been established, what the content of that right is, and when it can be infringed – and they do it all unilaterally, without dialogue or negotiation. In both senses, First Nations law is "captured" by the settler constitution, in that it is made to work according to the logic of, and subject to the authorities designated by, the settler legality.[110] In this way, the doctrines of Aboriginal rights and title continue the trend of absorption which has animated settler jurisprudence for hundreds of years.

Borrows's highly influential approach encourages a more fulsome engagement, with Indigenous law not only as a source of rights, but as an independent legal tradition equal to the common law or civil law.[111] By encouraging judges to draw on a multiplicity of legal sources, Borrows seems to envision transforming federal law into a sort of intersocietal legality that is not reducible to either settler or First Nations traditions. Such an approach would refuse the logic of constitutional capture, not by refusing engagement with the settler system, but by indigenizing the settler system from the inside out. Rather than Indigenous law persisting at common law, we might say that both Indigenous law and common law would persist at intercommunal law. Henderson takes a related approach, insisting that treaties, properly understood, recognize the ongoing authority of independent First Nations and settler legalities, acting as something of an inter-legal constitution informed by both traditions.[112] Here, too, capture can be avoided through appeal to a hybrid framework.

Scholars like Mills posit a more radical form of non-absorption. For Mills, First Nations legalities are not only distinct from settler legalities, they are so ontologically different that the two are essentially incommensurable.[113] Since it is not possible to hybridize the two systems, any inter-societal law must inevitably adopt either a settler ontology or a First Nations ontology. In other words, there can be no truly inter-societal law – one framework must necessarily displace the other.[114] If it is the settler frame, it will be based on the logic of sovereignty and individualism, and relations will inevitably be unilateral. Only an Indigenous frame, with its embrace of interdependence, makes space for multilateralism. Mills therefore envisions the absorption of settler legalities into what he calls a "rooted" ontological framework, in an act we might call "reverse constitutional capture" or perhaps "treaty capture."

Legal discourse therefore continues to revolve around questions of absorption and externality, as authors debate to what degree First Nations legalities exist within or outside of settler legalities. In this way, contemporary discourses can be understood as extensions of longstanding historical strategies of constitutional capture and constitutional refusal.

Case Study: The Barriere Lake Algonquin and the Quest for a Tripartite Agreement

A series of jurisdictional conflicts between the Barriere Lake Algonquins (BLA) and the governments of Canada and Quebec provides a good illustration of the trends this chapter has canvassed.

In the 1760s, the BLA negotiated a treaty with the French and British crowns assuring Algonquin neutrality in imperial struggles and signifying mutual respect and non-interference.[115] By the 1990s, over-hunting and logging on their territories made the Algonquins think that their agreement needed to be revisited. They approached the governments of Canada and Quebec, as heirs to the English and French crowns, to negotiate a trilateral framework for resource extraction, including comanagement and revenue sharing across the traditional territory.[116]

Settler governments, however, quickly began to favour the comprehensive land claims process instead.[117] Under this process, First Nations make ownership claims over their traditional territory and then exchange the Aboriginal rights flowing from those ownership claims for rights approximating fee simple title to a small percentage of their land. In the end, claimants are left with rights which are squarely internal to, and regulated unilaterally by, the settler legal system. In this sense, the CLCP is another mechanism of absorbing First Nations legalities into the settler authority system – reducing multiplicity to nested unilateralism. The BLA were emphatically uninterested in this process. Rather, they insisted on their status as an independent governing authority that must be negotiated with continually on a trilateral basis.

After prolonged conflict, settler authorities sought to impose a new leadership on the BLA that would not press the trilateral issue. A series of leadership battles and underhanded tactics ensued.[118] Ultimately, the federal government placed the BLA's finances under third-party management, effectively seizing financial control of the community.[119]

In response, the BLA launched a series of direct actions, including blockades to prevent logging on their territory, road checkpoints to regulate traffic in the territory, occupations of government offices to demand a return to trilateral negotiations, and reclaiming Victoria Island – a stone's throw from Parliament Hill.[120] Police responded with arrests, fines, property confiscation, and violence. In essence, settler governments had refused a multilateral legal frame and insisted on a unilateral approach, forcing the BLA to respond in kind with unilateral enactments of their own law in order to signal the continuing plurality of the legal landscape. The BLA also repeatedly took its case to the UN, especially the Permanent Forum on the Rights of Indigenous Peoples, where it insisted on the international nature of their relationship to Canada and Quebec and the binding international force of their original treaty.[121] Predictably, Canada relied on the exclusivity of territorial sovereignty to argue that any issues located within Canadian borders were necessarily a domestic concern.[122]

To this day, the BLA continue to insist that their relationship to Canada and Quebec is regulated by a treaty which is still in force, and that this treaty needs to be renewed in the form of the trilateral framework. In contrast, Canada and Quebec continue to claim that the BLA's rights and title are internal to Canadian law and subject to unilateral arbitration by Canadian courts, legislation by Canadian legislatures, and the discretionary acts of Crown ministers.

The approach taken by Canada and Quebec is consistent with the larger pattern of attempted absorption. From the imposition of *Indian Act* band councils in place of traditional leadership structures to the CLCP's domesticating structure to their non-engagement with

international fora, the Canadian strategy has been to deny legal pluralism and reposition the BLA and their lands as internal, and therefore
subordinate, components of the settler legal order. Likewise, the BLA
have engaged in a series of distance-maintaining manoeuvres, centring
their original treaty, appealing to international law, and directly enacting their own legal order in a variety of ways in order to signal their
continued independence and force multilateralism. In all these ways,
the BLA dispute illustrates the larger trends and strategies which animate the relationship between settler and First Nations legalities.

Conclusions

As we have seen, the relationship between First Nations and settler
legalities is complex and contested. Nevertheless, certain patterns
can be traced. Taken as a whole, these patterns suggest two broad
arcs.

First, settler legalities sought to absorb and internalize First Nations
legalities, bringing them gradually within their own conceptual and
institutional frame in a prolonged project of constitutional capture,
thereby subordinating First Nations law to a settler legality and creating a system based on sovereign unilateralism. Thus, settler authorities' perceptions of First Nations law slid gradually and inconsistently
from an external view of First Nations legalities as foreign nations to
an intra-imperial view which saw First Nations as autonomous units of
the empire to a customary law approach which saw First Nations law
as internal to domestic colonial law to an Aboriginal rights approach
which sees First Nations law as a source of rights within the settler
constitution.

Second, First Nations have sought to maintain distance and exterior-
ity from the settler legality, engaging in varied strategies of constitutional refusal, thereby affirming the presence of their own independent
legalities. By appealing to international law and imperial authorities,
centring treaties, taking direct action to define and protect their laws,
creatively using settler legalities to open spaces of relative autonomy,
and continuing their legalities independently, First Nations have sought
to assert and reassert their legalities as external, persisting, and coequal
with their settler counterparts, thus re-centring the need for multilateralism and forcing limited concessions from the settler judiciary.

Together, these patterned arcs have produced a number of limits on
settler authorities' discretion and preserved some space for First Nations
legal agency, as in the renewed recognition of treaties or the jurisprudence of Aboriginal rights and title. However, these concessions are

defined and enforced unilaterally by settler institutions, allowing settler authorities to understand them as internal to and consistent with settler sovereignty. Contemporary jurisprudence therefore combines elements of constitutional capture and constitutional refusal in complex and challenging ways.

Chapter Three

Economic Practices

The exercise of authority involves not only *imperium* – or authority over people – but also *dominion* – or authority over things.[1] The following chapter takes up this dimension of the relationship between First Nations and settler authorities, exploring how changing property relations are challenging and being shaped by sovereignty.

Following Nichols, I contend that shifting property relations can be fruitfully understood through two interwoven processes – alienation, or the dispossession of resources, and diremption, or the reconceptualization of those resources.[2] Tracing these two processes, I argue that conceptions of economic authority, like conceptions of political and legal authority, have gradually become more total and exclusive. As land and labour became commodified, they became subject to increasingly absolute control. At the same time, physical control over property has also been concentrated in a small settler elite. Together, the processes of alienation and diremption have produced what we might think of as the sovereignization of the material sphere, as economic practices produce private relations that increasingly resemble, support, and facilitate sovereign forms of authority.[3]

Alongside these processes of alienation and diremption, however, are notable counter-practices of persistence and adaption, as First Nations embrace, resist, withdraw from, and integrate new economic forms into their existing economic structures in complex adaptive acts, creatively maintaining distinct economic structures that continue to involve overlapping claims and negotiated forms of economic authority. The sovereignization of economic practice is therefore ongoing, partial, and contested.

Of course, each of these trends is subject to a great deal of local and temporal variation. Nevertheless, the connections between the conceptualization of property, the allocation of property, and the broader colonial frame can be traced through several lose phases. During the initial encounter, private authority was closely tied to political and social systems and ownership rights tended to be diffuse. Both First Nations and settlers were accustomed to overlapping property claims within their own economic systems and both accepted overlapping claims from the other. As the settler economy pivoted toward enclosed agriculture, however, land ownership became increasingly commoditized and ownership rights became more centralized. At the same time, First Nations and settler land uses came into conflict, driving processes of dispossession. Eventually, the alienation of First Nations land and resources facilitated a massive concentration of capital and simultaneously created a class of landless settler and First Nations labourers. Deprived of ownership rights in land, labourers were forced to rely on their ownership of their own bodies, selling their time to the rich. Labour, too, was being commoditized, further concentrating both material resources and private authority claims. As this dynamic matured, the owning class became less tied to particular places and thus even less embedded in political and social systems. As a consequence, private authority is increasingly unfettered and increasingly concentrated. First Nations, through fierce advocacy, have preserved some forms of economic authority and wrested new concessions in recent decades, making Indigenous consent increasingly relevant to economic practice. After centuries of dispossession, however, dire economic need puts many nations in a difficult negotiating position.

Ultimately, these intersecting trends have produced an asymmetrical relationship between a settler-dominated capitalist market and a multimodal[4] First Nations economy which persists alongside it, troubling sovereign forms of *dominion*. The following chapter will explore these processes, following their development through four historical phases before examining some of the most prominent practices and discourses that continue to drive these processes today.

Four Phases of Economic Relations

The Early Contact Period: Embedded Production and Mutual Subsumption (Contact—~1725)[5]

In examining early economic practices in the relation between settlers and First Nations, two things stand out. First, early economic practice was deeply embedded in political and social systems and characterized by overlapping, negotiated property claims that bear little resemblance to sovereignty. Second, early trade patterns do not revolve centrally around either alienation or diremption.

On both sides of the encounter, authority over property was, in large part, a function of political and social systems. English and French monarchs granted lands to lords in exchange for economic and military support, and those lords granted tenure to peasants in exchange for the same.[6] Each of these parties had certain rights in relation to land. The rights now associated with a property owner were then unbundled and widely distributed along the social hierarchy.[7] The colonial trade followed the same structure – monarchs granted trading monopolies to groups of investors, almost invariably lords themselves, who turned a profit in exchange for service to empire, much like feudal landholders.[8] These "companies" had all of the military, diplomatic, and governance authority needed to enforce their monopolies, and acted largely as independent geopolitical actors pursuing a combination of imperial expansion, mercantilist advantage, and personal profit.[9] Prices were often set by the government, certain trade items like brandy were prohibited while others were encouraged, and the state subsidized trade as necessary to offset potentially disruptive market fluctuations and maintain alliances.[10] Lines between state and corporation, politics and market were, in this sense, extremely fuzzy, and economic authority was layered.[11]

First Nations economies and property-holding practices varied widely, but lands and resources were typically vested in family groups or clans and held through some form of contingent proprietorship,[12] and kin and allied groups were frequently entitled to make claims on the proprietors' territory or resources.[13] As in Europe, ownership was tightly tied to social and political systems, with the gift economy serving to create social obligations, mediate disputes, conclude wars, consummate alliances, and, of course, meet material needs.

On both sides of the encounter, then, authority over property was a layered, conditional affair in which no one could claim absolute or exclusive authority. Settler–First Nations relations did little to change this, with overlapping claims and negotiated authority being the norm. English settlers, for example, commonly made annual gifts, perhaps understood as something like rent or tribute, for land that they "owned" under treaty, even making payments to multiple First Nations claimants for the same parcels.[14] Even then, proprietary rights rarely entirely excluded the sellers from continued use, with provisions for continued First Nations hunting, fishing, and travelling rights being common.[15]

Trade, too, initially fed existing economic institutions on both sides of the encounter, with neither economy displacing the other either materially or conceptually. On a material level, trade allowed each party to partially subsume the other into its own economic cycles and institutions.[16] For Europeans, fish and fur provided inputs and goods for resale across Europe, tying First Nations' economic production into existing networks of mercantilist, proto-capitalist circulation. For First Nations, European trade goods were largely incorporated into local gift-reciprocity economies, reinforcing existing economic structures.[17] Both sides retained meaningful control of their resources and modes of production.[18]

Conceptually, trade was typically an ad hoc mixture of gift-based exchange and proto-capitalist market exchange. Systems of advance payment, for example, were understood as loans by the French and as gift exchanges by their partners, with actual practice showing elements of both.[19] Likewise, pricing reflected both the kin duties of local Algonquin systems of exchange and the profit motive more familiar to European traders.[20] Ultimately, these compromises were ambiguous enough that each party could understand the relationship largely as an extension of their existing economic institutions and ideologies.[21]

Ince, drawing on Marx, calls this phase of interrelation "formal subsumption." In essence, "capital subsumes the labor process as it finds it," drawing on First Nations economic structures for material inputs which help grow the proto-capitalist settler economy but do not actively transform or usurp First Nations modes of production.[22] Contrary to Ince's progressivist narrative, however, processes of subsumption in this era were largely bidirectional. Even as First Nations labour and resources were feeding growing imperial economic systems, so too European labour and resources were incorporated into existing First Nations economies and lifeways. Thus, early practices of authority over property bear little resemblance to sovereignty, and neither alienation nor diremption appear as central features of the early encounter – or rather, both processes were loosely mutual.

The Middle Period – Serfs Up: Agricultural Enclosure, Commodification, and Dispossession (~1725–~1840)[23]

As time went on, a combination of increased expenses, over-hunting, and market saturation led to declining profits in the fish and fur trades,[24] and the settler economy began to pivot more strongly toward agriculture and resource extraction.[25] The shift from fur to agriculture would prove a major milestone in the economic relationship.

Changes in agriculture in Europe would also prove significant for the colonies. In Europe, the old feudal system was beginning to dissolve. Especially in Britain, previously common land and layered feudal holdings were increasingly being "enclosed" or transformed into privately owned parcels.[26] In this new system, property rights that were once diffused between lords and serfs became increasingly concentrated in the property owner. In that sense, land was transforming from a political good to something closer to a commodity under the total control of its owner.[27] As a result, economic authority was becoming less directly embedded in political systems, and *dominion* was becoming increasingly exclusive and absolute.

Enclosure also created a class of dispossessed peasants whose resistance threatened domestic stability in Europe.[28] Colonial settlements provided an outlet for restless, dispossessed labour, mollifying domestic unrest with the promise of cheap or even free farmland overseas.[29] The business of settlement also provided a place for newly enriched landlords to invest their excess capital, and the tax revenues it generated provided for national defence.[30] In mutually supporting cycles enclosure progressed, trade grew, and settlement expanded, following the same agricultural economic model being pioneered in the metropole.[31]

These two trends – the expansion of the settler population and the pivot toward enclosed agriculture and the exclusive conceptions of land ownership that enclosure entails – put settler economies into more direct competition with the economies of their erstwhile partners as newly arrived settlers enclosed First Nations' hunting, fishing, agricultural, and silvicultural lands for use as private farms. Alienation therefore became a major feature of the economic relationship.

As property rights within settler society became more centralized, so did ownership claims against Indigenous peoples. More and more, colonial authorities negotiated boundaries and limits to settlement, dividing the land into more or less exclusive First Nations and settler territories. As we have seen, the Royal Proclamation worked to conceptually divide the continent into increasingly exclusive First Nations and settler zones.[32] Where pockets of First Nations people remained within settler zones, reserves were created.[33] Indeed, three concurrent acts of demarcation – the establishment of private property through settler agriculture, the definition of international borders, and the creation of reserves – worked in a mutually reinforcing manner to support a logic of exclusive, bounded ownership.[34]

First Nations responses to these more concentrated forms of property ownership varied. Many communities moved away from growing settlements and continued with their economic production and land-holding much as they always had, while others – particularly those increasingly encircled by settlement – leveraged European economies strategically.[35] Haudenosaunee leader Joseph Brandt, for example, used the increasingly definite US/Canadian border to advocate for an Indigenous buffer state[36] while leveraging solidifying property norms to argue that his people should enjoy the same exclusive, absolute title over their lands that settlers claimed over their own parcels.[37] Many groups also contested the use of watertight territorial boundaries.[38] The same treaties that established reserves, for example, also frequently included guarantees that First Nations be able to hunt, harvest, and travel in settler zones as they had previously.[39] Even inter-settler treaties like Jay's Treaty, establishing the US-Canadian border, included provisions for the free movement of First Nations.[40]

Conceptions of property and economic authority also informed First Nations' geopolitical and military decisions. Many First Nations in the St. Lawrence valley, for example, allied with the French rather than the British at least in part because the former interfered less in local land-holding. The French economy was less agriculture and more rooted in the fur trade and so was more reliant on First Nations labour and less reliant on land dispossession.[41] French landholding also remained more feudal, and thus more easily amenable to overlapping First Nations claims. The British, in contrast, were increasingly displacing Indigenous peoples as dense settlements grew. Indeed, Miller attributes Pontiac's war in part to a preference for the French economic model.[42] British victory over New France and her allies thus represented a victory for their more bounded, exclusive conceptions of ownership, which would hereafter dominate the settler approach.[43]

In all these ways, the conceptualization of land was becoming increasingly commodified, such that land ownership increasingly amounted to total and exclusive authority. Along with these conceptual shifts, the distribution of ownership was also shifting, as land became more centralized in the growing settler population.[44] Thus, the shift from fur to enclosed agriculture marked a major turning point, making processes of alienation and diremption a more pronounced feature of the relationship between First Nations and settler authorities. Indeed, a memorial address given to Prime Minister Laurier by Shuswap, Okanagan, and Nlaka'pamux chiefs stressed the difference between fur-trade settlers and later settlers, noting that the former were economically interdependent and therefore cooperative and neighbourly, while the latter wanted only to dispossess Indigenous peoples.[45] Little wonder, then, that many First Nations consistently centre the shift from a fur trade to an agricultural economy as mapping a broader shift from mutual respect to coercion and assimilation.

The Late Period – Work/Force: Commodified Labour and the Wage Economy (~1840–~1970)[46]

Over time, cumulative effects of the colonial trade, the enclosure of both domestic and colonial agriculture, and the intensification of colonial resource extraction would again transform property relations. Together, these processes generated a massive accumulation of capital in a small settler elite, facilitating large investments in productive systems and fuelling an industrial and commercial revolution.[47] Second, with many former subsistence farmers pushed off of newly enclosed land, enclosure created a massive pool of dispossessed labour with no means to support themselves. Thus, wage labour began to emerge as a major component of settler production, as the poor sold their time to the rich. Like land before it, labour was becoming commodified – something to be bought and sold like chattel rather than organized accordingly to political logics. As a result, labour was increasingly subject to the sort of absolute control that property owners exercised over other commodities.[48] The relationship between settler and First Nations economies tracks these shifts as resources were increasingly captured by industrial wage-based production.

As excess capital accumulated in Europe, the need for profitable investments led to a dramatic surge in canal and railroad projects across the colonies.[49] Thus, colonization continued to play a crucial role facilitating the growth of contemporary capitalism, providing much of both the capital and the investment opportunities. In contrast to the independent farms that had thus far been typical of the colonial economy, these projects required wage labourers.[50] Imperial policy shifted to meet these shifting economic needs. Whereas cheap or even free land grants in the colonies had once been an important means of building an agricultural base, imperial administrators now pushed colonial governments to artificially raise the price of land.[51] Where land was dear, new settlers would be forced to accept wage labour until they acquired enough capital for land of their own, ensuring a class of workers subject to the absolute authority of factory and land owners.

Efforts to dispossess First Nations and discipline them into wage labour were particularly aggressive. On reserve, welfare provision became tied to school enlistment, forcing recipients to adopt a sedentary lifestyle which rendered many First Nations economic activities unviable, thereby pushing parents into the labour force even as children were prepared for the same fate through industrial schooling.[52] Social programs worked to lessen reliance on kin ties and encourage dependence on the state and employer.[53] Staple resources, like cod, beaver, bison, and salmon also saw rapid industrialization as settler factories displaced First Nations harvesting and monopolized access in massive, society-changing acts of resource alienation.[54] First Nations workers were often brought into these factories, which became a major site of diremption as well. Labour was thus increasingly alienated into the settler economy even as it was reconceptualized as an object of hierarchical control.[55] For Ince, this stage marks the point at which processes of formal subsumption, which accumulate capital by engaging with non-capitalist economies without transforming their modes of production, gave way to real subsumption, which is characterized by a conversion to wage labour.[56]

First Nations reactions to these shifts varied widely depending on local preferences, strategic considerations, and the viability of the local First Nations economy. Some groups (like the Tsilhqot'in) withdrew from populated centres or took steps to push out settler populations, while others (like the Lekwungen) relocated to be near industrial centres in order to take advantage of wage labour opportunities.[57] Even these groups, however, typically incorporated the new wage relation into their own economic systems. Labour was often undertaken seasonally, forming a new part of existing resource rounds.[58] Often, companies dealt with bands at the community level, contracting with chiefs to supply labour at negotiated rates.[59] On an individual level, too, First Nations people often used wages as inputs into their own prestige economies, giving the proceeds as gifts rather than for personal accumulation.[60] To some extent, wage labour replaced declining traditional activities, especially where ecological collapse had made First Nations economies less viable. Generally, however, wages, like the trans-Atlantic trade before it, were layered on top of existing economic activities, creating a flexible, multimodal economy which remained distinctively First Nations.[61] Thus, First Nations continued to incorporate settler economic practices into their existing economic structures and concepts even as they were incorporated into settler labour markets.

First Nations were also active in some early labour movements, joining settlers who were also contesting the new wage labour paradigm.[62] In the decades surrounding the turn of the century, First Nations participated actively in many unions, though they were also subject to racist exclusion from others.[63] These institutions created a degree of mutual need between capitalist and worker, facilitating an era of active, if asymmetrical, collective bargaining that meaningfully compromised the absolute control of capitalists over their assets.

In all these ways, the growth of the wage economy signalled another series of important shifts in the relationship between settler and First Nations economies. As capital accumulation birthed a wage-labour market in settler societies, conceptions and allocations of *dominion* became more exclusive and absolute.

The Modern Period – Invisible Hands: Neoliberalism
and Neocolonialism (~1970—~Present)[64]

As the colonization process and the capitalist economy coevolved and solidified, the massive concentration of capital resulting from the colonial encounter, and from the industrial revolution and the transition to wage labour in particular, gave rise to enormous multinational corporations. These corporations were increasingly mobile and less tied to particular states or workforces and thus even less embedded in political and social systems. As a result, both organized labour[65] and government regulation were drastically undercut by the threat that capital would simply relocate to more pliable areas. An era of deregulation, de-unionization, decreased social spending, and privatization ensued, facilitating in turn a further concentration of wealth. In other words, the growing concentration of wealth made possible more absolute control of economic production, undermining the influence of workers and governments. This in turn facilitated the concentration of wealth, as alienation and diremption continued to feed one another.

Even the colonial functions of the state were, in a sense, subject to privatization as colonization came to rely less and less on the "visible foot" of state coercion and more and more on the "invisible hand" of economic desperation to secure access to First Nations lands and labour.[66] Around the world, the relationship between former colonies and former colonizers has become "indirect" with imperial powers "able to govern the conduct of the former colonies by a host of informal means, from economic aid, trade manipulation, and debt dependency to military dependency, intervention, and restructuring … They exercise various forms of inducement, constraint, channelling, and response, and employ various means, from economic dependency to military intervention, to try to control or govern the way the former colonies or 'developing countries' exercise their powers of self-government."[67]

Like the relationship between colonies and the metropole, the forms of control that settler authorities exercised over First Nations are also becoming subtler, more indirect, and more reliant on market compulsion instead of direct coercion. Consider Impact-Benefit Agreements, for example – with settler governments having already impoverished First Nations, first by dispossessing them of their land and resources and then by undercutting state welfare policies, companies can now secure cooperation by offering a small share of the profits dispossession generates. Given their often dire economic circumstances, First Nations' "consent" to such arrangements is given – and withheld – in a context of economic coercion. The Modern Treaty process plays a similar role, inducing First Nations to offer a more predictable investment environment by forfeiting vaguely defined but potentially expansive inherent rights for more tightly defined treaty rights, along with a sizable cash settlement.[68] In all these ways, access to First Nations land and labour is increasingly secured not through direct state coercion, but through the creation and weaponization of economic need.

The processes of alienation and diremption therefore continue today, taking new forms as the concentration of wealth and the sovereignization of property continue to build on one another recursively. These new strategies, like the approaches that preceded them, have been only partially successful. To varying degrees, many Nations maintain multimodal economies which are in many ways distinct from the settler economy.[69] In this context, many Nations use participation in the capitalist economy as an expression of their agency or even as an input into their own mixed economies. Indeed, many Nations are self-consciously working to rebuild non-capitalist economic practices old and new.[70] At the same time, many Nations are also working to resist the commodification of their lands and resources altogether, with battles against pipelines, logging, fracking, mining, hydrological power, and urban expansion now among the defining features of the settler–First Nations relationship and indeed, of the Canadian economy. Processes of alienation and diremption, like other processes of sovereignization, therefore remain ongoing, incomplete, and deeply contested.

Practices of Note

The relationship between First Nations and settler economies can therefore be understood through a number of loose phases, each of which occurred in different ways and at different times in different geographic areas. In the earliest periods, economic authority was embedded in local political structures and ownership rights tended to be diffuse, rather than total or exclusive. As the settler economy pivoted toward enclosed agriculture, land became commodified and ownership rights central-ized. At the same time, conflicting land uses increased competition between settler and First Nations economic models. Settlers began dis-placing Indigenous peoples and productive processes more intensely, capturing their lands and reconceptualizing them as the object of exclu-sive ownership rights. As colonial dispossession provided the raw capital to fuel the industrial revolution, wage labour came to the fore of the settler economy. Like land before it, labour was commoditized and subject to more absolute control. At the same time, wage-labour processes monopolized many First Nations resources, alienating them into settler hands even as they were reconceptualized as the objects of exclusive control. As the imperial economy globalized and solidified, corporations became less tied to particular locations, and thus even less embedded in local political and social systems. This facilitated even more absolute control of productive processes and even greater con-centrations of wealth. As a result, private authorities are increasingly able to rely on indirect forms of economic compulsion to access First Nations labour and resources.

Polanyi describes such shifts as a "great disembedding" – as land, then labour, and ultimately money itself become commoditized, they are dis-embedded from political systems.[71] This makes economic authority increasingly autonomous, and thus increasingly absolute. Ultimately, these shifts have produced absolutist conceptions of eco-nomic authority which closely mirror the concepts and allocations of authority associated with the sovereign state – just as we have one all-powerful sovereign per state, so we have one all-powerful owner per property. In this sense, the shifts surveyed above represent the sover-eignization of the economic sphere. First Nations continue to contest this sovereignization, resisting both the appropriation of their lands and their commodification. In limited ways, they have succeeded in maintaining forms of layered ownership and contingent authority. The following section explores four practices which continue to be crucial to the soverigntization of the material sphere today.

Treaty

Treaty provides a helpful illustration of how intertwined the politi-cal, legal, and economic aspects of sovereignization really are. As we have seen, shifting treaty practices reflect the shifting political relationship between First Nations and settler authorities as set-tlers worked to gradually redefine Fist Nations from something like allies to something like subjects. This process allows settlers to understand their authority as sovereign. Treaties therefore were and are a central means of state building. However, treaties have also played an important role as market-building mechanisms, driving processes of alienation and diremption. Indeed, the evolution of treaty practices maps onto shifts in the overall focus of economic production over time.

Originally, the economic objective for both First Nations and settler authorities alike was control of trade against rivals. Hence, treaties focused on trade and military alliances, with little interference in the internal affairs or productive processes of either people. As land became the predominant site of economic concern, so treaties shifted from documents of peace and friendship to something more closely resembling deeds of land cession. As agricultural production, trade, and later industry came to depend on wage labour, treaties began to promote the conversion to agriculture and industry by providing agricultural implements and European-style education and training, and encouraging sedentary lifestyles that undermined traditional economies and increased dependency on wage labour.[72] Finally, as capitalism matured and Canada solidified as a resource economy, the Modern Treaty process arose as a means of creating legal certainty for resource extractors by both alienating large chunks of land to the Crown and by reconceptualizing what remains as private property.[73] Thus, treaties have been used to pursue a shifting battery of ends, working to re-allocate and redefine property with considerable, but limited, success.

The present phase of treaty making continues many aspects of earlier treaties, converting the layered ownership claims invoked by Aboriginal title into estates which more closely resemble exclusive, fee-simple lots, while at the same time reallocating the vast majority of the claimed land to settler governments. However, modern treaties also often contain provisions for comanaged land, spaces of concurrent jurisdiction, or land where government ownership is subject to certain continuing First Nations rights. To this degree, Modern Treaties are not only an instrument of alienation and diremption, but also a vestige of multilateralism and a partial exception to increasingly exclusive and absolutist property forms. Indigenous advocacy has been central in maintaining this limited space of shared or overlapping claims. Indeed, contemporary negotiations frequently feature proposals for more layered conceptions of ownership and jurisdiction.[74] In this way, the treaty processes illustrate both the shifting goals and the contested, incomplete, and partial nature of alienation and diremption processes.

Aboriginal Title and Land Ownership

One of the most foundational practices of alienation and diremption comes, ironically, in the conceptualization and recognition of First Nations property rights.

Voicing the dominant ideas of the time, theorists like Locke argued that ownership arose when a person used their labour to enclose and improve land.[75] This line of thought effectively equates enclosure with ownership itself, such that unenclosed land could also be understood as un-owned or "waste" land.[76] This move justified the dispossession of the English peasantry, re-conceptualizing their commonly held property as waste and facilitating its appropriation by private interests. As we have seen, this was a crucial driver of settler migration and of the consolidation of the capitalist class. At the same time, the equation of enclosure with ownership also justified the dispossession of Indigenous peoples, re-portraying their commonly held lands as unowned as well, and hence open to appropriation. Thus, a massive act of diremption, which worked to deny previously recognized forms of common ownership, in turn facilitated two massive and mutually reinforcing acts of alienation.

Building on this reasoning, settler courts found that First Nations did not own their lands but that they did use their lands and hence had some usufructuary rights. So conceived, actual ownership and sovereignty vested in the Crown, while Aboriginal title is merely a burden on the Crown's underlying title.[77] In other words, Aboriginal title conveys a proprietary interest in the land, while Crown title conveys sovereignty. The recognition afforded to First Nations and settler claims is thus deeply asymmetrical. The nature of the Crown's claim is that it gives rise to sovereignty, while the nature of First Nations' claims is that it gives rights and interests enforceable against the sovereign.

Still, each of these overlapping claims works to limit the other in asymmetrical ways. First Nations rights to title land include a right to exclusive use and occupation. However, this right is subject to inherent limits[78] and may be infringed for public benefit under a justificatory scheme in many ways looser than that involved in fee-simple expropriation.[79] Before it was constitutionalized in 1982, title could also be extinguished through legislative fiat.[80] Aboriginal title is also inalienable except to the Crown.[81] Thus, the range of permissible uses is narrower and potential infringements broader than those associated with fee-simple ownership, as Crown claims work to limit First Nations claims. Settler governments, for their part, can alienate title lands or infringe on title rights, but only subject to a justificatory test.[82] The government also

owes First Nations a fiduciary duty in managing title lands, obligat-
ing them to consult regarding land-use decisions and further limiting
their absolute discretion.[83] Even where title is unproven, certain limits
apply to government discretion.[84] Ownership of title lands is therefore
layered, and authority over them is not absolute. In keeping with the
presumption of Crown sovereignty, however, both sets of limits are
defined and enforced unilaterally by settler institutions.

Moreover, Crown title can be "perfected" by purchasing the Aboriginal proprietary interest; but First Nations' title can never be similarly
perfected by purchasing the Crown interest. Nor can new title interests
be purchased. Title therefore creates a unidirectional flow of land from
First Nations to settler authorities, and a unidirectional transformation
of title land into private property.[85] Indeed, the Royal Proclamation
recognized title not so much in order to secure a bundle of rights, but
rather to facilitate a process of purchase and enclosure. In all these ways,
even the recognition of First Nations proprietary interests was done in
such a way as to facilitate processes of alienation and diremption. It also
participates in a by-now familiar trend – First Nations claims are recognized, but simultaneously subordinated to Crown sovereignty. It is
also worth noting that, in practice, only one nation in the entire country
actually has legally recognized Aboriginal title.[86]

Reserve land is recognized in a similar way. Technically, even First
Nations reservations are owned by the Crown and only held in trust
for First Nations.[87] In fact, repeated efforts have been made to break
reserves up into parcels of individual property, both completing the
diremption of reserve land and facilitating its alienation through private sale.[88] First Nations have resisted such proposals, as well as the
Crown's authority over reserve lands, and have succeeded in imposing
a fiduciary duty on the Crown's management of reserve lands.[89]

The ways First Nations proprietary rights have been recognized therefore work not only to recognize competing claims but also to arrange
them hierarchically, and thus to facilitate both their alienation and their
conversion to private property. Such practices have had considerable,
but partial, success and remain ongoing today. Now, reserve and title
lands function as zones of partial exception troubling the Crown's ownership claims much the same way First Nations political agency troubles the Crown's sovereignty claims.

Marketization through Ecosystem Collapse

Settler authorities have also worked to incorporate Indigenous peoples
into the capitalist economy by causing the collapse of local ecosystems,

which in turn precipitates the collapse of the traditional economies that are based upon them. With ecosystem collapse, traditional economies become less and less viable, and Indigenous peoples are thereby forced into wage labour and resource extraction. Sometimes this process has been an unplanned side effect of colonial activity. At other times, eco-system collapse has been disturbingly deliberate.

In one fascinating study, Greer shows how roving farm animals acted as a major force of dispossession.[90] In the east during the Early Period, for example, private farm holdings were typically paired with com-mon grazing lands at their peripheries. Grazing animals dramatically changed the ecosystem of these areas, causing their First Nations habi-tants to relocate in pursuit of game and other sustenance. In this sense, ecological change acted as the forerunner of colonial expansion, con-tinually pushing the frontier one step past the actual settlements and facilitating their march west. As ecosystems changed and traditional First Nations economies became less viable, First Nations were forced to either retreat to more remote areas, participate in the growing agri-cultural and wage industries, or some combination of both.

Of course, the overhunting of fur-bearing animals was also a major contributor to the decline of the fur trade, marginalizing First Nations labour and feeding the subsequent redevelopment of the economy along agricultural and industrial lines. Indeed, by the early nineteenth century the Hudson's Bay Company was maintaining its profits by diversifying away from the fur trade, employing First Nations labour in agriculture and handicraft production.[91] While the collapse of fur-bearing ecosystems may not have been planned, it was a clearly foresee-able consequence of systematic over-exploitation.

Most dramatically, the commercial over-exploitation of staples – especially cod, bison, and salmon – for domestic settler consumption or export undercut the mainstay of First Nations production on the coasts and prairies, quickly putting formerly prosperous peoples in a desper-ate economic position.[92] Agricultural and later wage labour came to fill the gaps, being integrated in and in some cases becoming dominant parts of existing economic structures. In some cases, particularly on the prairies, settlers and governments deliberately decimated the buf-falo not only to trade their skins, but to weaken the resistance of First Nations rivals and forcibly open up their lands and labour supplies.[93]

In the contemporary era of resource capitalism, this trend continues. Resource extraction tends to scare off game. It also produces incredible amounts of pollution and disrupts local habitats. As a result, the pene-tration of the resource industry tends to undermine existing subsistence activities, tilting the balance in these mixed economies increasingly in favour of wage labour or government dependency.[94] In fact, even conservation efforts can reinforce this trend, undermining First Nations economies by preventing traditional harvesting activities.[95]

In sum, ecological destruction works to undermine First Nations economies and thus to reinforce emerging absolutist property forms.

Marginalizing Economic Inclusion

While the settler state has worked relentlessly to bring Indigenous lands, resources, and labour into the capitalist economy, it has also erected systematic barriers to successful participation in that economy. The result is a sort of marginalizing inclusion – one that works to keep Indigenous peoples on the margins of capitalism, tied to the system but often unable to thrive within it. This situation in turn creates structural poverty which is continually leveraged to open more lands, resources, and bodies to exploitation.

On the face of it, the overarching goal of government policy has been assimilation and incorporation into the workforce. At the same time, however, many government actions worked to limit the success of First Nations in the capitalist-market economy. Sometimes these acts came as a response to public pressure from settler competitors. At other points governments pursued their own interests, looking to channel resources toward tax-paying settlers as a means of lining state coffers. At other times it is doubtful that governments understood the effects of their policies at all. Nevertheless, legislation worked to simultaneously integrate and exclude First Nations land, labour, and production.

For example, as industrial agriculture took off on the prairies, settler negotiators used treaties to encourage agricultural settlement, channelling annuity payments into farm implements and instructors.[96] At the same time, governments, under pressure from local populations, refused to provide adequate machinery, delivered aid at inadequate levels, manipulated prices, and enacted legislation to disadvantage First Nations farmers.[97] Similarly, a myriad of federal and provincial laws limited the other types of occupations Indians could participate in, curtailed grazing and water rights, prevented the pre-emption of land, and excluded First Nations from acquiring fishing, timber, or trapping licences.[98]

The government monopoly on land purchases too was ostensibly designed to protect First Nations from economic exploitation. Instead, governments used their monopoly to suppress land prices. From 1860, they also took over management of the funds generated by land sales and, by and large, used them to finance broader government expenditures.[99] Reservations were often put on land of little economic value, and the communal nature of reserve property prevents First Nations from accessing credit.

Today, this tradition continues as Aboriginal rights are specifically held to protect only a modest, subsistence lifestyle and thus to preclude serious acquisition.[100] Modern treaties also take up this limitation. Schouls, writing of the BCTP, notes that "all resource harvesting rights are to be restricted to domestic uses only, cannot be sold to anyone other than Aboriginal persons, and are to be subject to federal and/or provincial measures necessary for conservation, public health, or public safety. There is to be no commercial Aboriginal right with respect to the harvesting of fish, wildlife, or migratory birds ... and, while the First Nations will possess treaty rights to harvest fish, wildlife, and migratory birds for domestic purposes, the annual total allowable catch per First Nation will be determined by the federal minister."[101] Thus, a process otherwise geared toward capitalist-market participation also includes significant barriers to that goal.

This sort of double-movement is confusing, but it plays at least two important roles for settler society. First, by deliberately impoverishing First Nations, the state undercuts their capacity to resist ongoing acts of colonization. In particular, entrenched poverty makes First Nations people economically dependent on state payments and corporate partnerships. Poverty also makes it easier for governments to buy off First Nations with desperately needed funds, putting many nations in the impossible position of choosing between their rights, laws, and traditions on the one hand and the material needs of their people on the other. Second, the ongoing marginality of First Nations helps ensure the continued concentration of wealth in settler populations.

Thus, a dynamic of inclusion/exclusion becomes as important to market-building and market-preserving processes as it is to state-building and state-preserving processes.

Multimodality, Persistence, and Resistance

As we have seen, First Nations have long participated in settler economies, both voluntarily as they seek opportunities and as a result of ecosystem sabotage, dispossession, coercive assimilation, and economic need. However, many Nations have also gone to extraordinary lengths to maintain traditional economic practices, gift economies, and landholding patterns. Many more are consciously regenerating economic practices based on uncommodified understandings of, and decentralized authority over, land and resources.[102]

In many instances, these two modes of private authority and economic production sit alongside one another, with many Nations drawing on both chattel ownership and gift exchange in dynamic ways to meet shifting needs and exploit shifting opportunities.[103]

Often, however, this persistent diversity remains a site of conflict. The clash between corporations and governments asserting absolute, exclusive property claims and commoditized understandings of land against First Nations, asserting uncommodified understandings of land and less absolute understandings of ownership has become one of the defining political and economic contests of our time.

These acts of persistence and multimodality continue to shape property formation, troubling both processes of dispossession and diremption. By maintaining and enacting their own forms of *dominion*, First Nations (re)create a situation of overlapping claims. By defending those claims, they render private authority less absolute and exclusive in practice.

Contemporary Economic Discourse: Progress or Theft?

Treaties and reservations, marginalizing inclusion, ecological destruction, Aboriginal title, and multimodal persistence have therefore proven to be important practices, continuing long-standing trends in the relationship between settlers and First Nations economies. In particular, these practices shape two contested processes: the alienation of First Nations resources into the hands of a small, predominantly settler upper class, and the re-imagination of First Nations resources, lands, and labour as capitalist commodities which are no longer subject to multiple, contingent ownership claims but instead are the object of more unilateral authority. Nevertheless, First Nations continue to enact economic practices which exceed the capitalist framework. In limited ways, they have succeeded in maintaining forms of layered ownership and contingent authority. As important as it is to understand these practices of transformation, the underlying discourses that legitimize and challenge them are equally important parts of the processes of economic colonization. In essence, the sovereignization of economic production and the associated absorption of First Nations economies is narrativized in one of two broad ways.

The first story comes to us from thinkers like Demsetz. This story argues that property regimes evolve toward efficiency over time in a spontaneous but inevitable manner.[104] Levmore calls this the "transaction-costs" explanation of economic change.[105] Basically, Demsetz argues that Europeans moved from decentralized, unbundled concepts of property and economic production toward increasingly spatialized, increasingly absolutist conceptions of property because the latter system had lower transaction costs and outcompeted the former. Once the new, more efficient model was introduced in the colonies, it outcompeted local decentralized economies as well. Demsetz uses the Innu[106] as an example. When colonial settlement gave rise to the commercial fur trade the value of furs rose sharply, which increased the externalities associated with open-access hunting. The Innu, Demsetz argues, began marking off their hunting grounds and allocating exclusive rights to hunt in certain places.[107] In short, they moved toward a private property regime voluntarily, for reasons of efficiency. Stories like this posit that the absorption of First Nations economies (and of the decentralized incarnations of settler economies) was largely voluntary, inevitable, and irreversible.[108]

Banner provides a second narrative, arguing that the costs associated with changing property regimes are so high that such transformations do not occur automatically, even when there are efficiency gains to be had. Rather, "societies [only] reallocate property rights when some exogenous political realignment enables ... benefits to be channelled disproportionately towards powerful and costs towards weak actors."[109] This set of political circumstances motivates the powerful to pursue changes in property relations that would otherwise not occur, often acting through the existing governing institutions which they control. Levmore calls this the "interest group theory" of property transition, revolving as it does around the ability of a particular elite to push for, and monopolize the benefits of, reorganization.[110]

This story relies on evidence that suggests common farming and other decentralized techniques are often quite efficient for their users.[111] Enclosing land as private property, however, allows the benefits of the land to be disproportionately captured by the wealthy title holders. Indeed, Banner notes that in Europe, in the colonies, and in First Nations communities, the distributional effects of the transition were typically highly skewed toward an emerging merchant elite.[112] In settler communities, private landholding also facilitated taxation, giving the state an incentive to support the merchant class in order to fund its own expansion and defence, as capitalist-market formation and state formation fed one another.[113] Similarly, some First Nations political systems may also have been captured by pro-enclosure elites whose wealth allowed them to monopolize existing political channels for private gain.[114] In this story, the changing economic relationship is not driven by diffuse efficiency gains for society at large, but rather by concentrated relative gains for the specific elites who pursue them.

There are three especially important differences between these accounts. First, if economic transitions are driven by efficiency gains then they are both desirable and largely inevitable. If, conversely, economic transitions are driven by the interests of powerful elites then they are contingent, resistible, and reversible. Second, the transaction-costs account suggests that First Nations poverty is the result of a stubborn refusal to fully modernize and will be relieved by overall efficiency gains once First Nations communities become fully capitalist. The interest-group narrative, on the other hand, suggests that First Nations poverty is the result of a political order which channels the benefits of economic production disproportionately toward powerful settlers and, to a lesser degree, to a small First Nations elite. It will be relieved only through structural reform to the colonial relationship. Third, the transaction-costs narrative suggests that First Nations economies are simply unviable in the contemporary era, that "there is no alternative" to the liberal-capitalist paradigm. Conversely, the interest-group narrative suggests that First Nations economic forms are still viable, and perhaps even superior in their distributional consequences.[115]

Today, governments and corporations continue to push forward and attempt to legitimize the processes of alienation and diremption by promoting versions of the transaction-costs narrative – arguing that bringing First Nations land and labour even more fully into the settler economy is the only way to alleviate poverty. Opponents resist dispossession and diremption on the grounds that they have created First Nations poverty by channelling First Nations resources to settler elites. The narrativization of the relationship between settler and First Nations economies is therefore contested, and this contestation remains crucial to contemporary patterns of property formation today.

Case Study: The Hudson's Bay Company

The remarkable existence of the Hudson's Bay Company (HBC), which spans nearly the entire history of intensive settler–First Nations contact on Turtle Island,[116] illustrates many of the recurring patterns that animate the economic relationship between settlers and First Nations.

In the early era of the fur trade, the Company was granted a trading monopoly to lands larger than all of Europe. Like many chartered companies of the era, the HBC was a profit-driven corporation but also a semi-autonomous agent of colonization with governance powers of its own.[117] Indeed, the Company maintained independent diplomatic and military relations, administered its own system of justice, and maintained its own system of governance for settler populations.[118]

The HBC was thus a "company-state," a sort of hybrid structure whose independent authority claims coexisted with imperial claims in complex and non-exclusive ways.[119] The Company also treated with local nations to secure lands for forts and settlements, despite pre-existing royal grants,[120] and initially made little attempt to extend their governing institutions to Indigenous peoples. The authority of the HBC was thus non-exclusive of First Nations claims as well. The result was a highly layered environment where no party enjoyed unilateral control and where politics and economics remained closely intertwined.

For the most part, early trade was mutually beneficial and land competition between settlers and First Nations was low.[121] The trade was a heavily "administered" mixture of barter and market exchange which could be easily incorporated into both European markets and local gift economies.[122] In particular, the Company began offering loans and supporting non-hunting members of the community, in an early use of welfare as a means of creating early relationships of dependency.[123] First Nations used seasonal employment and welfare benefits to supplement their own economic activities.[124]

In 1869–70, the HBC, under pressure from the imperial government, sold its charter rights to Canada, retaining only its trading posts, the areas around them, and a "fertile belt" of farmland stretching across the prairies.[125] The public and private functions of the Company were being separated, with the nascent nation of Canada assuming governmental functions and the HBC transitioning to a private fur-trading and agricultural land-speculating corporation.[126] Through strategic land sales in the fertile belt, the Company participated in a wider shift toward agricultural development which was now displacing First Nations' economies.

The end of the HBC's monopoly also signalled important shifts within the fur trade, as company paternalism declined, competitive markets emerged, and employment came to more closely resemble the wage relation.[127] Increasingly, government transfer payments and treaty annuities took the place of Company welfare,[128] maintaining relations of market dependence but now in a way that was not tied to a particular employer. First Nations traders responded to this newly competitive market, leveraging competition strategically in ways that showed both an understanding of the new price mechanism and also an ability to maintain distinct economic forms and logics.[129]

Over the course of the Late Period, the Company used well-timed land sales to supplement the fur trade and build up capital.[130] As the settler population in the West grew and the railroad and canal booms created a local wage-labouring consumer base, the Company invested its real estate profits into a massive expansion of its stores – now remodelled as department stores catering to the urban settler middle class instead of traders and trappers.[131] Like the broader economic relationship, the activities of the Company were becoming increasingly defined by wage labour and consumption.

At the dawn of the modern era, control of the company – like the Canadian constitution – was finally transferred from London to a board of Canadian governors.[132] In practice, however, powerful interests in London continued to exercise considerable indirect control[133] in ways that invoke the neocolonial tactics characteristic of the era. The welfare programs the company had pioneered also became an important tool of indirect settler rule in the North – one Paine has called "welfare colonialism."[134] In recent years, Indigenous peoples have also shaped these payment systems, as a series of land claims and treaties have created room to negotiate.

The story of the HBC is thus in many ways an illustration of larger historical processes. Initially, First Nations economies were incorporated into emergent mercantile capitalism even as settler economies were incorporated into local economic, political, and ceremonial systems. Ownership was layered, multilateral, and contingent. Over time, a transition to agricultural land-speculation created increased resource competition and alienation. The profits that land sales produced generated the necessary capital, and the land sales themselves generated the necessary consumer base for a transition toward wage labour and consumerism in the form of urban department stores. Over time, the corporate structure of the Company shifted to involve more indirect forms of imperial control, even as Company welfare policies were used to exert indirect influence over many First Nations. The history of the HBC therefore illustrates recurring patterns of mutual incorporation, displacement, discipline, and neocolonialism that have characterized the broader relationship between settler and First Nations economies, showing accelerating processes of alienation and diremption on the one hand and creative acts of adaptation, cooption, and persistence on the other.[135]

Conclusions

In sum, the economic relationship between Indigenous and settler peoples has historically been one of mutual, asymmetrical, and recursive transformation. Through this process, both the nature of property and its allocation would become far more centralized, exclusive, and absolute.

When the encounter between First Nations and settler authorities began, both social groupings organized production through unbundled, non-exclusive, and contingent forms of property ownership.[136] Early contact did little to change any of this. As the colonial economy became more agricultural, however, First Nations and settler economic forms were increasingly in competition. This triggered large-scale alienation, as settler farmers displaced First Nations and their economic modes. At the same time, enclosure popularized more total and exclusive conceptions of land ownership. Land was therefore being reconceptualised as a commodity, as well as reallocated. Over time, the accumulation of capital from cheap colonial resources and overseas monopolies fuelled an industrial and commercial revolution in Europe and eventually in the colonies themselves. Labour, too, became commodified, something to be sold and then subjected to the absolute control of the buyer. Industrial processes continued to displace First Nations economic practices, drawing Indigenous peoples into the wage relation in complex and uneven ways. Like land before it, labour was being reconceptualized even as control over it was redistributed. As neoliberalism developed, the wage-labour relation became more precarious, and the forms of alienation and diremption it facilitates became more intense and indirect.

Thus, First Nations and settlers alike saw disaggregated bundles of economic control centralize over time, gradually and unevenly giving way to a form of economic organization in which ownership is more exclusive and absolute. At the same time, actual ownership also concentrated in a small cast(e) of settler elites, whose newly exclusive claims gave them disproportionate control over the economic process. This control did not, however, flow to settlers in an undifferentiated manner. Rather, huge portions of settler society were also seeing their lands and independence eroded and their ideologies reworked in favour of the same elites.

First Nations have fought against dispossession and diremption alike, building multimodal economies, resisting dispossession, and asserting layered ownership rights. These acts of resilience and resistance have created or preserved limited forms of layered authority claims, and with them, limited spaces of multilateralism.

Nevertheless, there is a clear correlation between the conceptualization and allocation of private property and the broader relationship between First Nations and settler authorities. As economic relations became more centralized, absolutist, and asymmetrical, so too did the political and legal relationships between communities. In this sense, "European statehood did not emerge alone but as a political form specific to capitalist social relations that presumed a constitutive distinction between public power, exercised through claims of sovereign jurisdiction (imperium), and private power, exercised by private law ownership (property, dominium)."[137] Thus, Greer concludes that "owning and ruling, though analytically distinct, were intimately connected aspects of early modern empire building,"[138] and, we might add, they remain intimately connected aspects of the ongoing process of colonization today.

Chapter Four

Pluralism and Sovereignty in Canada

The preceding chapters have explored the political, legal, and economic dimensions of the relationship between settler and First Nations authorities in order to see how the lived practice of pluralism is reshaping, and being shaped by, concepts of sovereignty. The following chapter explores the connections between these three fields of practice, mapping the overall patterns they reveal.

Connecting Political, Legal, and Economic Practices in Canada

In all three fields, early practices modelled forms of shared authority as both parties engaged in one another's decision-making structures, created codecision structures, and negotiated the conditions of coexistence. Over time, however, settlers used force, fraud, and demographics to become physically dominant and gradually imposed more sovereign forms of authority.

Politically, settlers gradually re-imagined their authority as territorially exclusive and began purchasing or ignoring First Nations authority. First Nations have both leveraged exclusive forms of authority and fought to reassert shared forms. Settler authorities have been forced to offer concessions like self-government and comanagement regimes, but worked to make these subordinate to their own institutions and thus compatible with their sovereignty claims. Both the allocation of authority and the conceptual understanding of authority have therefore shifted as authority consolidates in settler hands, so too it is re-imagined as increasingly total and exclusive. These shifts have been, and continue to be, fiercely contested.

The legal dimensions of the relationship show a similar process of material and conceptual transformation. Where both parties once recognized one another as something like independent international actors and sought forms of shared authority, settlers gradually worked to re-imagine First Nations as subcomponents of their own empires and polities. In so doing, they sought to absorb First Nations institutions and thereby render them consistent with their sovereignty claims. First Nations have both made use of settler legal institutions and also maintained their own and appealed to international law in attempts to re-centre their independence. Today, Indigenous law exists both within and beyond settler legal institutions, creating a context that is both pluralist and deeply asymmetrical. Again, changes have occurred at both the conceptual level, as First Nations are re-imagined as domestic subjects, and at the material level, as settler courts monopolize *de facto* authority and again, these shifts continue to be contested today.

The economic dimensions of the relationship tell a related story. While economic practices were initially embedded in each party's broader political, social, and ecological systems, settler authorities have increasingly worked to dis-embed their own economy while simultaneously working to undermine First Nations' economic systems and draw First Nations into settler systems of production and ownership. As the settler economy became less embedded, it also came to reflect more total and exclusive forms of ownership. At the same time, systemic dispossession concentrated material resources in settler hands. Once again, both the conceptualization and allocation of economic authority has transformed over time. First Nations have both engaged in the settler economy and also persisted in their own, and their resistance to ongoing alienation and diremption remains a major feature of the Canadian economy today.

The result of these contested patterns is difficult to describe – the relation bears aspects of both sovereignty and pluralism, genocide and mutual support, occupying an ad hoc, dynamic, and contested space that draws on multiple forms of authority in pragmatic ways that do not map neatly onto either sovereignty or pluralism. Nevertheless, when taken together, the three dimensions of the relationship do suggest a broad historical arc – what I have called a sovereignization process, as settlers work to both reconceptualise authority as increasingly total and exclusive, and reallocate authority in increasingly concentrated ways. First Nations have contested this sovereignization process, exerting agency both within and beyond settler structures to force a continued degree of multilateralism. As a result, settler authorities have had to make a series of concessions, but they have done so in ways that seek to maintain both the self-image of sovereignty and the lived reality of deep power asymmetry. Aboriginal rights and title, the Modern Treaty process, comanagement agreements, and a host of other accommodations can all be understood in this light, as attempts to re-describe First

Nations authority as a component part of settler authority structures, thereby offering practical concessions in a manner consistent with both a self-understanding of sovereignty and a lived reality of physical dominance. As Richard Day puts it, "this context is *post*colonial, in the positive sense that the discussion is happening at all. But it is post*colonial* in the negative sense that the parameters of the discussion are still set by state peoples who are reluctant to give up the advantages they have gained through a history of domination and exploitation."[1] In the end, political, legal, and economic practices all suggest a relationship where authority is deeply asymmetrical but not quite total or exclusive enough to be properly termed sovereign.

The dispossession and displacement of First Nations' political, legal, and economic institutions and ontologies has been a major feature of the sovereignization process. However, settler conceptions of authority have also shifted in and through the encounter. Indeed, the pragmatic demands of colonization played a substantial role driving forward European concepts of sovereignty, bringing international law,[2] theories of property ownership,[3] and understandings of political community[4] to revolve more closely around the ideal of total, exclusive authority. At the same time, the colonization process worked to concentrate material wealth and power in certain segments of the settler population, greatly facilitating the rise of both the capitalist economy and the bureaucratic state.[5] The beneficiary elites used their power not only to usurp First Nations lands, laws, and political systems, but also to seize control of settler systems and remake them in their own image.[6] To say that settlers drew First Nations into a system based on sovereignty is therefore too simple – rather, sovereignty arose in and through the colonial encounter itself.

Academic discourse struggles to reflect this contested historical arc, working to capture the ad hoc, not-quite-sovereign, not-quite-pluralist nature of authority in the relationship between settler and First Nations authorities, and the blend of violence and cooperation, oppression and accommodation through which it has been pursued. Chief Justice Marshall, for example, concluded in 1832 that First Nations were "domestic dependent nations." By accepting a treaty relationship, and through the sheer reality of power asymmetry, he reasoned that First Nations had sacrificed some, but not all, of their original sovereignty, like vassal states of the European Middle Ages.[7] Here, both consent and coercion ground settler authority and the result is a situation somewhere between sovereignty and subjecthood. More than a century later, Alan Cairns echoes Marshal in arguing that settlers have already monopolized land and resources and, indeed, depopulated, impoverished, and traumatized Indigenous communities, leaving them too dependent on settler support to constitute nations of their own, and that many are proud Canadians anyway.[8] Instead, Cairns suggests we think of First Nations as "citizens plus" – that is, not as members of distinct polities, but as members of the settler polity who are entitled to special rights not afforded to other Canadians. Again, a mixture of force and consent gives rise to a situation somewhere between sovereignty and pluralism. Both authors seek to capture the asymmetrical multilateralism that defines the relationship. Where Marshal emphasizes a diminished form of nationhood, a century and a half later Cairns emphasizes an enhanced form of citizenship, illustrating the arc of historical development, as settlers work to transform First Nations from something like allies to something closer to subjects in a project deeply shaped by, but always at some distance from, sovereignty. Neither formulation, however, adequately expresses the relationship. Indeed, to ask if First Nations and settlers constitute two polities or one is to miss the complexity of lived practice and, crucially, both ignore the constitutive and ongoing contestation at its heart.

Thinking Sovereignization in Canada through Symbiogenesis

Sovereignty, then, and its cognates "nation" and "subject," are all poor descriptors of actual practice in Canada. Modifiers like "dependent nations" and "citizens plus" attempt to stretch concepts derived from sovereignty to capture these practices, but with limited success. If we want to understand the relationship between First Nations and settler authorities we need concepts that better capture the role of interdependence and plurality in the practice of authority – all without losing sight of asymmetry and oppression.

Haraway's use of the concept of symbiogenesis is helpful for thinking through this paradoxical coexistence and intermingling of pluralism and sovereignty.[9] As Haraway explains, it's not always possible to conceptualize a complex organism as a totally unitary, self-contained lifeform. Over time, as organisms coevolve in close proximity, they can become so entwined that they actually depend on one another to perform key biological tasks, even as each continues to pursue a quasi-independent course of development based on its own interests.[10]

Sometimes, a larger organism will attempt to absorb its partner(s) entirely, incorporating them into itself and thereby subsuming its partner to its own biological functions and interests. This process is not always successful. Sometimes, the partner organisms refuse to be absorbed, staking out their own independent existence in asymmetrical relation to their would-be host. The result is a coconstituted being, comprising two distinguishable beings, each constitutively shaped by their mutual interactions.[11] Over time, the two coevolve as a unit in relation to other units even as each continues its own independent evolution and maintains external relationships independent of its partner.

Similarly, we might say that the settler polity has attempted to absorb First Nations into itself, re-casting First Nations authority as something internal to settler institutions. First Nations, however, have refused to be absorbed. While they do participate in settler institutions and processes, they also exercise independent authority in ways that exceed and sometimes disrupt the settler system. This in turn shapes settler society. Indeed the settler state, its parent empires, and international law itself were all deeply shaped by their encounter with, and eventual exclusion of, First Nations diplomacy.[12] Likewise, contemporary First Nations are also deeply shaped by the encounter.[13] Yet each retains a separate identity with distinct, even contradictory needs. Rather than a body politic, we have been left with a holobiont politic: a community of asymmetrically related units who intra-act to constitute one another and their shared community in ways that can be both antagonistic and mutualistic.[14]

Symbiogenesis therefore provides a concept capable of holding at least some of the contradictions of this relationship in tension. The term allows us to think interdependence and impunity together, to see how each is a contingent, interactive, and intra-active function of the other.[15] In short, it helps us to cognize a complex interplay between pluralism and sovereignty – a situation shaped by both, but reducible to neither.

PART 2

Practices of Pluralism in Europe

Practices of Pluralism in Europe

Chapter Five

Political Practices

By the end of the Second World War, Europeans had for centuries experienced the extreme forms of international and domestic violence that a world of sovereign states can produce. The exclusive, total nature of sovereign power reached its highest expression in fascist and totalitarian regimes, and so too did violence and oppression. Desperate for a way to secure peace, protect human rights, and rebuild material prosperity, Europe's leaders were ready to countenance forms of multilateralism that challenge and exceed sovereign forms of authority. Thus, discussion of a European community gained new salience as European authorities contemplated an unprecedented set of multilateral institutions designed to prevent war, stifle totalitarianism, and promote commerce between European states.[1]

From the beginning, there were fierce debates about what such a union would look like, how expansive its powers would be, and how it would relate to the sovereign state. Supranationalists favoured a powerful Union positioned hierarchically above the state, while intergovernmentalists envisioned a voluntary organization subordinate to the state. In the face of persistent disagreement, the Union began with a modest set of institutions regulating the production of coal and steel in order to prevent any one nation from amassing the materials of war. Over time, these institutions grew and expanded, as diverse actors wrestled with divergent aspirations and shared needs. Those who favoured a strong Union and those who favoured strong states compromised recursively.

Alongside this contest between supranationalist and intergovernmentalist understandings of the Union, another axis of contestation has also shaped the EU's development. This contest pits a preference for technocratic decision-making against a preference for democratic decision-making. Here, too, the political structure of the Union reflects elements of each.

Together, these two cross-cutting axes of contestation have shaped the Union's development. I contend that this process has given rise to an ambiguous political entity that is neither sovereign over nor subordinate to its members. Instead, national and supranational actors have forged interpenetrating institutions where shared decisions can be reached and legitimized with neither a shared understanding of what sort of political community the Union represents, nor a shared understanding of where power does, or ought to, lie within it. In this sense, the political dimensions of the integration project can be understood as a de-sovereignization process that remains ongoing, incomplete, and deeply contested.

The following chapter explores the evolution of the European community's political organs, analyzes some key practices that political actors have used to navigate their interactions, and examines how the authority of the state and the Union have been narrativized in political science literature. Finally, I conclude with a case study showing how Europe's failed Constitutional Convention illustrates both many of the tensions and practices that drive the integration process and the ways that once-sovereign powers are increasingly shared, divided, and pooled.

An Overview of the Political Relationship (~1950–2020)

Describing an Elephant: Two Positions on the Nature of European Integration

Since the inception of the European Steel and Coal Community in 1955 – and, indeed, even before[2] – attempts at European integration have been marked by two conflicting positions, one seeking a federal or quasi-federal "United States of Europe" and the other envisaging an international community of independent states more akin to the League of Nations or the UN.[3]

The supranationalists, as I will call proponents of the first position, come in many stripes. Some were ardent federalists, advocating the immediate establishment of a popular, European- level government complete with all or most of the hallmarks of a traditional state.[4] Others suggested the gradual extension of functional agreements overseen by apolitical technocrats, with minimal public input, as a means of slowly binding nations together.[5] Seeing an outright transition to a sovereign European government as impractical, these functionalists suggested that mutually advantageous deals on specific issues would, over time, create spill-over effects, leading supranational structures to accumulate more and more power and legitimacy until a continental government had been achieved.

While the former saw political legitimacy as essential to overcoming parochial nationalism and forging a European demos, the latter favoured depolitizing integration as much as possible precisely in order to avoid needing to meet such a challenge head on. Garnering elite support for particular projects would be less demanding than popular support for a new federation. Nevertheless, both functionalists and federalists advocated an integration process which would create a distinct, sovereign political entity above and independent of the nation states.

On the other side of the debate, the inter-governmentalists – defenders of the national state – fought for forms of integration that privileged and preserved state sovereignty.[6] They saw integration as a form of coordination between state parties who would retain ultimate authority rather than transferring it, all at once or gradually, to a supranational structure. They argued that absent a European demos, only the state could provide a forum for democracy and human rights, and that any continental union must necessarily consist of voluntary cooperation between fully sovereign states.[7]

Thus began a long debate over the shape and nature of the European project – would states feature as minor actors within a new continental sovereign, or would states remain the central actors, using the union as a mere tool to achieve their autonomous ends? This debate is clearly reflected in the integration process itself.

From World War to Tug of War: A Brief History of European Integration

In many ways, the evolution of the EU treaties can be read as a tug of war between supranationalist and inter-governmentalist positions over time. As the respective academic and political potency of these two visions of integration waxed and waned, different periods were marked more strongly by one or the other.[8] Yet at no point has either position ever been totally dominant; even the most inter-governmentalist periods of the EU's development also helped to create and strengthen independent European institutions, and even the most supranationalist steps made concessions to the continuing sovereignty of member states.

As a result, the EU has come to reflect a complex and sometimes contradictory compromise between these divergent positions. To this day, there is enough of both positions in the treaties that debates about how best to understand the nature of the EU as a political community continue unabated. In the end, the prevailing wisdom is that the EU is politically *sui generis*, what Delors famously described as an "*objet politique non-identifié*," lying somewhere between a traditional federation and a typical international organization.[9]

The early European Coal and Steel Community, for example, featured a supranational Commission empowered to make binding decisions which state parties were obligated to obey and a supranational court to settle disputes.[10] Yet the arrangement also created a strong Council comprising state governments to steer the process and another to wield legislative power. This mixed institutional arrangement and the ideological tension it expresses have been central to the European community ever since.

Indeed, subsequent moves toward a European Economic Community shifted the continent closer to a supranationalist vision by dramatically expanding community competences, but did so only by taking the issues its member states found most sensitive – for example, defence – off the agenda.[11] The EEC also fulfilled federalist ambitions by creating a nascent European Parliament, yet at the same time strengthened the role of the Council in community decision making.[12]

Compromises in the treaties themselves were also borne out in practice. In 1965, inter-governmentalists led by French President De Gaulle pushed for consensus decision making in the Council, while supranationalists preferred qualified majorities[13] which could push integration forward over the objections of reluctant states. The result was the famous "Luxemburg compromise" – Council decisions would formally require only a qualified majority, but in practice no decisions would be taken unless full consensus could be achieved.[14] This de-facto veto swung the balance of power within the community in favour of national governments. Yet this period also saw the EEC gain control of its own budget (1970) and led to the first direct elections of the European Parliament (1979).

The Maastricht Treaty is widely seen as swinging the balance toward supranationalist ambitions once more.[15] In a move to help build a European demos, it created European-level citizenship and coined the name European Union, rather than European Community. It also created codecision mechanisms between the Parliament and Council, empowered the Parliament to block appointments to the Commission, and enabled it to request the initiation of new legislation. Furthermore, Maastricht created new supranational institutions like the European Central Bank (ECB) and European System of Central Banks (ESCB), set in motion the creation of the euro, and expanded Union competences into new areas. At the same time, however, it enshrined the much-celebrated principle of subsidiarity, whereby EU programs are always implemented by the smallest level of government capable of doing so.[16] According to this principle, member states implement the majority of Union policies themselves, according to domestic institutions and policy priorities. The Union only acts directly when member states would be unable to act effectively on their own. This strategy gives member states a continuing role even in areas that are technically Union competencies, making EU supranationalism less top-down and drawing state apparatuses into pursuing Union goals. This important principle was paired with the principle of conferral, stating that the Union only had such competences as the member states conferred on it.[17] Together, these doctrines worked to protect national sovereignty, ensuring that supranational bodies could only act where states had empowered them, and even there only to the degree that supranational solutions were truly necessary.

Even more tellingly, Maastricht established a "pillar" structure for the community, separating competencies into three areas, each governed by different rules.[18] The Economic Pillar would be more strongly supranationalist, driven primarily by the Commission and controlled by qualified majorities in the Council. The Social and Security pillars, however, would be driven by the Council and require consensus. This structure allowed states to cede more power in areas perceived of as peripheral to their own sovereignty while retaining a greater degree of inter-governmentalism in the areas that concerned them most. In fact, even the more heavily supranationalist developments were balanced by a number of opt-outs and exceptions, allowing states to determine their degree of integration according to local political preferences.

The subsequent Constitutional Treaty failed when French and Dutch voters rejected it in referenda, but its content was largely carried forward into the Treaty of Lisbon. Lisbon further consolidated the Union, but it was deeply shaped by the failed Constitutional Treaty and consciously shunned more ambitious federalist language and content.[19] Provisions regarding the primacy of European law over national law were made deliberately ambiguous, and Article 347 established a sort of reserve sovereignty for member states, safeguarding their supremacy in areas that had not been delegated up to the EU. Lisbon also consecrated the emerging "Open Method of Coordination" approach, a system of non-binding benchmarks and monitoring processes which allowed the Union to suggest wide-ranging policy goals but fell short of actually empowering it to enforce them. Instead, these goals would take the form of suggestions, to be implemented or ignored at the pleasure of the member states. While Lisbon dissolved the pillar structure established in Maastricht, it retains separate decision-making processes for security and foreign policy.[20] In the end, critics attacked Lisbon from both sides, with some claiming it was too supranationalist and others decrying the resurgence of inter-governmentalism.[21]

Similarly, the United Kingdom's dramatic exit from the European Union shows how hotly contested the issue of supranational control can be. With significant portions of the population feeling a loss of control stemming from EU influence, migration, and the globalization of capitalism more generally, nationalist politicians were able to argue that Britain needed to take back its sovereignty. Prime Minister Cameron, however, was able to leverage the ambiguous nature of the Union to propose something short of outright separation – a newly negotiated deal that would make UK membership more inter-governmentalist in nature. While the public ultimately voted against this proposal by slim margins, the topic has continued to define British politics for years. Indeed, even negotiations over how to leave the Union became a sight of struggle, with some suggesting a more nationalist approach and others supporting some degree of continued integration. In the wake of Brexit, many on the continent hope the United Kingdom will act as a warning to the Union and push it in a more inter-governmental direction before more countries decide to leave.[22] Others, however, see new potential for a deeper supranational Union now that the Council has lost one of its most consistently nationalist and inter-governmentalist members. Others still see the peaceful exit of a member as a sign that existing institutions work well.[23] Thus the meaning of Brexit remains ambiguous. Likely there is some truth to all three narratives. So far, at least, it does not appear that Brexit has heralded seismic changes in the EU-state relationship more broadly.[24] Rather, Brexit represents an especially high-profile episode in an ongoing series of contests that have always been inherent to the integration process.

In retrospect, then, the development of the EU treaties reflects a long ideological struggle between inter-governmentalist and supranationalist positions. During the initial period, supranational trends seemed ascendant, while the period between the EEC and the Single European Act (SEA) seemed to signal the victory of inter-governmentalism before Maastricht saw the pendulum swing back the other way. The defeat of the constitution, Brexit, and the recent euro and migration crises may suggest that the tide could be turning yet again. Yet even within each period, the dominant theory coexisted uneasily with, and made serious concessions to, its competitor. In this sense, the European integration process has been a process of compromise, one which has allowed fundamental questions about the very nature of the process itself to go unresolved.

Consider the current legislative balance. Only the supranational Commission may introduce legislation. Once proposed, legislation follows a variety of decision procedures based on the subject matter at hand. In the Ordinary Procedure,[25] also known as the Co-decision Procedure or Community Method, Parliament considers the Commission's proposal and offers amendments before sending the bill to the inter-governmentalist Council. The Council may then either pass the law or send it back to Parliament with amendments of its own. Parliament can accept these amendments or make further changes. The Commission then expresses its opinion on those changes. If it objects, the Council can only pass the law through unanimous consent. If the Commission assents, ordinary qualified majorities will suffice. Thus, the Commission acts as an agenda setter and gatekeeper, while Parliament and the Council fill the legislative role jointly.[26] Decision-making authority is therefore shared, requiring the support of both inter-governmentalist and supranationalist bodies.

This Ordinary Procedure is, however, also subject to a wide spectrum of variations. Certain issues require only a Consent Procedure, meaning Parliament must agree but cannot offer amendments.[27] In other areas, Parliament must be consulted but its opinion is non-binding.[28] In certain rare areas, the Council and Commission can legislate without any parliamentary involvement at all.[29]

Overall, this system can be characterized as a hybrid authority structure supported by a system of dual legitimacy, blending inter-governmental and supranational institutions and theories of legitimacy in a dynamic, shifting, and asymmetrical manner that allows the fundamental tension between them to persist unresolved.[30]

Technocracy, Democracy, and European Integration

While state and EU actors are playing out an important contest between supranationalist and inter-governmentalist visions in Europe, citizens, NGOs, and social movements are also actively contesting and influencing how and where authority operates. These struggles often transcend supranationalist and inter-governmentalist stances, geographic divisions, and even traditional left/right political cleavages, revolving instead around the contested nature of political authority. For technocrats, authority is legitimate when it produces desirable outcomes – growing economies, personal security, etc. For participatory democrats and populists, authority is legitimate when it flows from legitimate inputs – that is, from the preferences of the people. This contest between "output legitimacy" and "input legitimacy" is essential to understanding the development of the EU.[31] This axis of contestation focuses not on how authority is distributed between EU and national governments, but rather on the nature of authority itself, regardless of where it lies. Like the contest between supranationalism and inter-governmentalism, this contest has also shaped the Union over time.

From the beginning, the development of the EU was marked by a profound mistrust of democratic politics.[32] In the wake of popular fascist dictators and communist revolutions, many felt that democratic publics were simply too ill-informed, too emotional, and too easily captured by rent-seeking special interests or populist demagogues to reliably set good policy.[33] As a result, securing adequate output-legitimacy requires a degree of elite rule. The Union was deliberately designed with this idea in mind and often favours decision making by national elites and technical experts. The leading role of the Commission, for example, reflects not only supranational motivations, but also technocratic ones, as unelected experts hold an exclusive right of legislative initiative. Likewise, the early Parliament was purely advisory; decisions were reached in Council. Parliament's power has since grown, but it remains in a relatively weaker position.[34] This is both a means of ensuring inter-governmentalist influence and a means of insulating the integration process from direct democratic pressures. Thus, both supranational and inter-governmental processes often act as technocratizing processes at the same time, insulating political processes from direct democratic input, oversight, or control.

For a time, this strategy appeared to enjoy broad support. Indeed, the early stages of European integration have been called the era of the "permissive consensus" as the public, presumably satisfied with the substantive achievements of the Union, seemed largely unconcerned with how decisions were being reached and by whom.[35] Indeed, many Europeans remain "euro-instrumentalists" – they support integration when it serves their interests or suits their policy preferences, and defend national sovereignty when it does not.[36]

As time went on, however, the democratic credentials of the political system have become more salient and the issue of inputs has been re-politicized. Indeed, the following decades saw Danish voters reject the Maastricht Treaty, Danish and Swedish voters reject introduction of the euro, Irish voters reject the Nice and Lisbon treaties, and French and Dutch voters reject the Constitutional Treaty.[37] In many cases, these rejections came despite the support of major parties, unions, and business associations and, tellingly, despite the fact that integration was otherwise popular.[38] A substantial share of the "no" vote was motivated not by substantive objections, but by disapproval of the elite-driven integration process.[39] Clearly, the permissive consensus had collapsed. In its place, the so-called democratic deficit has become a major focus of contestation and debate.[40]

Institutional actors have responded to these sentiments. Most obviously, the power, and in particular the oversight abilities, of the European Parliament have been consistently growing.[41] In the 1990s, just as contemporary populism was gathering steam across the political spectrum, the Commission also undertook a large-sale effort to incorporate civil society actors into EU decision-making practices – what is often called the "participatory turn" in European politics.[42] The Commission proceeded to make consultation with civil actors widespread, inviting their participation in committees, aggressively funding European-level groups, and working to both cultivate public debate and provide points of contact with decision-makers.[43] The Constitutional Convention embodied a similar ethic and was explicitly mandated to bring Europe closer to its citizens,[44] with the drafting process consisting not only of an Inter-governmental Conference between the member states, but also a Constitutional Convention engaging a variety of interest groups, NGOs, regional representatives, and ordinary citizens. The text of the Constitutional Treaty, and the later Lisbon Treaty, also provided for elements of direct democracy, including a European Citizen's Initiative (ECI), through which citizens could ask the Commission to legislate on any issue within its competencies.[45] Member states, too, have responded to increasing pressure to involve the public in the integration process. While only nine referenda were held on EU issues before 1992, more than thirty have been held after, despite the significant complications such campaigns can present.[46]

In many ways, however, this package of democratic reforms remains largely in keeping with the technocratic vision of the Union. While civil society has been brought into the policy process, its role is purely consultative – actual decision-making power continues to rest with EU and state officials.[47] Similarly, the real power shaping the European constitution lay at the inter-governmental conference, with many participants in the Constitutional Convention feeling that the pretense of input was simply used to generate legitimacy for pre-determined ends.[48]

The ECI, too, is a rather weak form of democratic participation. Even if a Citizen's Initiative is successful in gathering enough signatures to suggest legislation, the Commission is under no obligation to actually propose the suggested legislation; and even if it did, the Parliament and Council are under no obligation to pass that legislation. Thus, citizens cannot legislate directly without the approval of all three central institutions. Actual authority remains concentrated in political and bureaucratic leaders. As a result, the participatory turn fails to really speak to the vision of democracy that civic actors are voicing.[49] Unsurprisingly, these reforms have done little to calm talk of the democratic deficit.[50] Indeed, the idea that Brussels bureaucrats were thwarting the will of the British people was a major theme of the Brexit campaign.[51] More broadly, this concern is at the heart of the contemporary "populist zeitgeist"[52] or "populist moment,"[53] as European politics is increasingly framed as a contest between a corrupt but powerful elite and a virtuous but disenfranchised people who must reclaim power, either through participatory measures, as with left-populism, or through an authoritarian leader who embodies the ordinary people, as in right-populism.[54]

Contests between technocratic and participatory visions of integration therefore represent a major axis of contestation, one that has shaped the Union in ongoing ways. This contest sits alongside the supranationalist v. inter-governmentalist contest, the two cross-cutting in complex ways and bringing both the distribution and the nature of authority into question. As with supranationalist v. inter-governmentalist debates, the contest between technocratic and participatory or populist understandings of the Union has never been resolved definitively, giving rise instead to mixed institutions, hybrid approaches, and ongoing contestation.

Practices of Note

Political institutions in Europe therefore reflect at least two cross-cutting contests, one between supranationalist and inter-governmentalist visions, and one between participatory and technocratic visions. These contests concern both the allocation and the nature of authority, and partisans of each position have proven able to shape the integration process. Over time, these contests have produced a series of mixed authority structures which mediate between multiple sites and kinds of authority. As a result, Europe has gradually and unevenly moved from a political context defined by state sovereignty toward less exclusive, total forms of authority. This de-sovereignization process has been iterative, uneven, and contested. It remains incomplete and ongoing to this day.

This process relies in important ways on its own ability to leave important questions about the exact locus and nature of authority unresolved. The following section explores a number of practices that have facilitated this ambiguity and thus, the de-sovereignization process itself.

Functional Bracketing

The remarkable accomplishment of constructing the most integrated region in the world without a clear consensus on exactly what was being built – where authority does, would, and should lie within the Union – has relied in part on an explicit strategy of setting the most contentious issues aside.

The founders of the ECSC, many of them committed functionalists, had faith that integration could begin in the least controversial areas and gradually spill over into more difficult issues as citizens' interactions with, and loyalty to, the international level increased.[55] This approach was reaffirmed with the Spaak Report of 1956, in which the Inter-governmental Committee decided explicitly to focus negotiations on less contentious issues like trade barriers while leaving more controversial political issues aside.[56]

This theme has been a hallmark of European integration. In general, policy integration has far outpaced political integration. Even in the policy domain, issues perceived as tangential to state sovereignty have seen more integration than areas like foreign affairs, defence, criminal law, languages, etc. Perhaps the most notable discrepancy in this regard is the robust trade and economic integration in contrast to relatively weak social policy and service provisions. While there have long been calls – both official and unofficial – for a "Social Europe," social policy remains largely the purview of individual member states.[57] These areas, which both require and reinforce bonds of solidarity and identity within political communities, lie closer to the core of state competencies. They are also deeply controversial, both within the member states and especially at the European level, where issues of redistribution and burden-sharing tend to arouse strong passions on all sides. As a result, these areas have seen relatively little integration, with social policy continually deferred to future negotiations.

Even economic integration has been primarily focused on trade barriers and monetary policy, with the more sensitive issue of budgetary control remaining almost entirely untouched until the recent euro crisis forced leaders to take action. Indeed, the Eurozone had long been, and still is, criticized for being lopsided – characterized by monetary union and budgetary nationalism.[58] Once again, we see that more difficult, more controversial issues are often set aside in order to facilitate progress in other areas.

The Syrian refugee crisis illustrates this trend well. Thus far, the EU has given enormous amounts of aid to Syria's neighbours in exchange for their help settling refugees before they reach Europe's shores.[59]

They have signed agreements with Turkey, providing money and policy incentives to the Turkish government in exchange for their help re-settling refugees already in Europe.[60] They have strengthened external borders and stepped up naval patrols.[61] All of these are relatively uncontroversial steps for an affluent continent faced with a politically volatile situation. As of yet, however, European leaders have not been able to reach effective agreements on the most critical issues – how many refugees to settle, where in the Union to settle them, and how to manage the process.[62] In a context where the migration decisions of one country effect outcomes in others – Greece can open its borders and Germany will see increased migration – a common policy on the right of refugees to enter, travel around, and settle in member countries seems like an obvious candidate for supranational resolution. Yet public passions run high and are not uniform throughout the Union. As a result, responses remain fractured, with policy developments occurring almost exclusively at the national level.

In light of the EU's history, this is hardly surprising. Bracketing controversial issues and setting them aside for later has long been an important strategy in the integration process. At times, it has facilitated progress when disagreements threatened to undermine the integration process. However, as the refugee crisis, and perhaps the near dearth of social policy, illustrate, this strategy can also threaten the integration process. Seen in this light, the fact that inter-governmentalist, supranationalist, technocratic, and participatory positions all remain viable interpretations, and potent shapers, of the integration process seems less flabbergasting. In many ways, the EU is a Union that survives, prospers, and grows precisely by harnessing its own ambiguity.

Multispeed Integration

Another key practice which has allowed the integration process to proceed without settling fundamental questions regarding the locus and distribution of sovereignty is what has been referred to as the EU's "variable geometry" or "multi-speed integration."[63] In essence, integration is not uniform – some countries are integrated more or less depending on local preferences.

One benefit of a functional, issue-by-issue approach to supranational governance is that different groupings of countries can agree on different issues. Thus, the borders of the EU, the Eurozone common currency area, the European Economic Community, the Common Defense Policy (CDP), and the border-free Schengen Area, to take just a few examples, are not totally coterminous. To illustrate, the United Kingdom was, until recently, an EU country outside of the Schengen Area[64] which did not use the euro;[65] Monaco, despite not being a member of the EU or Schengen, does use the euro;[66] while Switzerland, a non-EU state that does not use the euro, is within the Schengen.[67] In this way, European integration is not a one-size-fits-all arrangement. Different countries are able to integrate differently and to different degrees.

To this end, opt-outs have been an important feature of the integration process. The Danish, for example, received opt-outs concerning defence policy, among other things.[68] In exchange, Denmark agreed to recuse itself from decisions on these matters. British objections to Union social policy similarly led the other member states to conclude an agreement on that matter between themselves.[69] Each round of enlargement also saw transitional measures designed to allow certain portions of community law to be delayed or accepted gradually.[70] Eventually, the Maastricht and Amsterdam treaties formalized this strategy, establishing a series of opt-outs and "enhanced cooperation procedures" that allowed states to conclude agreements which, although part of EU law, would not apply uniformly throughout the territory.[71]

These provisions, designed to keep a handful of reluctant states from paralysing the integration process, have been seen as a backdoor for European federalism – a means for a vanguard of committed countries to lead the way toward an ever deeper Union.[72] For others, opt-outs and enhanced cooperation procedures are a means of ensuring member state sovereignty over the pace and extent of the integration process – a way to keep the states in the driver's seat.

The procedures themselves reflect this ambiguity. While nation-states can use them to shape the Union, the Commission and Parliament also play a decisive role in deciding whether to proceed and governing when countries can join or leave such arrangements.[73]

The Open Method of Coordination (OMC) is another key feature of this variable geometry. In essence, the OMC is a voluntary mechanism whereby the Council sets policy goals and monitors their implementation by the members, without enforcing them directly or prescribing specific ways in which those goals should be pursued.[74] It is therefore up to the members to choose whether, and in what way, to pursue those goals.

In fact, even more traditional, hard-law mechanisms which apply throughout the entire Union are subject to considerable variation by virtue of the principle of subsidiarity.

Directives and regulations, although passed at the supranational level, are implemented at the national or even sub-national level. As a result, these acts are incorporated into domestic law in different ways in different countries, according to national traditions and policy preferences.[75] The presence of sub-national actors only complicates matters further, as the authority and status of these regions vary wildly.[76]

Ultimately, the result of these side agreements, opt-outs, enhanced cooperation procedures, transitional agreements, OMCs, subsidiarity variations, and treaty concessions is a highly variable, non-uniform sort of integration which, at least to an extent, allows states to position themselves along a spectrum of sovereignty. This allows each state to view its relationship with the Union, and the distribution of sovereignty between them, slightly differently. Such arrangements make *a priori* agreement on the fundamental nature of the integration process less important – in a very real sense there is no one single integration process or, for that matter, one single distribution of authority within it.

The recent drama surrounding the United Kingdom's membership in the Union provides an example. When British voters expressed discontent with the extent and specific contours of the integration process, Prime Minister Cameron set out to re-negotiate the terms of the United Kingdom's membership, seeking particular opt-outs, changes, and concessions which, in his view, would allow the United Kingdom to reassert key aspects of its own sovereignty while nevertheless participating in the integration process. In essence, he sought to adjust the United Kingdom's position on a sliding scale between national sovereignty and supranational participation. That he was unable to sell these concessions to the British public should not distract from the fact that the Union was able to offer such flexibility. Even the decision to leave the Union has not exhausted the multispeed dynamic, but rather triggered a series of negotiations designed to decide how far, and in what ways, the United Kingdom would remove itself from the Union.

Like the strategy of bracketing off broadly contentious areas, the strategy of allowing some states to integrate more than, or differently from, others allows the integration process to proceed without ever settling the question of whether the EU is a mere agreement between states, or something closer to a super-state.

Functional Legitimacy

While the EU's reliance on output legitimacy rather than input legitimacy has itself been heavily contested, it has also played a crucial role in allowing both the contest between supranational and intergovernmental visions, and the contest between technocratic and democratic visions to go unresolved.[77] In essence, such questions are decided on functional, rather than or alongside, principled grounds.

Consider, for example, the principle of subsidiarity. Member states implement Union policy according to local institutions, traditions, and priorities wherever possible, and the Union only acts directly when member states would otherwise be ineffective. In other words, the division of authority is functional, designed to meet policy goals as much as to balance political principles. In essence, authority lies wherever it needs to, fluctuating issue by issue, with its particular configuration at any moment justified relative to the desired output. Similarly, the Commission describes the participatory turn not only or even primarily in terms of democratic principles, but in terms of improving policy deliberation and therefore delivering more popular outputs.[78] Here, too, the role of the public in policy setting is justified largely on functional grounds.

Indeed, Isikel has argued that the integration process has become dominated by a logic of functional legitimacy, where discourse focuses on the tasks performed and goals accomplished by the Union rather than the nature of the Union itself or any principled arguments therefore.[79]

Rather than rallying citizens, or governments for that matter, around a theory of political legitimacy, elites have been rallying around particular policy goals.

For example, a 2016 pamphlet produced by the UK government to advocate for EU membership during Brexit discussions makes not a single mention of democracy, peace, political community, or individual rights (except the right to study and work abroad), but instead dedicates lengthy sections to the instrumental value of EU membership to the UK economy and its impact on the cost of living, opportunities to study and work abroad, and security cooperation.[80] Similarly, counterpoints place heavy emphasis on the uncertain economic results of leaving the Union. There is scarcely a principled argument to be found.

In this way, the overall ambiguity as to the precise nature of the EU and the exact grounds of its authority have been facilitated by a focus on functional achievement, as deciding issues on pragmatic grounds allows principled issues to go unresolved.

Contemporary Political Discourse: "Pooled" or "Shared" Sovereignty

The political development of the Union has therefore reflected several cross-cutting cleavages, as different actors hold different understandings of what the EU is and where it is going. Supranationalist, intergovernmentalist, technocratic, and democratic understandings of the EU have all shaped its development over time, each with their own understandings of where and how authority is distributed. Rather than resolving this fundamental ambiguity, the EU has gradually developed a series of power-sharing practices that allow it to leave fundamental questions about its own nature unanswered. As a result, the EU increasingly defies traditional political categories – it is neither a sovereign state nor a non-sovereign international organization, but something in between. Scholars are struggling to develop language to describe this situation. Some favour terms like "divided sovereignty" or "disaggregated sovereignty," reminiscent of federal theories where each level of government remains sovereign in its own policy domains.[81] As Burca points out, however, this conception is increasingly tenuous. As Union competencies expand, there are virtually no policy fields which do not require joint action in some sense.[82] Authority may be divided, but not in ways that facilitate unilateralism. Other scholars are thus embracing various concepts of "shared sovereignty" instead.[83] Exactly how authority is being shared, and between whom, however, remain subjects of debate.

Lord and Magnette argue that rather than resolving questions of authority, the EU has essentially created different institutions drawing on different accounts of authority.[84] Thus the Commission, Councils, and Parliament give supranationalists, inter-governmentalists, technocrats, and democrats respectively reasons to support EU authority. Together, these institutions operationalize "legitimacy chains," each contributing to the overall authority of the Union by appealing to different blocks of constituents. "These, in turn, support [overall] political systems that are not configured for the articulation of any one view of legitimacy but for the mediation of relationships between several."[85] In this way, the EU is built around a foundational multiplicity of political legitimacy claims.[86] In fact, such chains are variable – influence varies functionally, as certain bodies are more influential in some fields and less in others; it also varies temporally, with different bodies involved in different stages of the decision-making process. This allows the EU to prioritize different constituents in the areas and policy phases most important to them. As a result, the EU generates support for different, even contradictory reasons in different constituencies. On this account, sovereignty is shared in the sense of being pooled or exercised jointly – multiple actors cooperate to support a single, unified authority claim.

Bellamy, taking a sort of neorepublican position, argues that this strategy can be understood as a return to pre-sovereign practices, drawing analogies to the balance struck between estates,[87] guilds, churches, and other power-brokers before the rise of the centralized state.[88] This arrangement, he contends, is inherently polyarchic and revolves around a balance of powers, a version of republican checks and balances, which prevents any single actor from operating unilaterally. In this way, each site operates as a quasi-autonomous body in conditions of non-domination and cooperation. Accordingly, to Bellamy, Europe's multilevel governance and mixed authority structures extend this logic, updated as "mixed-sovereignty."[89] He describes the result as a "mixed commonwealth"[90] or "bricolage" dividing power between both communitarian/inter-governmentalist and cosmopolitan/supranational authority structures, each of which works as a check on the other.[91]

Discourses of "multi-level governance" (MLG)[92] offer a different, and more expansive, take on the diffusion of authority. MLG suggests that, in an increasingly globalized world, no single actor is able to exercise effective governance alone. Rather, effective governance occurs through issue-specific networks, as not only EU and national bodies, but also municipalities, regions, corporations, civic actors, and others share authority.[93] Each network is highly specific, characterized by different combinations of actors and norms of interaction.[94] Networks overlap both geographically and functionally, and the same actors are often members of many networks. As a result, there is no one locus of authority. Sovereignty, to the extent that it can be said to exist at all, can only be exercised jointly.[95]

While both accounts emphasize the diffusion of previously centralized power, Bellamy's account focuses on state, regional, and supranational power and foregrounds how the division of power prevents unilateralism, while MLG includes a broader array of private actors and foregrounds how the pooling of power enables authority that would otherwise be unavailable to any single actor.

Walker, on the other hand, introduces the term "late sovereignty," seeking to capture both the diffusion of power and the continued influence of sovereign forms of authority.[96] In crisis situations, where power-sharing breaks down, he argues, European actors continue to rely on state sovereignty.[97] Insofar as sovereignty consists of final decision-making power, then, states arguably retain important elements of sovereignty – not least through their ability to leave the EU entirely. Nevertheless, the fact that ordinary governance occurs in decidedly non-sovereign ways is significant. Late sovereignty therefore captures both the continuities with sovereignty and the distinctive power-sharing of the European system, as well as the potential for evolution into an even less sovereign system. Thus, Walker shows not only how sovereignty is fading, but also how traces of it remain, all while emphasizing the evolutionary nature of the de-sovereignization process.

Each of these discourses, in its own way, points to forms of authority that reject the inter-governmentalist/supranationalist dichotomy, with its presumption that authority rests either with the state or the Union. Whether Europe is moving toward post-sovereignty or returning to its pre-sovereign past, authority is increasingly shared – divided, pooled, and networked. As a result, the explanatory power of sovereignty is waning as Europe undergoes a de-sovereignization process that is ongoing, incomplete, and deeply contested.

Case Study: Unity in Diversity – Sovereign Ambiguity in the Constitutional Treaty

The saga surrounding Europe's failed constitution provides an excellent example of the ambiguous nature of political authority in the EU and the ongoing compromises this ambiguity produces. The drafting process included both a Constitutional Convention engaging a variety of interest groups, NGOs, regional representatives, and ordinary citizens at the European level, and an Inter-governmental Conference between the member states. While the Convention was designed to be, and touted as, participatory and deliberative, participants debated under the shadow of the coming governmental negotiations.[98] Even within the Convention itself, inter-governmentalist and supranationalist camps were readily identifiable, leading Convention President Valéry Giscard d'Estaing to "call on the conventioneers to seek to keep the best of both approaches."[99]

The content of the treaty was also highly ambiguous, with both sides making gains.[100] For example, it would have affirmed, for the first time, the supremacy[101] of Union law, while at the same time stressing that the EU was a Union of states and could act only in areas voluntarily conferred on it by those states.[102] Similarly, the competencies of the Union would have been expanded, but reserve powers would have been allocated to the member states.[103] While the powers of the European Parliament were expanded in a number of ways and the document introduced provisions for ballot initiatives at the European level, the Constitution also provided for legislative scrutiny by national parliaments[104] and created, for the first time, a formal exit mechanism for national governments[105] as well as a series of procedural safeguards, vetoes, and opt-outs for member states.[106] The text also recognized the role of sub-national governments and would have given them standing before the ECJ. Thus, the content of the treaty was a blend of inter-governmental and supranational proposals.

The ratification process, too, included parliamentary procedures typical of international treaties in some countries, while others held referenda more reminiscent of supranational constitution-making. Semantically, the document claims that it reflects the will,[107] and serves the interests,[108] of both the people and states of Europe. Academic reactions mirrored this ambiguity, and, in the end, the treaty was criticized for being both too federalist and not federalist enough.[109]

Even the slogan associated with the constitution, "Unity in Diversity," is wonderfully ambiguous. Indeed, this statement captures the dynamic of political contestation around issues of sovereignty nicely; in the end, the Union would be neither supranationalist nor intergovernmentalist, and both at the same time.[110] Nicolaïdis, for example, presents the constitutional text not as a contradiction but as a third way, between inter-governmental and supranational visions; a Hegelian synthesis of a Cartesian dichotomy.[111] She argues that the constitution is best seen as a demoi-cracy; "a vision of the EU grounded in a double legitimacy of states and citizens."[112] As in discourses of "pooled" or "shared" sovereignty, the authority of the Union would come precisely from its mixed structure. Rather than creating a hierarchy or defining watertight compartments, then, the Constitution is best seen as a framework for the joint exercise of sovereignty.[113]

When the Constitution was put to a vote, however, both French and Dutch publics rejected it, despite the support of major parties, unions, and business associations and, tellingly, despite the fact that the EU was otherwise popular in both countries.[114] A substantial share of the "no" vote was essentially a protest vote, motivated by disapproval of the elite-driven integration process, rather than an objection to integration itself.[115] The Commission's attempt to generate popular legitimacy through dialogue had failed, in part because civic actors were not seeking dialogue. They were seeking actual decision-making power – power which remained deliberately elusive. Rather than contesting the balance of power between the state and union, many civic actors were contesting what the state and the Union share – a representative model of technocratic, low-intensity democracy where power remains perennially removed from public participation.[116]

After the defeat of the Constitution, state and EU actors re-packaged its content into the Lisbon Treaty – a text which is substantively nearly identical to its constitutional predecessor.[117] Only the sweeping constitutional language and the grand attempt to involve citizens and civil actors were gone, allowing elites to keep a lower profile and push through much of the same content without engaging in the same risky public process. In essence, state and EU actors moved to narrow the range of sites of authority and theories of legitimacy which had to be managed. By cutting out civil society, state and EU leaders were better able to forge compromise. Once again, however, they had to reckon with civil society, as Irish groups defeated the treaty over the strong support of all major political parties.[118] Recognizing that civic actors could not be cut out so easily, EU and Irish authorities invested huge sums into civil society groups of their own, held a second referendum, and secured passage of the treaty.

The saga of the Constitutional Treaty therefore highlights the multiple axes along which political power is contested in Europe. It also speaks to the messy, even contradictory, and often unsuccessful ways in which various actors seek to manage conflicting sites of authority in Europe.

Conclusions

The political dimensions of EU integration are therefore deeply marked by contestation. Indeed, it was the increasingly violent character of international and domestic contestation that motivated European leaders to take the initial risk of forming an international community whose authority claims might rival their own. The advent of the EU has not abated political contestation. Since the beginning, there have been conflicting positions on the exact nature of the European integration process. Some favour a strong Union and subordinate states, others the reverse. Some favour a technocratic Union, while others envision a more direct role for public participation. These axes of contestation cross-cut one another in complex ways. The very nature and distribution of political authority is at stake in these questions. Yet rather than resolving them one way or the other, the story of European integration is one of ambiguity and compromise, contradiction and synthesis, as actors move away from total, exclusive forms of authority and embrace a variety of power-sharing practices.

As these practices evolve, spread, and deepen, the relevance of sovereignty to European politics is beginning to wane. Increasingly, the EU has no body which wields total, exclusive authority – no "power to keep them all in awe."[119] Nor does it revolve around a single narrative of who *ought* to have political authority or how that authority ought to function. Interestingly, however, the resulting competition between sites of and conceptions of authority has not given rise to war or oppression. Rather, it has birthed practices of compromise and bracketing, multi-speed integration and functional legitimacy claims – practices which allow state and Union to interpenetrate, coordinate, and even codecide. These practices have allowed a shared political community to survive, indeed flourish and grow, without any agreement on the very nature of the community itself.

We can therefore understand European politics as undergoing a de-sovereignization process that is ongoing and deeply contested. The resulting structures can be unstable, contestation and crisis are a near-permanent state of affairs, and predictions of the Union's imminent demise are frequent. The role of war, genocide, and totalitarian repression within these conflicts has, however, been greatly diminished.

Chapter Six

Legal Practices

This chapter explores the relationship between national and supranational courts in Europe, asking how their practices of interrelation challenge, and are shaped by, sovereign conceptions of authority. The topic is vexed. The early treaties provided little guidance on how European and national law should relate. As the Union grew and expanded, however, the issue of sovereignty took on increasing salience and the European Court of Justice (ECJ) boldly proclaimed the supremacy of European law over national law. Various national courts, however, forwarded a series of counterclaims asserting national sovereignty. Both national and supranational courts have therefore made conflicting sovereignty claims. Rebutting one another's claims directly could, however, have the potential to scuttle the integration process entirely. As a result, each court has an incentive to find ways to cooperate even in the face of persisting disagreement about how and where authority operates.

Rather than seeking joint institutions through which to reach shared decisions, as in the political sphere, legal actors have gradually developed practices of conditional cooperation, where each court recognizes and accommodates the authority of the others subject to certain conditions. As a result, each actor's authority is autonomous, but contingent upon their meeting certain minimal standards imposed by the others. This system of "constitutional pluralism" allows the legal dimensions of the integration process to proceed without any single actor exercising total or exclusive authority. In this way, the development of constitutional pluralism can be thought of as a de-sovereignization process.

As in the political dimensions of the relationship, these practices of de-sovereignization are full of ambiguity, variability, and dynamism. Each court maintains its own distinct understanding of the trans-systemic relationship, setting parameters derived from their own local contexts and traditions. As a result, there is no uniform relationship between central and national courts, but rather a broad variety of specific relationships that can and do vary substantially. Each of these specific relationships also varies over time, as participants adjust their claims and counterclaims in ongoing practices of dialogue. The presence of multiple competing claims has not, however, jeopardized the legal dimensions of the integration project. In fact, just the opposite, the resulting practices of contestation, adjustment, and coordination have made law into a major driver of the integration process.

The following chapter explores the historical evolution of the relationship between national and European courts, examines some notable practices that courts have used to regulate their relationships, and explores how legal authority has been narrativized in academic discourse.

An Overview of the Legal Relationship (1952–Present)

The View from the Mountaintop: Sovereignty in
the European Court of Justice

The original EEC treaties contained no provision dealing with the relative status of national and European law.[1] This was likely at least in part because community law was, at the time, a relatively minor and discrete field of law. In part, it likely reflects the EU's strategy of leaving the most contentious issues deliberately unaddressed. As the Coal and Steel Community expanded into a nascent European Community, however, EU law expanded and its relationship to national law became increasingly important. During the 1960s, when the inter-governmentalism of the Luxemburg Compromise had paralysed political actors and all but halted the integration process, the European Court of Justice (ECJ) decided to take matters into its own hands and ruled that EU law is supreme over national law. According to the ECJ, the treaties establish a new political community, sovereign in its own domains, independent of its member states, and bearing a direct relationship to the people of Europe.[2] Member states, the ECJ claims, have forgone a portion of their original sovereignty in order to create the Union, and can therefore be compelled and overruled by it. In this sense, community law reigns supreme. The Court's declaration shifted the balance of power in favour of the Union and buttressed supranationalist understandings of the European project. Indeed, it has been credited with quietly reinvigorating the integration process.[3]

The first major step toward this position came in the landmark decision *Van Gend en Loos*.[4] Here, a Dutch corporation claimed that tariffs applied to its imports violated the EEC treaty. A Dutch Court subsequently referred the matter to the ECJ, asking whether the treaty was directly enforceable in national courts. Among other things, the Dutch, Belgian, and German governments protested that only member states and the Commission could bring suits based on the treaty, and only the ECJ could consider them.[5] This position suggests that European courts are a mere tool of the states, there to be used or not as suits their interests. The ECJ rejected this logic, proclaiming that the treaties had created a new political community, the subjects of which were both states and citizens, and that the EU therefore had a direct relationship to the people of Europe, unmediated by their governments.[6] Accordingly, citizens gained direct rights under the treaties, rights which could be asserted by individuals and heard by national courts. This principle of "direct effect" positioned EU law as something that exists independently of, and is capable of being enforced against, its member states. It also empowered national courts to apply EU law directly, effectively recruiting them as enforcement partners.

Shortly after, the Court followed this ruling with its decision in *Costa*.[7] In this case, Italy had nationalized its energy sector and a shareholder complained that this action violated the Treaty of Rome. Under Italian law, the most recent expression of parliament's will implicitly repeals any older, conflicting laws. Thus, Italian courts held that the nationalization was valid and repealed any conflicting portions of the Treaties as they applied to Italy. This stance positions the Union as a mere voluntary commitment, to be complied with or set aside at the pleasure of the state. In this sense, it constituted a strong claim to national sovereignty. The ECJ once again rejected this logic, arguing that states had ceded a portion of their sovereignty by signing the treaties and were no longer at liberty to act outside of them.[8] As a result, it proclaimed that Union law was supreme over national law, regardless of which had come first, and that national courts were therefore under an obligation to set aside any national laws which conflicted with the treaties.[9] With this new doctrine of "supremacy," the court solidified its aggressively supranationalist position, portraying the Union as not only an independent political entity, but one positioned hierarchically above the member states.

The years that followed saw the ECJ gradually expand and solidify both supremacy and direct effect. In *Solange 1*, it extended its claim of supremacy over national legislation to cover national constitutions as well.[10] In *Simmenthal*, it ruled that lower courts, not ordinarily empowered to set aside national law, could and indeed must, do so if it conflicted with EU law.[11] In *Foto-Frost*, the ECJ ruled that national courts could not review Union law for constitutionality, or even for compliance with the treaties themselves.[12] Only the ECJ could rule on the validity of Union law, which national courts were obligated to apply.

Likewise, the court also expanded its doctrine of direct effect. Under *Van Gend en Loos*, only treaty provisions and EU regulations were directly effective. Directives, which ask a member state to achieve a particular result without prescribing a mechanism and are generally seen as a less intrusive legal instrument, were not directly effective. In *Van Duyn*, however, the court held that directives could also be directly effective.[13] Thus, the direct effect doctrine came to encompass all expressions of EU law, even those deliberately designed to afford states more discretion. In *Defrene*, the Court further found that direct effect operates not only vertically, in that courts are obliged to enforce EU laws against their own governments, but also horizontally in disputes between private citizens.[14]

The doctrines of direct effect and supremacy have made the law into a major driver of the integration process, arguably pushing it far beyond what political actors had envisioned or agreed to.[15] Indeed, at first glance they effectively federalized the Union, making the treaties into a constitution and the Union into a sovereign entity. There is, however, more than one side to every story.

Voluntary Servitude: Sovereignty in National Courts

National courts throughout the Union have, in different ways and to different extents, contested the ECJ's claims of supremacy and the supranationalist vision they imply.[16] These counterclaims take a variety of forms, each rooted in their own national legal traditions and cultures, and can themselves be internally complex. A few simplified examples will serve to illustrate the point.

Of all the member states, Belgium perhaps comes closest to affirming the ECJ's claims. In *Le Ski*,[17] its Cour de Cassation accepted EU supremacy based on the very nature of international law. Belgium has a monist legal culture where international law is generally seen as inherently higher than national law, making it easy for Belgian courts to accept EU supremacy. However, even here matters are not quite so clear. In *Orfinger*, the Conseil d'État found supremacy to be rooted in Article 34 of the constitution, which allows for the transfer of sovereign powers to international institutions.[18] Although clearly friendly toward the ECJ and accommodating of its claims to supremacy, this argument suggests that, should Article 34 ever be amended, EU law may no longer be supreme. In effect, it says "you are supreme ... because we say so." In this perspective, *kompetenz-kompetenz*, or the authority to decide where authority rests,[19] is located in national law. *Orfinger* also suggested that transfers of sovereignty made under Article 34 cannot violate the core of Belgium's constitutional identity, suggesting there may be limits to what Belgian courts would accept from EU law.[20] This interpretation draws some support from the fact that the Court of Arbitration is empowered to review treaties *post facto* for constitutionality, suggesting that treaties are not inherently supreme, but rather acquire that status as a result of national law.[21] While this logic is community-friendly, it also suggests that whatever supremacy the Union may have was freely delegated, could presumably be withdrawn by the member states and may be subject to limits. Thus, even within a national judiciary friendly to the ECJ's supremacy claims, latent challenges exist.

Poland sits on the opposite end of the spectrum. While EU law is supreme over statutes under Article 90(1) and by virtue of a successful accession referendum, the national constitution remains the supreme law of the land.[22] The constitution is to be interpreted as far as possible in accordance with EU law, but in the event of an unresolvable conflict between EU law and the Polish constitution, the latter takes precedence. Thus, the court proclaims: "the principle of interpreting domestic law in a manner sympathetic to European law ... has its limits. In no event may it lead to results contradicting the explicit wording of constitutional norms or being irreconcilable with the minimum guarantee functions realized by the constitution."[23] In the event of such a conflict, Poland must either amend its constitution or leave the Union.[24] Furthermore, the Court has held that certain key competencies and rights are so central to the identity of Poland that they cannot be delegated to international organizations.[25] These positions imply a strong counterclaim against the ECJ – for the Poles, sovereignty rests with the member state and EU authority is dependent upon their ongoing consent. In fact, the Polish Constitutional Tribunal has recently ruled that *de facto* changes to the Union's operation have rendered certain aspects of the EU treaties unconstitutional and thus unenforceable in Polish courts.[26] In so doing, the Constitutional Tribunal has mounted the most direct challenge to EU supremacy that the Union has ever seen. At the time of writing, it remains to be seen how this conflict will be resolved. It is worth noting, however, that this unusually direct confrontation between courts comes as a direct result of the Polish government stacking domestic courts with party loyalists in the face of opposition from the European Commission and Parliament, as well as the ECtHR and the ECJ.[27]

In this sense, the conflict has taken on extra-legal dimensions which may be impeding the normal processes of mutual adjustment that otherwise tend to prevail between European courts.

German courts have accepted EU supremacy.[28] Like Poland and perhaps Belgium, German courts have also placed limits on supremacy. In fact, they have been particularly explicit and detailed in this regard. In a now famous pair of cases, the *Solange* decisions, the Constitutional Court first ruled that, because the EU did not provide human rights protections, it was incumbent upon German courts to review EU laws for compatibility with the basic human rights.[29] In this way, EU supremacy was subjected to certain limits – Union measures which violated basic rights would not be applied. Thus, while accepting supremacy in its day-to-day operations, the German Constitutional Court simultaneously positioned itself as the ultimate authority and the locus of *kompetenz*. Years later, in *Solange 2*, the Constitutional Court found that the EU had since developed an impressive human rights jurisprudence that provided internal protections essentially equivalent to those in the German law.[30] As a result, German courts would no longer review EU laws unless evidence could be presented that the EU system as a whole no longer provided equivalent human rights protection. These decisions have been euphemistically referred to as the "So-long-as" decisions – so long as the EU does not systematically violate the basic rights enshrined in the German constitution, it will be considered supreme.[31]

The Constitutional Court has since added additional conditions. In *Maastricht*, it held that EU law may not be treated as supreme if German courts found that the EU had exceeded its jurisdiction, directly refuting the ECJ's position in *Foto-Frost*.[32] In *Lisbon*, it ruled that EU law could not affect the core identity of the German federation, including by intruding into such policy areas as the use of force, core fiscal decisions, social programs, or issues of cultural importance like education and family law.[33] These "locks," as they are commonly known, represent a clear counterclaim – while the ECJ believes that member states are no longer at liberty to set aside EU law, the German Court clearly believes otherwise. It considers itself to be in a position to accept or reject the ECJ's supremacy claims based on its own conditions.

This issue came to a head in the *Outright Monetary Transactions* (OMT) case.[34] Here, the German court made a reference questioning the legality of the European Central Bank's bond-buying program. In the reference, the German court indicated that it found the legality of OMT dubious and suggested that if the ECJ did not find it to be contrary to EU law the German court may find it to be contrary to one of its "locks." The ECJ responded that OMT was legal, provided it met certain criteria.

Ultimately, the German court accepted these criteria and declined to follow through on their threat to declare the program unconstitutional. In this way, Germany was able to leverage its locks to encourage the ECJ to introduce certain limits on the OMT program, in exchange for which it continued to support ECJ supremacy in practice. This conditional approach to supremacy claims has since spread around the continent,[35] with most courts adopting conditional postures of assorted varieties toward the ECJ.[36]

As these examples show, the principle of supremacy has been contested, resisted, and limited in dialogue with national courts. The same can be said of direct effect.[37] Here, too, the result has been a conditional acceptance – national courts embrace direct effect but also police its limits. The ECJ accepts this policing in exchange for national cooperation. The system depends on mutual accommodation between the two.

In fact, in *Celmer*, the ECJ extended the logic of conditional acceptance and mutual policing to relations between states.[38] The ECJ ruled that Ireland does not have to honour extradition requests made by another member state if that state's justice system is systemically deficient in ways that threaten the defendant's rights. Thus, the acceptance of extradition requests between states is conditional – it turns on the extraditing party's assessment of the requesting party's legal system. This creates a system of peer review between national courts, with each monitoring the others and cooperating only on a conditional basis.

As a result of this evolving system of mutual accommodation, the European legal environment is able to function despite the fact that its participants hold wildly contrasting, even contradictory, understandings of their shared relationship. The fact that German, Polish, Belgian, and European courts all have different visions of where authority does and should rest does not prevent them from developing shared norms and tackling complex problems. Rather, it occasions a constant dialogue by which courts collectively find solutions that are mutually acceptable from each perspective, without the need to resolve their underlying differences. Instead, each court enjoys a sort of conditional authority, wielding autonomous powers subject to the minimal conditions of their peers.

Three's Company: Sovereignty and the European Court of Human Rights

As a separate international legal order to which all EU states are parties, the presence of the European Court of Human Rights (ECtHR) in this environment adds yet another level of complexity, as the ECtHR also makes and elicits its own sovereignty claims vis-à-vis national and European courts. Interestingly, the ECtHR and the ECJ have developed practices of conditional authority similar to the "So-long-as" approach.

Much like the ECJ, the ECtHR holds that violations of the European Convention on Human Rights (ECHR) are to be rectified, regardless of whether their source is domestic legislation, international treaties, or national constitutions.[39] In this way, the national constitution is not a shield from obligations under the ECHR, which is in a certain sense "supreme" over national law. However, the ECHR is not directly effective and does not require direct, hierarchical incorporation of the ECHR into domestic legal orders. In fact, it does not specify any particular method of realization, requiring only that the rights in question be protected in some way.[40] Thus, the ECtHR is supreme, but not directly effective. When the ECtHR declares a state to be in breach, the state itself is left to rectify the problem under the supervision of the inter-governmental Council of Europe – a system which has been called "weak judicial review."[41] The ECtHR has also introduced a "margin of appreciation" doctrine, ruling that national courts and legislatures enjoy a degree of discretion or latitude in the manner in which they discharge their obligations under the ECHR.[42] Where there is widespread disagreement among the member states as to the importance or meaning of a given right, the margin will be wider; where there is widespread consensus, the margin will be more narrow. In this sense, the strength of the Court's supremacy claims hinges, in part, on the practices of the member states themselves.[43] In all these ways, it is a very different supremacy claim from that made by the ECJ.

For their part, member states have generally given Convention rights effect in national legal systems through enabling legislation, constitutional provisions, judicial activism, or simple constitutional monism.[44] Positions regarding the supremacy of the ECHR vary according to the method of incorporation.[45] In the Netherlands and Moldova, the Convention out-ranks even domestic constitutions. These courts essentially accept the ECtHR's claims that international law has an inherently superior status. In other countries, the ECtHR's role is defined in reference to domestic legal norms and methods of reception.[46] In Austria, the Convention has constitutional status. In other states, including Spain, Portugal, and France, the Convention ranks above ordinary legislation but below the national constitution. Germany and Italy accord the Convention normal legislative status, although both judiciaries have given it a special interpretative significance that effectively raises its profile to a supra-legislative level. Once again, we see a legal relationship that is highly variable.

The relationship between the ECJ and ECtHR is also complex. The EU is not a member of the ECHR and vice versa. In this sense they are separate, parallel legal orders, each with no claim to direct supremacy vis-à-vis the other. However, given that all EU members are bound by both sets of laws, supremacy questions arise indirectly regarding which set of rules a member would have to follow in the case of a conflict. For its part, the ECtHR has conducted indirect review of EU laws by holding member states accountable even in areas where their competences have been delegated to an international organization.[47] In this sense, the ECtHR can be seen to consider its rulings supreme over other international commitments, including those made to the EU. However, it has also held that it will not review specific acts so long as the organization in question provides an equivalent degree of rights protection to that provided in the Convention. Since the EU has been found to provide such protection, the ECtHR does not review EU acts directly.[48] So it seems that, like Germany's Constitutional Court, the ECtHR considers itself technically supreme but has decided to waive that supremacy subject to certain conditions, allowing *de facto* ECJ supremacy in its own sphere.[49]

The ECJ has struck a similar posture. Under *Kadi*, it will review the acts of EU institutions or member states for compliance with EU law even if those acts give effect to international treaties or laws.[50] It also indicated that it might waive that right if the relevant treaty itself provided comparable protections.[51]

Here, too, European courts have managed the presence of multiple supremacy claims through condition-setting practices that allow them to coordinate without actually resolving the question of sovereignty.

Constitutional Pluralism

As we have seen, the ECJ considers European law supreme over national law. However, various national courts employ a variety of locks or conditions in order to place constraints and conditions on the ECJ's claims, suggesting that domestic constitutions are supreme in the case of conflict. Rather than resolving these conflicting claims one way or another, national and European courts each express their claims in ways that accommodate the claims of their peers. Thus, the ECJ claims that it is not bound by national conditions, but nevertheless avoids violating them in practice. National courts insist that they *could* overrule EU law, but treat European law as supreme in practice.

As a result, neither party enjoys unfettered authority – national law is valid only to the extent that it conforms to EU law, but EU law is recognized only if it meets nationally imposed conditions. The ECJ and ECtHR place conditions on each other's authority as well. Thus, each court enjoys only a conditional level of authority, but each court also enjoys the ability to place conditions on the authority of others.

Whereas traditional legal systems can be conceptualized as a hierarchy, with a supreme court at the top exercising total and exclusive authority over lower courts, the European legal environment is more of a heterarchy – "a form of management or rule in which any unit can govern or be governed by others, depending on circumstances, and hence no one unit dominates the rest."[52] Scholars have called this system "constitutional pluralism."

Practices of Note

The development of EU law has therefore been marked by contrasting positions regarding where sovereignty lies. The ECJ claims broad supremacy for EU law, but national courts have signalled that this supremacy claim is contingent upon meeting certain standards derived from their national legal systems. In short, national authority is recognized only where it does not conflict with EU law, but EU authority is recognized only where it meets national conditions. Since both courts have a vested interest in having their authority recognized by the other, each has an incentive to act within the conditions laid down by its peers. As a result, neither court enjoys total or exclusive powers in practice. We might therefore understand the gradual development of condition-setting practices as a process of de-sovereignization. This system, aptly described as constitutional pluralism, relies on a number of important practices which allow the parties to accommodate one another without needing to fundamentally resolve the question of where and how authority functions.

Mutual Advantage through Judicialization

It is notable that, despite fundamental differences on core questions of relative authority, direct conflicts between national and European courts are extremely rare. Rather, each court finds ways to accommodate one another's concerns. This reality depends, at least in part, on the fact that both courts stand to benefit from cooperation.

Indeed, the doctrines of direct effect and supremacy may have occasioned a power struggle between courts, but they also work to strengthen both national and European courts relative to legislative branches of government. By empowering national courts to enforce EU law directly, the ECJ was able to piggyback off their domestic legitimacy.[53] Where national governments may have been able to defy or ignore a fledgling ECJ, they could not defy or ignore their own courts. Violating the conditions national courts lay down would risk jeopardizing this support. Similarly, national courts have accepted direct effect and supremacy in part because it strengthens their hands against national governments – in essence, EU law provides a new tool which national courts – especially lower courts – can use to challenge their governments.[54] This is especially true for lower courts, which are often not empowered to set aside laws on the basis of their domestic constitution, but who are empowered to do so on the basis of EU law. To deny ECJ supremacy would mean giving up a potent tool. Thus, the system of mutual accommodation can be explained, at least in part, as a function of mutual advantage, as each actor tries to maximize its own power relative to national governments. In this sense, the relationship between national and European courts is not only part of the struggle between supranationalist and inter-governmental interpretations of the integration – it also participates in the contest between technocratic and democratic visions, as courts cooperate to enlarge their own power at the expense of elected institutions. The judicialization of European politics is also a form of technocratization.[55]

Mutually Assured Destruction

Cooperation is also facilitated by the simple fact that upsetting the apple cart would be risky in the extreme for either party. If the ECJ were to produce a ruling that national courts simply would not enforce, for example, its own authority would be radically undercut. After all, EU law only has "direct effect" in practice as long as national courts are willing to directly apply it in the cases they hear. Without the cooperation of national courts, the ECJ would be reliant on national governments and EU institutions to bring cases directly before it, essentially reducing the ECJ to an optional conflict resolution tool. Moreover, national courts typically enjoy a high degree of domestic legitimacy. If they were to openly deny the legitimacy of EU law, a political crisis for the ECJ would be sure to follow.

Conversely, if national courts were to reject the supremacy of EU law outright, they would essentially be empowering national governments to pick and choose which EU laws they wanted to follow. This would drastically undercut the integration process. Given that integration, on the whole, enjoys substantial popular support across most EU countries this would risk undercutting popular support for the offending court. The national government, too, would very likely feel the court had overstepped, tanking an integration process that is properly a matter for political, rather than legal, authorities. As a result, the national court would face a legitimacy crisis of its own. Even if the national court weathered such a crisis well, it would find itself deprived of the ability to use European law to curtail its national government and would, at least to that extent, find its domestic standing diminished.

Thus, a direct conflict between courts would be potentially catastrophic for both parties, as well as for the integration process. No court wants to risk being blamed for killing European integration. This gives both parties a substantial incentive to accommodate one another's claims in practice.

Variability

Another striking feature of the European legal environment is how evidently non-uniform it is. As we have seen, each national court understands its relationship to the ECJ and ECtHR differently, based on its own legal culture, institutional structure, and constitutional traditions. The ECJ and ECtHR understand this as well. As a result, the practices of dialogue that prevail between each national court and its central interlocutors differ substantially from one another. Rather than establishing a single, standardized relation between central and national courts, the European system allows each national court to think about authority in its own way and to act accordingly.

In Ireland, for example, EU membership is often seen as a potential alternative to English colonialism. In Poland, conversely, EU law can be reminiscent of Soviet impositions. These two historical-political contexts demand distinct responses, and the European legal environment is flexible enough to accommodate that.

Variability also makes the system dynamic – because there is no established way that national and EU courts must relate, each is able to make adjustments in response to changing circumstances. Variability also facilitates experimentation, allowing courts to test out their positions and revisit them over time. Courts can even observe their peers and borrow approaches that seem to work.

Perhaps most importantly, however, variability allows all courts in the European legal environment to avoid definitively answering the fundamental question: "what is the relationship between national courts and the ECJ/ECtHR?" Rather than needing to build consensus around one particular vision, actors are able to coexperiment with a range of provisional answers that are neither final nor binding on their peers. Much like the strategy of multispeed integration, this technique allows integration to proceed and, indeed, provides opportunities for ambitious courts to lead the way while preventing hesitant courts from stalling overall progress. For all these reasons, the fact that the relationship between national courts and the ECJ and ECtHR is not uniform has been an important means of facilitating legal integration.

Interpenetration

Another interesting feature of the relationship between European and state legal systems is that it can be difficult to tell exactly where one ends and the other begins.

The human rights jurisprudence of both the ECJ and ECtHR, for example, are rooted in the common constitutional traditions of the member states.[56] Similarly, the ECJ treats the ECHR as a "minimal standard" in its own human rights discourse, and many national courts give it special consideration in their own rights jurisprudence.[57] Just as EU law is based in the constitutional traditions of the member states, so too it is based in the ECHR, such that the three systems are not totally discrete.

The degree of interpenetration is variable. For example, the ECJ gives ECtHR judgments "special significance" and authority in its own jurisprudence,[58] essentially importing the entire jurisprudence of the ECtHR as a source of authority within EU law. Conversely, the spread of the *Solange* approach shows how national courts can borrow specific jurisprudential approaches, ideas, and lines of reasoning from one another without necessarily giving one another's jurisprudence direct authority.[59] Indeed, Slaughter contends that European judges increasingly constitute a single community, drawing on and wrestling with a common body of trans-systemic precedent and doctrine[60] and autonomously applying it to their specific circumstances.

The principle of direct effect and the use of reference questions between EU and national courts also facilitates a sort of interpenetration. Through direct effect, EU law is applied by national courts, drawing it into their own legal reasoning. Reference questions even allow national courts to invite the ECJ to directly participate in ongoing legal cases at the national level. This is not exactly a codecision structure or a shared institution, but it does allow the ECJ to exert autonomous influence within the legal reasoning of the national courts, such that the resulting decisions are independently shaped by both actors in ways that blur the lines between systems.

In all these ways, various European legal orders interpenetrate one another while also retaining their distinct decision-making processes and identities. This interpenetration helps facilitate constitutional pluralism in at least two ways. First, by providing a degree of overlap[61] or common ground between courts, interpenetration helps ensure that contestation stays within bounds that all parties find acceptable.[62] In essence, courts are able to engage in dialogue about particulars and to leave these dialogues unresolved in part because they feel secure that the most fundamental issues are already the subject of substantial agreement. Second, interpenetration allows each court to accommodate its peers without deferring to them directly, thus facilitating compromise while allowing each court to treat itself as supreme. In *Tarrico* and *Solange*, for example, the ECJ reacted to claims of national supremacy by declaring that the impugned national norm is in fact a part of EU law, because EU law is based in national traditions. This allows the ECJ to uphold the results sought by national courts, but to do so on the basis of EU rather than national law, thus preserving its broader supremacy claim. In essence, each court can draw on its peers without venturing outside of its own body of legal precedent because the systems are not conceptually discrete. In both these ways, the interpenetrating nature of European legal systems is an important practice through which legal actors avoid conflict while still maintaining competing supremacy claims.

Contemporary Legal Discourse: Conflict or Cooperation

The practices of the ECJ, national courts, and the ECtHR are therefore characterized by conflicting claims to and accounts of authority. Over time, European courts have developed unique practices that allow them to manage this uncertain legal environment. Rather than creating joint institutions to wield joint authority, like political actors have, European courts act autonomously, but under conditions set by their peers. Authority is not shared in the sense of being exercised jointly, but rather shared in the sense that each actor influences, and is influenced by, each of its interlocutors. In this sense, no actor enjoys total or exclusive authority. The development of constitutional pluralism can therefore be understood as a de-sovereignization process. Nevertheless, this process is contested and questions of sovereignty continue to shape the ways constitutional pluralism is theorized. Indeed, the field is both haunted by a dogged insistence that someone must be sovereign in the final instance and also actively experimenting with new conceptions of authority which deliberately leave sovereignty behind.

An enormous amount of the scholarship on constitutional pluralism revolves not around the everyday practices of accommodation that characterize the system, but rather around the question of who *would* have ultimate authority if those practices ever broke down. The lack of a sovereign to resolve disputes is thus a major site of concern, even among those who generally celebrate the practice of judicial dialogue. Some would vest ultimate authority in either the ECJ or the national courts.[63] Others, like Joseph Weiler, for example, seek middle positions. Weiler praises Europe's constitutional "sonderweg," or special way of doing things, defined precisely by its capacity to foster cooperation without erasing difference, and stresses the productive role of "constitutional toleration."[64] Nevertheless, the potential for conflict between courts leads Weiler to argue for a new Constitutional Council, with members drawn from both EU and national courts, to resolve potential conflicts.[65] In essence, Weiler would create a codecision body similar to those that characterize the political sphere so that courts could wield authority jointly. What all these accounts share is the presumption that, if push were ever to come to shove, someone must wield sovereign authority.

Other scholars, like Maduro, suggest that any such body, by resolving the question of where sovereignty lies, would undercut the distinctively pluralist nature of the European legal system and the practices of dialogue and accommodation on which it is based.[66] On this account, the sort of authority that characterizes the European system is fundamentally different from the logic of sovereignty in that it presumes heterarchy as the normal state of affairs, rather than a crisis to be solved.[67]

Maduro describes this heterarchy as a "contrapuntal" system, in that different courts speak in different rhythms, but also work to harmonize their outputs with the others. The same way a symphony does not revolve around any one instrument, but rather the interplay between instruments, so legal authority arises not through any one source of law but through the interplay of several. Authority is, in this sense, partially a function of harmonization – a court's pronouncements gain authority precisely when, and to the degree that, they resonate with those of its peers. This system does not require uniformity – a symphony would be boring if everyone played the same notes – rather, it requires that differences be constrained by considerations of the whole. Similarly, Kumm and MacCormick, in their own ways, both argue that the current system of dialogue and accommodation does a better job realizing the underlying principles and ideals of constitutionalism than either national supremacy or European supremacy would.[68] Recourse to sovereign forms of authority would therefore impoverish constitutionalism itself.

Europe's constitutional pluralism is therefore challenging, and challenged by, concepts of sovereignty in important and dynamic ways. On a day-to-day basis, this system functions with no clear sovereign, and yet it remains deeply shaped by the perceived need for sovereign authority if and when practices of accommodation break down. As a result, some see constitutional pluralism itself as little more than a set of conflict-of-laws provisions which, at best, defer the question of sovereignty to extraordinary circumstances. Others present constitutional pluralism as a new form of constitutionalism revolving around new, non-sovereign forms of authority. Both the allocation and the nature of legal authority are at stake in these debates. Both accounts concur, however, that sovereign forms of authority have, at the very least, receded into the background of European legal practice. To this extent, the contested development of constitutional pluralism represents a de-sovereignization process.

Case Study: Constitutional Dialogue and European Human Rights

As we have seen, the European legal environment is characterized by multiple conflicting sovereignty claims. Rather than resolving these conflicts, European courts engage in practices of dialogue and mutual accommodation. The development of Europe's human rights discourse illustrates these practices well.

Originally, the ECJ's position was that fundamental rights were the purview of national and ECHR – but not EU – law.[69] Initially, this division of competences suited national courts and the ECtHR well – they would ensure fundamental rights, while the ECJ would enforce EU treaties.[70] As the doctrine of supremacy evolved, however, the ECJ declared EU law, with no human rights protections whatsoever, to be supreme over national law, even national constitutions. This left open the possibility that EU law could violate basic rights, potentially exposing citizens to grave abuses.[71] German courts raised this concern in the *Solange 1* decision.

In response, the ECJ proposed a new arrangement; it declared that although constitutions themselves were subordinate to EU law, respect for the constitutional principles of the member states was an integral part of EU law, which therefore provided human rights protections of its own.[72] It proceeded to analyse whether there was an infringement of these rights and replied in the negative.

The German Constitutional Court, however, was not convinced by this newfound and as-yet untested commitment to a somewhat vaguely defined body of principles emerging from the varied constitutional orders of the member states. *Solange 1* made this clear; the Court would review EU law on constitutional grounds *so long as* the EU itself lacked comparable and proven rights protection.[73] In this sense, it can be read as an invitation for the ECJ to prove its credibility. Here, too, the Constitutional Court found that no violation had, in fact, occurred in this case.

The ECJ responded with its decision in *Nold*.[74] It knew it had to give its rights jurisprudence greater credibility and specificity in order to satisfy the Germans. It also knew that doing so created a possible conflict with the ECtHR – then a much more established entity – which could undermine its legitimacy even further.[75] The ECJ fed two birds with one hand, declaring that treaties signed by the member states, including the ECHR, were a part of EU law. In so doing, it was able to piggy-back on the credibility of the ECtHR, already accepted by the Germans, while also preventing conflicts with it.[76] If both German and EU law conformed to the ECHR, after all, then the two systems would offer essentially equivalent rights protections. The ECJ proceeded to demonstrate its commitment by drawing on the ECHR in a number of subsequent cases.[77]

The German Constitutional Court was convinced – for the most part. It responded by softening its position, agreeing not to review EU acts so long as EU rights jurisprudence remained, on the whole, comparable to Germany's.[78] Rather than refuting the German court's suggestion that EU law was not, in fact, supreme over the German constitution, the ECJ chose to resolve the conflict between them. With the conflict gone and German courts signalling their willingness to uphold EU law in practice, it became unnecessary to decide who, if anyone, was really supreme.

However, the ECJ's entry into the field of human rights created a new problem, in that its rights jurisprudence might depart from or conflict with national or ECtHR interpretations. In response, the ECJ signalled that it would generally follow the jurisprudence of the ECtHR. It also borrowed a page from the ECtHR's playbook by allowing national courts a margin of discretion in *Schmidberger* and *Omega*.[79] The ECtHR, too, had to adjust to this changing legal environment. Reacting to the ECJ and drawing inspiration from the Germans, its *Bosphorus* judgment effectively endorsed a version of the *Solange* approach.[80]

In this way, the community transitioned from a functional model, based on a division of labour between the ECJ, the ECtHR, and domestic courts, toward a model of overlapping competencies and mutual coordination, as the result of an ongoing process of claim and counterclaim. This transformation illustrates how constitutional pluralism works; one court suggests a given arrangement, others object and react or forward counter-suggestions of their own, and the issue ping-pongs back and forth, each court adjusting its position vis-à-vis the others until a mutually acceptable solution is found.

Importantly, each court seemed careful to make its interventions in a manner accommodating of the claims and authority of its interlocutors. Note also that no consensus has actually been reached on the fundamental question of sovereignty. Rather, these practices allow each court to consider itself supreme in the final instance, while at the same time providing practices of negotiation which prevent supremacy claims from coming into conflict. As a result, various actors are able to coordinate action on complex topics without any actor enjoying total or exclusive authority over the others.

Conclusions

The legal dimensions of the relationship between the EU and its member states has been characterized by competing authority claims and, indeed, competing understandings of the European legal system. In the 1960s and 1970s, many national courts were forwarding intergovernmentalist understandings of the Union – understandings which presumed that sovereignty lay at the national level. The ECJ rejected these positions and declared the supremacy of Union law over national law, thereby forwarding an assertively supranational understanding of the Union. National courts have responded in a wide variety of ways, some essentially accepting the ECJ's position, others rejecting it, and others still placing conditions on their support for EU supremacy. This approach quickly spread through a number of national courts, and to the ECJ and ECtHR, which have adopted a similar strategy in relation to one another.

As a result, the authority of each party effectively depends on satisfying conditions laid down by the other – national law is recognized on the condition that it does not conflict with EU law, and EU law is recognized on the condition that it does not conflict with certain core constitutional provisions of the member states. Because each side has a strong incentive to secure the recognition of its peers, each tends to respect the conditions placed upon it. When conflicts do arise, courts engage in processes of dialogue, each adjusting its position until both are satisfied. Each party is therefore able to understand itself as in some sense supreme, while neither party exercises total or exclusive forms of authority in practice.

This system of constitutional pluralism remains deeply marked by sovereignty, and indeed, questions of sovereignty are almost an obsession of the field, with scholars and judges alike relentlessly focused on what would or could happen if practices of mutual accommodation ever broke down. The day-to-day reality of the system, however, is one of dialogue, compromise, and mutual adjustment over time.

We can therefore understand the development of constitutional pluralism as a de-sovereignization process, albeit one that remains incomplete and deeply contested. However, the de-sovereignization practices developed by legal actors are quite distinct from those developed by political actors. Rather than forming codecision structures, each court retains its separate institutional structure and makes independent decisions, accepting certain conditions on its own authority and placing conditions on the authority of others in turn.

Nevertheless, EU law has proven an extremely effective and influential driver of the integration process, sustaining and facilitating integration even in the face of persisting disagreement about how and where authority operates.

Chapter Seven

Economic Practices

This chapter explores the economic dimensions of the relationship between the European Union and its member states, asking how economic authority is structured, distributed, and contested and how these contests challenge, and are shaped by, concepts of sovereignty.[1]

Of course, the distribution of control over the economy has important implications for the distribution of sovereignty between the Union and its member states, participating in the ongoing contests between supranationalists and inter-governmentalists. What is most striking about the contest for economic power is not, however, a transfer of sovereignty from the state to the Union, but rather a transfer from representative institutions to technocratic ones. This reconceptualization of economic power as an object of technical management, rather than political decisions, has the effect of shielding economic decisions from popular control, thereby concentrating economic authority in a small class of technical experts.

European economic practices therefore depart from the trends that animate political and legal practices. While political and legal actors have used codecision structures and conditional forms of authority to distribute power and facilitate contestation, economic structures work to concentrate authority and pre-empt contestation instead.

The following chapter explores the changing distribution and conceptualization of economic authority, discusses some notable practices that work to make economic authority more technocratic in nature, and examines how the relationship is narrativized in academic discourse.

An Overview of the Economic Relationship

Post-War Reconstruction and the "Economic Constitution" (~1950−~70)

At the end of the Second World War, Europe's governments were swollen from war-time growth, but its major economies needed to be totally rebuilt. This situation proved fertile ground for a form of liberal economic theory called ordoliberalism, particularly in Germany.[2] Like classical and neoliberals, ordoliberals see a competitive market as the key to economic growth. However, while classical and neoliberalism focus on restraining state interference with "natural" market dynamics, ordoliberals see markets as non-natural phenomenon that need to be created by state intervention.[3] Ordoliberals therefore envision a strong state capable of intervening decisively to build a stable and, above all, competitive market.

However, the wars had also left many European officials deeply suspicious of democratic politics, which many saw as both intellectually unsophisticated and prone to capture by demagogues and rent-seeking special interests.[4] This would lead the government to pick favourites in the marketplace, undermining competitiveness and fostering patronage and corruption. The state must build the market, but democratic governments cannot be trusted to do this without corruption, incompetence, and volatility. Ordoliberals therefore promoted an "economic constitution" – a set of economic ground rules which would be deliberately insulated from popular political control.[5] To safeguard these rules, society would require a number of unelected, arms-length bodies to make key economic decisions in a rational, apolitical manner. Particularly in Germany, but also in Italy and the Benelux[6] countries, ordoliberalism became a defining feature of the reconstruction period.[7] Unelected, independent public bodies began to proliferate and entrenched rules were the order of the day.[8]

In this context, many saw the integration process as a means to construct an ordoliberal system that would be beyond the reach of any national government.[9] In this way, the growth of the Union as a supranational entity and the entrenchment of a technocratic economic order have always gone hand in hand. For example, consider the leading role played by the unelected Commission and Court in the ECSC, compared with the constrained consensus requirements that paralysed the Council and the merely advisory power of the Parliament. The institutional structure of the Union, especially in its early form, was in many ways designed to give unelected bodies a leading role which could only be loosely shaped by political actors. To this day, only the unelected Commission can propose legislation – the Council and Parliament are confined to approving, modifying, or rejecting those proposals. Likewise, the Coal and Steel Community, the Atomic Energy Community, and the Economic Community that followed were all acts of state-led market building – proactive attempts to (re)establish the conditions of competitive enterprise. By entrenching a supranational market in these goods, the nascent Union effectively prevented any one government from intervening to regulate them.

The EEC, in particular, enshrines four fundamental freedoms: the freedom of goods, people, capital, and services. By prohibiting interference in these areas, the EEC denied states many of the traditional tools with which they intervened in their economies.[10] Without tariffs or capital controls, states could no longer nurture domestic industries or use trade as a geopolitical tool against rivals. Without hard borders, states could no longer control local labour markets. Thus, the early institutions of the EU reflect an attempt to entrench economic ground rules and insulate them from popular control by member governments.

Ordoliberalism's supposedly "apolitical" economic vision was, however, pursued in a political context. At the European level and at the German level, ordoliberals found themselves compromising with Keynesians, social democrats, and corporatists.[11] To a certain degree the resulting compromises were congruous – ordoliberals prized a competitive market, but many could see how a certain level of welfare provision, social services, and regulations could work to safeguard consumption and worker competitiveness overall.[12] In other cases compromises were needed. The (in)famous Common Agricultural Policy (CAP), for example, can be read as a concession to politically powerful special interests at the national level, and thus a departure from ordoliberal orthodoxy.[13] The early era of the EU's post-war economy was therefore defined by a blend of social market interventions and ordoliberal economic constitutionalism but characterized overall by a transfer of power from representative state institutions to unelected technocrats at both the national and supranational levels.

The Crisis of the 1970s and the Neoliberal Turn (~1970–~2008)

As post-war reconstruction progressed, simply rebuilding could longer provide an adequate basis for economic growth.[14] The European economy began to stagnate.[15] In response, the Keynesian and social democratic elements of the European economic structure fell into relative disfavour and the neoliberal ideas that were more fashionable in the Anglosphere began to gain currency.[16] Alongside ordoliberal market building, which often required de-commodifying interventions, the EU began to display a more marked propensity for commodifying interventions – interventions which privatized public goods and services as a path to competitiveness. The nature of the economic constitution remained mixed, but the ideological mix was shifting. All the while, the insulation of economic choices from public control was continuing.

First, consider the continued entrenchment of the original ordoliberal vision. In 1985, the Schengen Agreement established the free movement of people, while in 1986 the Single European Act set in place a plan to complete the internal market and to move incrementally through a system of pegged exchange rates toward a common currency. The creation of the Euro, which flowed from this, is perhaps the most important ordoliberal feature of the EU. Crucially, the European Central Bank took on much of the authority formerly held by national central banks, but with an explicit mandate not to use this power to manage national economies, as national central banks had long done.[17] Rather, the ECB would maintain price stability and nothing more.

Moreover, in order to be eligible for the shared currency, countries had to agree to stringent debt and deficit limits.[18] These requirements undercut governments' ability to use deficit spending to stimulate depressed economies or manage macroeconomic cycles. The EU, however, has a budget of only about 1–2 per cent of European GDP and has not replaced the state as a major deficit-spender.[19] Without the ability to run large deficits at either level, governments become dependent on attracting an influx of private capital to stimulate depressed economies – rather than spending public funds, governments must deregulate or lower taxes in order to attract private investment.[20] This, in turn, shrinks states' revenue and regulatory reach, further reducing national governments' capacity for economic intervention. In this way, the monetary union and its associated budgetary criteria constitute a major entrenchment of the economic constitution, further tying the hands of elected governments.

Alongside these ordoliberal policies, commodifying neoliberal policies were also gaining prominence. Beginning in the 1970s and gaining momentum through the 1990s, European economies undertook large-scale privatization of government assets and services.[21] In large part, these reforms were driven by the Maastricht debt criteria, along with the pressures of free capital and the persistent, detailed, and sector-specific efforts of the Commission.[22] These commodifying shifts in the European economy reflect a novel neoliberal ideology, yet they also participate in the broader shift in power toward actors who are not directly subject to popular control.[23] At the same time, the Commission took steps to bring private actors more prominently into the policy process.[24]

Once again, more corporatist and social democratic influences are also discernible in this period. The Single European Act expanded community competences into social policy, economic and social cohesion, research and technological development, and the environment, reflecting a more pro-regulatory approach. More importantly, it included a range of social cohesion funds, structural funds, agricultural funds, regional funds, and other forms of industrial policy measures reminiscent of the rent-seeking behaviours which ordoliberals despise.[25] The economic structure of the EU therefore remained mixed – a product of various political manoeuvres and compromises over time. Increasingly, though, the overall character of the economic relationship between the EU and national governments was being defined by entrenched, EU level rules and unelected actors setting economic parameters which could no longer be easily contested by representative institutions at either the national or supranational level.

The 2008 Financial Crisis and Post-Ordoliberalism (~2008–~20)

The financial crisis of 2008 marked another major turning point in Europe's economic system, intensifying the entrenchment of the economic constitution considerably. In essence, bad debts threatened Europe's banks, and their combined debt load was more than some governments could backstop.[26] In this way, it was not only a banking crisis but a sovereign debt crisis as well. Both in its goals and in its chosen methods, Europe's response was deeply shaped by ordoliberalism.[27]

Biebricher argues that the overarching goals of the various measures taken was to restore competitiveness via pro-market reforms and fiscal policy.[28] He also points out that the chosen methods are deeply technocratic. For example, indebted countries were offered conditional loans that forced national governments to adopt economic reforms dictated by unelected experts in the Commission, the IMF, and the ECB.[29] Second, the system of fiscal constraints introduced earlier was dramatically expanded with new regulations giving the Commission expansive supervisory powers over all national budgets.[30] Third, technocratic governments were installed in several countries to implement the economic reforms that their democratic governments had refused.[31]

Even this period, however, is not uni-dimensionally ordoliberal, and certain elements of the EU's crisis response suggest a Keynesian influence. For example, the ECB began printing money to cover bad debts – much to ordoliberal chagrin. In other areas, different economic visions coincide – for example, social democrats and ordoliberals alike can agree on strong anti-trust measures and even environmental regulations, which continue to characterize European regulatory approaches. Nevertheless, the overall goal of economic reforms was to make indebted countries more competitive by imposing entrenched economic rules that representative bodies could not easily contest. Cerny calls the resulting mixture of neoliberal, ordoliberal, and Keynesian policies "post-ordoliberal" to signify a complex blend of partially overlapping policy prescriptions which, while not theoretically coherent, have the practical effect of both entrenching the economic constitution and of transferring power away from representative institutions and toward a range of technical experts.[32]

Economic Constitutionalism and the Fourth Branch

Overall, then, we might say that the economic structure of the EU has a strong and persistent ordoliberal foundation, coexisting in a range of semi-comfortable compromises with social-democratic, corporatist, Keynesian, and neoliberal economic visions over time.[33] Given the relatively strong social state in most European countries, the net effect has been liberalizing.[34]

The most significant dimension of the economic relationship between the EU and its member states is, however, the pronounced commitment to economic constitutionalism – that is to say, a commitment to using supranational institutions and rules to insulate economic policy from popular control. Authority is not merely being shuffled around in this process, it is also being confined within a set of capitalist market–based rules. As a result, the expression of popular sovereignty through member states and EU institutions alike is circumscribed.[35] As this system evolves, an array of unelected public and private actors have come to play growing roles in economic decision-making. Vibert refers to this as "the rise of the unelected," arguing that such bodies are now so heavily implicated in economic governance that they effectively constitute a fourth branch of government.[36]

In both these ways, representative institutions are seeing their economic authority fettered, as the economy is reconceived from a subject of political debate to an object of technical management. The populist and nationalist resurgence across Europe is, in part, a reaction to this narrowing of public control.[37] In all these ways, the economic relationship between the EU and its member states participates in larger contests over how power should be distributed between actors, but it also reveals another line of contestation regarding how power should be limited and structured.

Practices of Note

The economic structure of the Union has always shown the influence of an ordoliberal preference for both entrenched economic rules and technocratic decision-making, gradually building an economic system which representative institutions cannot easily contest. The following section explores a number of diverse practices that have facilitated these two processes.

Structural Asymmetry in the Integration Process

One major practice which shields the economic structure from effective institutional contestation is embedded in the structure of the integration process itself. Indeed, integration is marked by what Scharpf, drawing on Hayek, has called two "asymmetries."[38]

First, the barriers to action are much higher for political actors than for legal actors. Court decisions require only a majority of a panel of judges, while European-level legislation requires a qualified majority of member governments (each of which must maintain a legislative majority domestically) plus a majority of the European Parliament and the support of the Commission. Moreover, once a judicial decision has been made it can only be reversed through treaty changes, which once again requires a high degree of political consensus. The system therefore structurally favours legal over political forms of integration.[39]

Second, legal action necessarily favours negative integration.[40] There are several reasons: EU law is primarily concerned with free trade, the ECJ's caseload comes largely from a corporate litigative elite who pursue a coordinated continental attempt to push the law in a more liberal direction, and most importantly – courts are empowered to strike down existing laws but not to create new, European-level regulatory regimes.[41]

The dual asymmetries Scharpf describes work to both concentrate power in the hands of unelected judges and to entrench a set of rules which are difficult for political actors to contest. In both ways, the very structure of integration constrains legislative intervention. This is not, of course, to suggest that integration is automatically de-regulatory – political actors can and do take regulatory action. Rather, it is to say that integration makes such action require a higher degree of consensus than deregulation.

The Law of the Market

EU law revolves around the "four freedoms" – the free movement of goods, services, capital, and people. Its founding purpose was and remains preventing governments from interfering with that economic framework. When the ECJ declares the supremacy of EU law over national law and even national constitutions, it is not only pushing the Union in a more supranational direction, it is also moving the Union in a more ordoliberal direction – effectively constitutionalizing an economic framework and empowering itself to enforce that framework.

The Court's landmark supranationalist stances in *Van Gend en Loos* and *Costa*, for example, were not only supranationalist victories – they also meant exposing market-intervening legislation to challenge by private actors and reducing tariffs designed to protect local industries. Both decisions subordinated the social priorities of national governments not only to the authority of the courts, but also to the economic order enshrined in the treaties. In this way, the court's determination to deepen what began as a trade deal and transform it into a true supranational entity is also effectively a commitment to insulate the economic structure from national intervention.

Subsequent rulings like *Dassonville* and *Cassis* similarly expanded the scope of community law substantially, but primarily as a negative instrument which could be used to keep social policies and regulations consistent with an ordoliberal framework. In *Dassonville*,[42] the ECJ interpreted a treaty ban on import quotas as prohibiting any national legislation that had any effect on the movement of goods, even if this effect was unintended and, indeed, even if it was only a potential and not an actual effect.[43] Thus, the court dramatically expanded its own authority from the power to strike down tariffs to a much broader power to review essentially all national legislation. As Menéndez puts it, this move transforms "the power of review of the validity of national laws ... from a mouse, restricted to the national norms through which the economic border is established and reproduced, to an elephant, extending to the whole national legal order."[44] At the same time, however, it undermined the economic discretion of national states dramatically. The ECJ went on to apply this framework to challenge everything from national tax and pension systems to labour and protest rights, extending its own reach and insulating the market from state intervention at the same time.[45]

Thus the courts, in expanding their own power vis-à-vis national law, have also entrenched an economic framework and empowered themselves to police it, shifting power from elected bodies to unelected bodies and effectively constitutionalizing the economic structure of the Union.

It's All about the Benjamins: Sovereignty, Currency, and Monetary Union

The euro is perhaps the most visible, evocative achievement of the supranationalist vision of the European Union. However, this landmark in the contest over the distribution of sovereignty between the state and the Union also works to circumscribe the sovereignty of popular actors in important ways.

In many ways, the struggle to establish the euro was not about supranationalism or inter-governmentalism at all.[46] Rather, the euro has its foundation in the way capital flows in Europe. In essence, surplus countries, notably Germany, export far more to the rest of Europe than they import, leaving them with a sizable trade surplus relative to deficit countries, like France or Greece. Before the euro, this created two diametrically opposed economic interests. It was in the interest of deficit states to use low interest rates and deficit spending to stimulate domestic production and close their trade imbalance. Yet these very policies deprived surplus nations of their foreign markets. Europe was therefore locked into a mercantilist monetary competition. Deficit states worked to stimulate their domestic economies through deficit spending, and surplus states worked to prevent this by periodically raising their own interest rates, thus raising the cost of borrowing and forcing deficit states to abandon their now too-expensive economic interventions.[47]

After several rounds of this cycle, the French concluded that the sort of economic interventions France needed were impossible at the national level. Accordingly, they decided to change their focus to the supranational level.[48] As a result, successive generations of French authorities developed an ambitious plan: they would pursue monetary union, creating a new European Central Bank which, they hoped, would be willing to use monetary policy to support deficit economies.[49]

The surplus nations, however, were wise to the plan and used their considerable economic clout to hijack the project. Under threat of yet another engineered recession, they made sure that the new ECB would be the most independent central bank in the world[50] and that its mandate would be to pursue currency stability, not prop up deficit regions.[51] The currency would contain no mechanism for helping out struggling deficit nations – in fact, it would explicitly forbid bailouts.[52] The creation of the euro therefore transformed monetary policy from a political instrument to an entrenched economic structure.

In this way, the development of a supranational monetary policy reflects a contest between divergent economic interests and ideologies, but it also shows how both sides were committed to using supranationalism as a means of entrenching their own economic preferences, deliberately insulating them from popular contestation.

Big Brother Is Watching: Economic Surveillance and Criteria

The economic constitution also finds expression through fiscal policy. In fact, one of the most important practices through which sovereignty is delimited in Europe comes through the Fiscal Compact and the corresponding European Semester.[53]

Eurozone states have long been subject to the European Stability and Growth Pact (SGP), which obliges member states to maintain budget deficits of less than 3 per cent of GDP and overall national debt levels under 60 per cent of GDP.[54] If countries violate these criteria they risk substantial fines and sanctions. In order to ensure compliance, member states submit annual fiscal reports to the Commission, detailing their plans to meet the SGP criteria. These criteria represent a form of structural negative integration in the fiscal sphere – they work to prevent government spending, but not to enable EU spending. Indeed, because the EU's budget comes from the member states, the SGP represents an indirect limit on Union budgets as well.

After the euro crisis, the European Fiscal Compact (EFC) tightened these macroeconomic monitoring and enforcement mechanisms, requiring GDP targets to be incorporated into domestic law and supervised by an independent domestic monitor, providing for earlier and more consistent corrective action, and requiring every state to submit their national budgets to the Commission in advance.[55]

In practice, however, the Commission's "advice" is not limited to maintaining proper debt and deficit levels. Rather, it extends to every corner of economic policy, even areas in which the Union does not have authority – including, for example, tax policy.[56] In this way, all national budgets are pre-screened to ensure that they match the vision of the economic constitution.

Interestingly, the ability of the Union to compel policy changes is directly linked to the state of a member's economy – the more indebted a country is, the more stringent the surveillance and the more punitive the sanctions. In this sense, fiscal sovereignty exists as a sort of gradient – to the extent that states voluntarily limit their fiscal policies, they remain sovereign; to the extent that they exceed fiscal limits, sovereignty is curtailed.[57] This distribution of sovereignty serves less to empower one level or the other, and more to structure how power is used – and how it is not.

Commons Wealth: Contestation, Occupation, and Alternative Economies

In the face of structural, monetary, and fiscal constraints which limit the ability of representative institutions to shape the economic sphere, economic contestation has come to involve an array of extra-institutional, direct-action tactics. Sometimes, these tactics have even enacted alternative economic practices directly. These grassroots innovations constitute an important site of pluralism and an important practice of economic contestation in Europe.

The Italian Commons Movement provides an excellent example. The movement began in response to mass privatization, particularly of water utilities.[58] Activists began in local political fora with a series of citizen's initiatives, but regional and national governments alike refused to even debate their proposals.[59] Under public pressure, the Italian government formed a commission which recommended that certain resources be seen as "common" – that is to say, neither state-owned nor privately owned, but rather owned directly by the community of resource users and managed according to their needs and the needs of future generations.[60] The government, with the EU's support, ignored this recommendation and proceeded with privatization. Citizens organized a referendum to declare water a "common" resource. All major parties opposed the referendum, and the government also challenged the campaign in court.[61] Nevertheless, the referendum passed with a record 95 per cent and an unprecedented absolute majority of Italian citizens.[62] Parliament worked to ignore and limit the referendum results, prompting courts to intervene.[63] Nevertheless, privatization continued, pushed by Commission bureaucrats and the technocratic Monti government as a way to help meet the Maastricht criteria.

In response, activists organized the first successful European Citizens Initiative, far exceeding the requirements with 1.9 million signatures in thirteen member states.[64] Like the Italian government, the Commission's response was lacklustre, refusing to make access to water a human right and citing a need to remain "neutral" on questions of privatization.[65] Water services were omitted from a later directive on service liberalization, but privatization continued.

Having exhausted traditional institutional channels at both the state and EU level, commons activists took extra-institutional action. Theatres in Rome, Venice, Catania, Palermo, and Milan were illegally or semi-legally occupied as "cultural commons" and administered through participatory structures.[66] In Naples, activists established a participatory system of public governance for the local water corporation, taking control away from the city council and handing it directly to a community of resource users.[67]

These economic alternatives are deliberately participatory, rather than technocratic. Rather than relying on entrenched rules policed by experts, they rely on open-ended dialogues where communities of resource users are able to experiment in flexible, dynamic ways to suit their respective needs. In this sense, they represent a decidedly non-ordoliberal vision.

Similarly, much of Europe has a rich history of politicized squatting.[68] When the 2008 financial crisis hit, millions saw their homes foreclosed as political institutions struggled to respond from within the confines of an ordoliberal system. In response, activists in Spain and elsewhere began directly re-occupying repossessed homes, supporting families illegally staying in their erstwhile residences through dense networks of community aid.[69] Many occupied residences became directly democratic community hubs, complete with public assemblies and a rich relationship with the broader anti-austerity movement.[70] Like the commons, politicized squatting enacts an economic vision in which decisions are made directly by ordinary citizens, rather than technical experts, and where such decisions are not bound by predetermined rules.

Similarly, activists in the United Kingdom and across Europe have been contesting the economic system based on its unsustainable relationship to the living earth. Frustrated by the major political institutions' shared lack of action to tackle climate change, Extinction Rebellion has organized massive direct-action campaigns[71] to push for a citizens' assembly on climate change.[72] Likewise, French activists in the yellow-vest movement engaged in massive protests and even property destruction, calling not only for increased social programs and market intervention, but also for direct democracy. Demands varied widely but often included citizen initiatives, citizens' assemblies, and legislatures filled by lottery from the general population.[73] In both cases, activists want to take decision-making power away from technocrats and impotent legislatures and hand it to ordinary people, freed to act beyond the confines of ordoliberal economic policy.

These experiments are significant in at least three ways. First, they eschew technical management of the economy in favour of various forms of direct, participatory control of resources and economic decisions. Second, each of these sites contests the delimitation of sovereignty, positioning the people as a constituent power that is not bound by the existing economic structure.[74] Finally, they show how institutions which limit popular control over economic policy can also encourage extra-institutional forms of contestation.

Contemporary Economic Discourse: Embedding and Dis-Embedding

The economic structure of the EU is therefore shaped by an ordoliberal preference for technocratic decision-making and entrenched economic rules designed to insulate the economy from popular contestation. Because of these preferences, supranationalism has been closely tied to the entrenchment of an economic constitution. Structural, monetary, and fiscal constraints all fetter the authority of elected actors, transforming economic policy from an object of political debate to an object of technocratic management. In these ways, economic practices are redistributing power toward supranational and technocratic actors and also subjecting the authority of elected actors to limits that cannot be easily contested.

Discursively, the link between sovereignty and the de-politicization of the economy is pronounced. It has led some to herald an era of new corporate and financial sovereigns – powerful transnational elites, cross-cutting every conceivable level of power, whose own interests shape the exercise of authority more profoundly than any political process.[75] Others speak of the installation of technocratic governments in Italy or the imposition of loan conditions on Greece as "coups,"[76] and it is not uncommon to hear the dominance of German monetary policy spoken of as the "Fourth Reich."[77] Even the moniker of the latest economic crisis – the "*sovereign* debt crisis"[78] – suggests evocative links.

Stephen Gill describes this system as "disciplinary neo-liberalism" or "embedded neo-liberalism" – a series of electoral, legal, and fiscal punishments designed to keep elected officials playing by pre-determined "rules of the game."[79] As the economy is reconceptualized from an object of legitimate political debate to an object of technical management, for example, the political costs of departing from expert prescriptions grows. At the same time, an array of diverse national and transnational structures work to impose costs ranging from being shut out of credit markets to sanctions, tariffs, fines, asset seizures, conditional loans and strings-attached rescue packages. The "free" markets this infrastructure supports also enables highly mobile investors and employers to punish and reward economic policies by making or withdrawing investments.[80] The end result is that state decision-making becomes less responsive to citizens and more responsive to market forces, allowing capital to discipline governments while at the same time becoming increasingly free from discipline by those governments.[81] For Gill, it is not so much that political actors lack the formal capacity to depart from ordoliberal economics, but rather that the electoral costs are so high that few politicians would survive the attempt.[82] Disciplinary neoliberalism therefore creates what Sitrin and Azzellini call the "extreme center" – a basic core of economic policies that are shared by all major parties, left and right, at all levels of governance, such that even voting for the opposition does little to change macroeconomic choices.[83] Ordoliberalism is, in this sense, entrenched into the political system itself.

Hayek, and scholars building off his work, similarly emphasize structural biases, arguing that the creation of a transnational government inevitably undermines market intervention.[84] This is so for two reasons. First, transnational union undermines the interventionist capacity of national states.[85] Because corporations are free to move around the Union, they will seek the most favourable (least interventionist) conditions. This incentivizes a race to the bottom as countries compete to attract mobile capital. Similarly, since workers are also mobile, they too have an incentive to migrate to favourable countries, namely those with a high degree of social support, draining welfare systems they did not pay into. This, too, creates anti-interventionist pressures. Finally, national states are deprived of the use of tariffs and monetary policy. In these ways, and others, the capacity of the national state to manage its economy is dramatically undermined. Second, the interventionist capacity that has been lost at the national level is not necessarily re-created at the transnational level.[86] In fact, the diversity of national welfare, taxation, and corporate governance regimes, along with diverging economic interests, mean that any shared policies would have different effects in each member state. This in turn makes it incredibly demanding to garner the necessary consensus for transnational market interventions. As a result of these conditions, transnational union undermines the capacity of national states to intervene in the market without recreating comparable capacity at the European level. "The conclusion that, in a federation, certain economic powers, which are now generally wielded by the national state, could be exercised neither by the federation nor by the individual states, implies that there would have to be less government all round."[87] Scharpf, Streeck, and Cutler all offer complementary contemporary analyses, arguing that the ways authority is divided between state and Union work to make market-intervening exercises of authority structurally more difficult than market-entrenching policies.[88] In this sense, the contest between supranationalist and intergovernmentalist visions coincides with, and indeed masks, a contest between market-intervening and market-entrenching forms of governance.[89] This latter contest is not primarily about how authority is distributed, but rather how the total store of authority is limited or diminished.

Taking a different tact, Polanyi, and scholars building off his work, argue that liberal and neoliberal economic theory also involve an attempt to dis-embed the economy.[90] For these scholars, the emphasis is not on how a particular economic theory is embedded in political and legal structures, but rather how the economy is being separated from social and ecological concerns and transformed into an autonomous sphere of activity, responsive to no logic but its own.[91] Indeed, modern economic theory is based on the abstraction of the individual from their ecological and social surroundings.[92] Workers and consumers are treated as atomistic, their behaviour determined by market incentives alone and totally unaffected by their political, social, and natural relationships. Natural resources are treated as commodities, abstracted from the ecosystems and social relationships that produce and reproduce them. The social and ecological aspects of economic activity therefore become externalities that play no direct role in economic thought. As a result, economics can be reconceived as a pseudo-science, a purely technical sphere rather than an object of social debate.[93] So conceived, political intervention can be cast as inappropriate meddling, justifying – indeed necessitating – the insulation of economic decision-making from democratic control.[94] Seen in this light, economic constitutionalism not only compromises the autonomy of representative institutions, it ensures the autonomy of economic processes. Inevitably, this attempt to render the economy autonomous produces pushback, as political actors work to reassert control. Any such attempt, however, undermines economic output and undercuts its proponents. The result is a sort of "double movement" as society seeks to free the economy and re-embed it at the same time. Consider, for example, the EU's relatively robust environmental and anti-trust regulations and plentiful structural funds, or the participatory economies promoted by social movements, both of which coexist uneasily with broader trends toward liberalization. In Polanyi's time, the resulting tension gave rise to fascism. Contemporary far-right populism raises the spectre that this history may yet repeat itself.

Each of these accounts stresses how economic choices are increasingly insulated from public control and subject to entrenched limits which cross-cut institutional divisions and levels of government. These rules are complemented by a range of unelected public and private actors who are now influential at every level of the policy process. Considered in the context of the preceding chapters, this appears to be something of a countertrend. While the political and legal domains are increasingly characterized by revisable, contestable rules which are never quite settled, the economic sphere is increasingly organized around rules that are insulated from contestation. Similarly, while political and legal actors are sharing authority in ways that make them responsive to the concerns of others, economic authority is being concentrated in a small array of technocrats in a way that makes them less responsive to the concerns of others. This suggests that economic authority is not only being reallocated through the integration process; more profoundly, it is also being subjected to new limits as the very act of reallocation increasingly places some tasks beyond the power of any actor.

Case Study: Sovereign Debts and Democratic Deficits – The Euro Crisis

All of this can be illustrated in reference to the Greek financial crisis of 2009. As we have seen, patterns of economic exchange within Europe are dominated by a flow of goods from the Germanic centre to the eastern and Mediterranean peripheries, and an inverse flow of capital from the peripheries into Germanic and French banks.[95] This creates a surplus of cash in the surplus nations and a scarcity of it in deficit nations, making lending highly profitable in the periphery compared to the centre.[96] As a result, banks in the centre use their surplus cash to make lucrative loans in the periphery. The resulting loans finance the continued purchase of goods from the surplus countries, while locking the deficit countries into ever deeper debt.

Such was Greece's position in 2008. This, in combination with some serious internal problems in Greek tax collection and public spending, led to an accumulation of unsustainable debt, causing lenders to suddenly shut Greece out of the credit market. This meant that the Greek government could no longer cover its own expenses. Normally, countries have both monetary and fiscal options to respond to such crises. The monetary option is to print more money, allowing the country to pay its debts while simultaneously devaluing the currency and encouraging foreign investment. Because it was bound to the euro, however, this option was not available to the Greek government. The fiscal option is deficit spending, borrowing cash and using it to stimulate the economy, thereby increasing tax revenues and allowing the government to cover its debts in the long term. Because it was bound by the EU's debt and deficit criteria, however, this option too was unavailable. This triggered fears that Greece would have to either leave the euro or suffer economic collapse. With several other countries experiencing similar crises or debt levels, this possibility raised the spectre that the Eurozone could collapse entirely.[97] In light of the functional legitimacy claims on which the Union was built, such a crisis had the potential to throw the entire integration process into question.[98]

In an effort to safeguard the integration process, three technocratic institutions, the European Commission, the European Central Bank, and the International Monetary Fund – collectively nicknamed the Troika – offered a loan to help Greece meet its obligations. In exchange for the bailout, they demanded an aggressive package of ordoliberal reforms aimed at cutting government spending, privatizing state assets, and deregulating the market in order to encourage investment and competition. In other words, loans were conditioned on accepting an entrenched economic vision, locking Greece into a series of economic choices which no subsequent government could challenge.

After weeks of public protests and occupations, a snap election was held and Greek voters overwhelming rejected the pro-bailout government. A left-wing party formed government on a promise to use government spending to stimulate the economy. In essence, the Greek government preferred a social-democratic economic policy to an ordo- or neoliberal one. For months, the Greek government and the Troika negotiated. The Troika refused to offer a loan without ordoliberal conditions, portraying the crisis as a problem of technical management rather than a matter of political choices. In an attempt to re-politicize the issue, the Greek government put the Troika's offer to a referendum. Greek voters rejected it by substantial margins. However, the Troika refused to compromise and used its leverage as Greece's last remaining source of credit to force the government to accept its conditions.[99] Under considerable duress, the Greek government accepted the terms of an agreement that was arguably even harsher than the one their voters had rejected. The Troika proceeded to release its funds bit by bit, keeping Greece barely solvent, and thus keeping itself in a position to supervise the Greek economy on an ongoing basis.[100] Critics claim the result is a veritable coup, with the Troika – rather than Greece or the EU – exercising sovereignty and with loan conditions acting as a *de facto* Greek constitution.[101] When established institutions failed to provide a viable vehicle for popular concerns, the protest movement became as much about a rejection of technocratic rule and, indeed, of low-intensity representative democracy, as it was a rejection of austerity.[102]

In a very real sense, the combination of debt criteria, supranational monetary policy, conditional loans, and powerful unelected actors worked to constrain the ability of the Greek voter and even the Greek government to make their own economic choices. Instead, these choices are constrained by an economic constitution which is backed by a host of disciplinary measures and enforced by unelected, arm's-length institutions. The Greek crisis therefore illustrates, in dramatic fashion, how economic authority is flowing not only from state to Union, but also from representative institutions to technocratic ones. In the process, economic authority becomes more concentrated and less contestable – in other words, it comes to resemble sovereignty more closely.

Conclusions

As we have seen, the contest between supranational and inter-governmental visions of the EU has important economic dimensions, as economic power flows from the state toward the Union. Because of the ordoliberal nature of the EU, however, this also means that economic power is flowing from representative actors toward technocratic actors, being subjected to entrenched economic rules, or both. As a result, economic authority is increasingly concentrated in the hands of experts and increasingly insulated from contestation – in short, it is increasingly total and exclusive.

Indeed, the history of the EU's development has also been a history of economic entrenchment. From the start and still today, the specific form of supranationalism developed by the EU has been shaped by an ordoliberal ideology that favours technocratic decision-making and entrenched economic rules that popular actors cannot easily contest. With the development of entrenched economic rules, a range of unelected actors, both private and public, have also become involved in the governance process. In both these ways, the growth of the EU has also meant the growth of technocracy. This has resulted in both a redistribution of economic authority toward unelected actors and a reconceptualization, as economic matters are re-cast from objects of political debate to objects of technical management. Both processes work to insulate economic policy from contestation.

Because institutional channels of contestation are increasingly closed, economic contestation often takes on a populist and eurosceptical character, and dissatisfied actors frequently engage in forms of contestation that exceed formal institutional channels.

In this way, economic practices in Europe both mirror and depart from the patterns of practice than animate legal and political spheres. Like the political and legal spheres, economic actors have developed interpenetrating institutions, like the European semester, and forms of conditional authority, like the SGP and EFC. They have also brought private and technocratic actors into existing policy processes. None of these actors controls the economic sphere unilaterally. However, these interpenetrating institutions and forms of conditionality work together, not to facilitate contestation – as in the political and legal spheres – but rather to prevent it. Instead of creating an open-ended dialogue, economic constitutionalism has resulted in a shared silence.

Chapter Eight

Pluralism and Sovereignty in Europe

If sovereignty is defined by total, exclusive forms of authority designed to monopolize power and thereby provide order in a chaotic world, the novelty of the European project is immediately clear. Instead of vesting power in a singular, total, exclusive authority, European actors have dispersed authority, slowly building a multipolar system that provides order through compromise rather than fiat.

This system emerged gradually and in a deliberately piecemeal fashion. In the wake of centuries of ceaseless and escalating conflict, Europeans sought to stich previously sovereign states together by reaching a series of functional agreements. Some understood these agreements as a way to recue state sovereignty, while others foresaw the rise of a new supranational sovereign. Europeans, however, chose to leave such questions un-answered, focusing instead on developing an infrastructure of cooperation between authorities. Since each authority has a stake in continued cooperation, and since each can read cooperation in a manner compatible with their own authority claims, the system was able to progress without any single site of sovereignty. Instead, diverse parties were able to develop novel practices and hybrid institutions which allow them to share authority in heterarchical ways. This experiment has succeeded entirely in preventing war between European powers and, arguably, in curbing the worst forms of authoritarian abuse within them.

In particular, European actors have developed interpenetrating authority structures, codecision processes, and forms of condition-setting. These practices allow a variety of actors to coordinate their actions without ever reaching agreement on where authority does, or ought to, lie. Order in Europe is therefore a function of contestation rather than an alternative to it.

At the same time, however, European governance has become increasingly technocratic, as unelected actors take prominent roles in political processes, the power of judges relative to legislatures expands, and economic policy is subjected to entrenched rules that work to suppress rather than harness contestation. Technocracy works to stifle contestation and concentrate power and, to that extent, embraces the logic of sovereignty. European pluralism therefore represents a limited but nevertheless significant challenge to the practice of sovereignty, and one that continues to shift and evolve over time.

Connecting Political, Legal, and Economic Practices in Europe

I have argued that the political dimensions of European pluralism can be understood in large part as a contest between supranational and inter-governmental visions of the Union, and a parallel contest between technocratic and democratic visions. Rather than resolving these contests, political actors have developed a variety of codecision mechanisms. Of the four major political institutions, for example, two are supranational and two are inter-governmental. One is technocratic, one is democratic, and two are indirectly democratic or executive-led. To accomplish anything of note, the support of all four is needed. Thus, the political organs of the EU work to facilitate joint exercises of authority. This is not to say that each actor is equal or that the system is necessarily balanced. It does mean, however, that asymmetrically arranged actors can compete and cooperate without any of them exercising something like sovereignty over the others.

The legal dimensions of European pluralism display a similar logic but a different set of responses. Here, too, the relative power of elected and unelected actors is at stake, and here, too, supranationalist and inter-governmental visions collide as national and European courts make conflicting supremacy claims. As in the political sphere, these contests have gone pragmatically unresolved. Rather than developing codecision mechanisms to facilitate shared decisions, legal actors have turned to practices of condition-setting. By subjecting one another's authority to conditions, European courts are able to retain their autonomy while nevertheless coordinating their actions and preventing conflict between them. Because each court is both a condition-setter and a condition-receiver, neither exercises total or exclusive forms of authority. As in the political sphere, these arrangements are dynamic and evolving and commentators predict crisis constantly. In practice, however, the legal aspects of the integration process have been highly successful and surprisingly durable.

The economic dimensions of European pluralism are also characterized by contestation between supranational and inter-governmental visions, and especially between technocratic and democratic visions. Rather than leaving these questions unresolved, however, European actors have gradually entrenched a technocratic economic system. To the extent that codecision and condition-setting practices are present, these are designed to empower technocratic actors and thus to insulate economic policy-making from contestation. It would perhaps be an exaggeration to say that technocrats exercise sovereignty, but they do embrace a governance strategy based on the logic of sovereignty – ensure order by preventing contestation.

Several cross-cutting trends emerge across all three dimensions of authority. First, authority is being diffused to more and more sites and to more and more different kinds of sites (national, supranational, regional, corporate, bureaucratic, civic, etc.). Second, the various sites of authority at work in Europe do not share a common understanding of where authority does or should rest. Their relationships are therefore characterized by ongoing, perpetually unresolved contestation. Third and relatedly, each actor holds only a portion of the authority needed for collective action, such that the ability of any one actor to pursue its ends depends critically on the cooperation of others. Each actor therefore has an incentive to cooperate even in the face of ongoing disagreement about fundamental questions. As a result of this cultivated codependence, European governance is not a matter of watertight units, each governing its own jurisdiction unilaterally according to its own logic. Rather, European institutions tend to foster forms of codecision, sharing and distributing authority rather than concentrating it.

A number of practices facilitate such sharing. In particular, the use of interpenetrating authority structures and codecision structures has emerged as a prevalent alternative to sovereignty. The hybrid structure of the EU's institutions, the dual strategy of the Constitutional Convention as an inter-governmental conference and a constituent act, and the various decision-making procedures of the Union all represent notable attempts by two or more authoritative actors to regularize processes of codecision. Where authority sites have remained distinct, rather than developing shared institutions, they have often turned to strategies of conditionality instead. The *Solange* approach, characterized by the conditional acceptance of EU supremacy, is surely the paradigm case. Yet this logic is pervasive. The ECtHR's margin of appreciation works, in its own way, to reinforce that trend, making power contingent upon meeting certain standards. The Fiscal Compact draws on a similar logic, acting as a conditional, revocable recognition of budgetary autonomy. Even the principle of subsidiarity can be seen in this way, as imposing a condition on the Union's political authority. All of these arrangements function to create mutual flows of influence – one party accepts the influence of the other, but only on the condition that it be able to exert influence in return. Together, these practices help enable forms of action-coordination and conflict-management that do not require questions of authority to be settled definitively.

It is notable, however, that similar practices have been used to very different effect in the economic sphere. To the degree that the Commission exercises supervisory authority over national budgets, for example, national and EU institutions interpenetrate. The ECB represents a sort of codecision mechanism, and the fiscal parameters set by the EFC and the SGP represent a form of conditional authority. In all cases, however, the effect of these practices is to empower technocratic actors to influence other actors without being subject to influence in return. These practices redistribute authority to new actors, but they do not work to share authority. They operate in a context of persistent contestation, but they work to exclude rather than tolerate competing economic visions. As a result, these practices embrace the basic premise of sovereignty – that order is most secure where authority is most concentrated and contestation is least present. Economic practices are therefore an important reminder that European pluralism remains deeply and unevenly shaped by practices of sovereignty, embracing them in some places even as it works to transcend them in others. This countertrend can be read as a site where European pluralism is incomplete or underdeveloped. On the other hand, it can also be argued that the pluralist model of the political and legal spheres actually relies on the presence of a unitary model in the economic sphere, such that European governance represents a particular type of constrained, capitalist pluralism.

Together, these developments suggest that Europe is undergoing a deeply contested and fundamentally incomplete, but nevertheless significant, de-sovereignization process. Indeed, the integration process consists precisely of a gradual, piecemeal attempt to induce once-sovereign states to share authority with one another. Each actor loses a little bit of its autonomy to its neighbours, yet each receives an ability to influence those neighbours in return. As a result, no one's authority is quite as total or exclusive as it once was. This process is subject to countertrends and exceptions. Nevertheless, Europe is in the process of developing forms of social order whose logic is more heterarchical than hierarchical, and this system seems to provide social order at least as effectively as sovereign states. Indeed, Europe today, whatever its flaws, is considerably more peaceful, more prosperous, and more stable than it was when the integration experiment began.

Thinking Pluralism in Europe through Sympoiesis

Dempster's ideal-typical distinction between autopoietic and sympoietic systems can be helpful for understanding the European experiment.[1]

Autopoiesis means self-producing. Autopoietic systems are therefore self-referential systems, immune from outside influence.[2] Computer programs provide a classic example – they are organizationally closed; sequences of 1s and 0s determine their function and no amount of external persuasion or coercion will ever change them. The classical account of state sovereignty displays this character – isolated states, each contained in well-defined borders, making decisions as if they were radically separate, autonomous units. In contrast, sympoiesis means coproducing. Sympoietic systems are not self-referential; rather, they are collectively created by the systems that surround them.[3] For example, a healthy forest is ordered according to complex internal relationships in interaction with the prairie, costal, alpine, or tundra ecosystems that might surround it. If any of these surrounding systems changed, so too would the forest. Such systems have no sovereign. Instead, they display what Dempster calls "distributed control" as each actor influences the others.[4]

In such systems, order is a result of "emergent properties" – properties which do not inhere in any one system, but rather arise from the contested interactions between them.[5] Consider, for example, the relationship between courts and legislatures in a checks-and-balances system of government; the interaction of the two systems produces a rough balance between individual rights and collective goods despite – indeed, precisely because of – the fact that each branch of government leans decidedly in one direction or the other. Balance is not a characteristic of any of the component parts; rather, it emerges from their interaction and contestation. As Dempster puts it, "structures or behaviours emerge at critical points of tension ... [and] rely on the system poising at this position of dynamic tension, held by counteracting influences. If the tension is lost, so is the emergent structure or behaviour."[6]

Taking up this frame, we can see sovereignty as emulating autopoiesis, in that it envisions a world of discrete, unitary, and autonomous units.[7] Here, order is a function of non-competition – order becomes possible only when a system becomes closed to outside influences and subject to just one influence. In other words, order comes when authority is exclusive, and therefore total. In contrast, European pluralism appears closer to sympoiesis. It is made up of multiple, mutually interpenetrating actors who both enable and constrain one another. Here, order is a function of contestation, emerging precisely because various actors influence one another and are influenced in turn. In other words, order arises because authority is not exclusive, and therefore not total. Indeed, the functionalist development of the EU is in many ways similar to an emergent order, creating novel structures unpredictably in an environment of disequilibrium and contestation. All of this suggests that we miss something crucial about the integration process when we seek to understand its component actors as autopoietic, or when we try to arrange them according to a sovereign/subject binary. In the focus on each component part, we lose sight of the ways patterns of contestation and cooperation create emergent properties. From an autopoietic perspective, the ambiguous, contested nature of European governance appears as crisis, but from a sympoietic perspective, it appears as the engine of European governance.

The autopoietic/sympoietic distinction can also help us make sense of some of the countertrends in European integration. In effect, the market remains more autopoietic, self-referential, and institutionally shielded from the influence of surrounding social systems. Similarly, consider the technocratic nature of European governance and the democratic deficit. We might say that the sympoiesis emerging between European institutions has, for the most part, yet to emerge within these institutions. The Commission, for example, relates heterarchically with the Parliament and the Council. It remains, however, relatively insulated from the influence of ordinary citizens.[8] From the point of view of an institution, perhaps the system has become sympoietic. From the point of view of the average citizen, however, the system remains deeply hierarchical. In this sense, the system displays both sympoietic characteristics at the inter-institutional level and autopoietic characteristics at the intra-institutional level.

The distinction between sympoiesis and autopoiesis therefore allows us to recognize that different components of the European system may display different internal logics while also allowing us to recognize that these systems are neither discrete from one another nor internally coherent – rather, they are layered and interpenetrating on the one hand and shot through with counter-dynamics and contestation on the other. Indeed, different parts interpenetrate to different degrees, such that the European order is both a function of sovereignty, a function of pluralism and mutual influence, and above all, a function of the tension between these principles.

PART 3

Practices of Pluralism in Comparative Context

Chapter Nine

A Comparative Analysis of Pluralism in Europe and in Canada

[S]ome attempts towards Sovereignty, not long ago, was one of the principal causes of all our troubles.

          – Sir William Johnson, Superintendent of Indian Affairs[1]

The problem which must be solved in the first place, and without whose solution there will be no real progress, is the definitive abolition of the division of Europe into national sovereign states.

          – Altiero Spinelli and Ernesto Rossi, Founding Fathers of the EU[2]

Introduction – A Bridge Too Far

When you spend years of your life thinking about a concept, it starts to infuse your existence. You begin to see your objects of analysis everywhere, in everything. During the middle of the night, while taking a shower, or as you stroll down the street – something triggers a connection and suddenly the constellation of ideas that you obsess over as a profession appears to you more clearly.

    One such moment occurred for me in the middle of a bridge. I wasn't on my way to the office. In fact, I wasn't on my way to anywhere. Weeks earlier, Canadian police had once again moved to forcibly open Indigenous lands to resource extraction, this time on Wet'suwet'en territories. Settler authorities had approached local, *Indian Act* band councils and in many cases secured their consent.[3] Leaders from traditional Wet'suwet'en governance structures, however, were making their own sovereignty claims and they were challenging the pipeline. In a show of solidarity, a group of activists had occupied the BC legislature grounds, using it as a base of operations for marches, pickets, bank disruptions, and today, an occupation of the main bridge in downtown Victoria. Years after my encounter at the Kwekwecnewtxw, scenes like this one were becoming all too familiar. A grey-vested officer from the police force's community relations team approaches our liaison. The first question is always the same: "Are you in charge here?" The expectation of sovereignty. The critical entry point into understanding this gathering – comprehension begins by sorting participants into those who give orders and those who follow them. The reply is also standard: "Nobody is in charge, we make decisions collectively." His disbelief is evident. Sovereignty is a strong presumption.

"You have to move off the road," he says bluntly, hand resting on his sidearm. Traffic is not the real concern. There is another bridge a few hundred metres from where we stand (and another a few hundred metres past that one). Safety is not the concern either. The bridge has been safely closed off for hours now. No, the real concern is that the Wet'suwet'en chiefs, in denying the sovereignty of the pipeline company over its "property" is also denying the sovereignty of the Canadian state. By acting in solidarity, so too are we. Thus, our presence becomes a challenge to the sovereignty of this officer, his department, and the government for which they stand. Our presence raises the spectre of multiple sites of authority. In other words, it raises the question of pluralism. The officer, and his heavily armed colleagues in Wet'suwet'en territory, are enacting the response that sovereignty provides to the question of pluralism: where there are multiple authority sites, they must be subordinated to an order-giving sovereign. In order to maintain its vision of social order, the state must demonstrate that its authority is total and exclusive.

Eventually, the officer does just that. Police close in and the bridge is cleared. Sovereignty has been reasserted, but the cycle of conflict continues. It was a bridge today, tomorrow it will be an intersection, a ferry terminal, an office building. Across the country, others block railways, highways, ports, and more. Indeed, the wave of protests ends only when the federal government recognizes the authority of the hereditary chiefs and announces they will enter into negotiations.[4] Years later those negotiations have born limited fruit and conflict has resurged. Indeed, over the course of revising this manuscript, blockades and arrests accelerated, police conducted at least two more large-scale militarized raids,[5] a construction site was destroyed, and four police cruisers were torched.[6]

As I leave the bridge my mind drifts back to this book. From the European Union to the brutal colonization of Canada, from the Tsleil-Waututh to the Wet'suwet'en to this standoff on a bridge, the same lessons seem apparent. Maintaining sovereignty requires an enormous amount of violence, and in the end, this violence does not buy peace. Conversely, negotiation between multiple authorities does not threaten order, it facilitates it. In all these cases, the actual practice of pluralism puts the lie to the narrative of sovereignty.

Still, many decried negotiations with the Wet'suwet'en, just as many decry the Modern Treaty process or the EU or just about any other form of multilateralism that challenges the idea of sovereignty. We are taught that unilateralism is stable, safe, and desirable, while contestation is uncertain, risky, and threatening. As a result, we are frightened by the prospect of contestation and negotiation and this keeps us "captives of sovereignty."[7]

If writing this book has convinced me of anything, it is this: there are effective alternatives to sovereignty. In Canada and in Europe, there have been times when actors have found ways to coordinate conflicting authority claims without any of them exercising total or absolute authority over the others. In fact, actors in both settings have employed a remarkably similar set of practices. These practices are tried and tested in two profoundly different contexts. They show us that pluralism works, if we let it.

The following chapter works to make this case. I begin by summarizing my analysis of Europe and Canada and then mapping the patterns that connect them. In both settings, I show that actors have developed interpenetrating authority structures, codecision mechanisms, and condition-setting practices which allow them to navigate pluralism without recourse to sovereignty. I attempt to theorize these practices, showing how they rely on mutual need and contestability, and how sovereignty frustrates those conditions. I conclude that we need not fear practices that challenge the idea of sovereignty. Indeed, we should seek them out every opportunity.

Summary – A Tale of Two Agonisms?

An Overview of the Relationship between the EU and
Its Member States

In many ways, the relationship between the EU and its member states is quite remarkable. In the wake of centuries of escalating warfare and civil violence, European leaders adopted a strategy to gradually bind former antagonists together through shared institutions and mutual interests. From the beginning, different actors held profoundly different views about where authority does and should lie. With multiple actors claiming and exercising authority, systems based on sovereignty became impossible. Instead, Europe developed a variety of ways for actors to share authority or exercise it jointly without ever resolving their fundamental differences. In this context, each actor needs the support of its peers. Thus, each has an incentive to cooperate even in the face of persistent disagreement, conflict, and contestation. Some seventy years on, this system continues to broaden, deepen, and expand, facilitating governance and responding to crises with limited recourse to sovereign forms of authority.

Politically, the Union mediates at least two foundational tensions. One is between supranationalists, who see the EU as sovereign over the states, and inter-governmentalists, who see the states as sovereign and the EU as a mere tool to serve state interests. The other is between technocrats, who see the Union as way to place guard rails on democratic politics, and democrats who see the Union as a vehicle for popular input. Rather than resolving these differences, political actors sought narrow forms of cooperation where agreement could be reached and set contentious concerns aside. In this way, European actors took steps to gradually cultivate interdependence, many hoping that this would slowly produce shared institutional structures. Over the years, this founding ambiguity has been extended, as partisans of each ideology compromise in order to pass treaties. The EU maintains balance through complex and evolving interpenetrating authority structures and codecision practices at nearly every level of bureaucratic and political decision-making. In effect, the EU's political organs operationalize legitimacy chains, drawing on multiple actors at multiple levels in order to put forth a multifaceted account of legitimacy which has something to offer ideologues of every stripe.[8] As a result, no actor exercises anything like total or exclusive authority. Instead, authority is increasingly shared.

Legal practice displays a similar dynamic. The initial treaties were silent as to the relation between EU and national law. When the European Court of Justice first positioned itself, and by extension the EU, as the dominant partner by claiming independence from and supremacy over domestic legalities, national courts responded by placing limits and conditions on the ECJ's supremacy, effectively reasserting their own dominance.[9] The ECJ, deeply conscious of its need for the support of national courts, chose not to challenge this move directly. As a result, each legal order has gradually come to act as a check on the other – the ECJ must secure the support of national courts, and national courts must secure the support of the ECJ.[10] In this sense, the authority of each court has become contingent upon certain minimal conditions set by its peers. These conditional authority claims allow each actor to retain its own understanding of the relationship, while at the same time providing a powerful incentive to take other positions into account. Thus, legal actors have also developed ways to contest and coordinate their relationship over time without a sovereign to reign over them. Where political actors have largely used codecision mechanisms, legal actors have largely turned to condition-setting practices instead.

Economic practices are also contested, with supranationalist, intergovernmentalist, technocratic, and democratic actors vying for control. Rather than leaving these questions unresolved and subject to continual contestation, however, Europe has entrenched a particular economic vision and deliberately insulated it from contestation. Where codecision and condition-setting practices exist, they are mostly unidirectional, allowing technocratic actors to influence others without being subject to influence in return. Thus, Europe's remarkable ability to tolerate ad hoc and multipolar political and legal arrangements does not extend to the economic sphere, where actors work together to limit contestation and impose finality. Here, the strategy is to ensure order by limiting contestation, rather than harnessing it.

Politically and legally, Europe began as a collective of sovereign states, each claiming total and exclusive authority. Over time, however, European actors have cultivated a diverse set of interpenetrating institutions, codecision mechanisms, and condition-setting practices. These institutions put each nation in need of the others, motivating cooperation even in the face of deep and persistent contestation – and, crucially, in the absence of sovereign. In essence, each actor has sacrificed a little of their autonomy, opening themselves to the influence of the neighbours. In return, each receives the ability to influence its neighbours as well. Authority, in other words, is becoming less total and exclusive. The mutual influence that characterizes political and legal practices, however, is notably absent in economic practice. Instead, technocrats are increasingly exerting influence and increasingly insulated from being influenced. Here, the logic of sovereignty remains more pronounced. We might therefore conclude that Europe is undergoing a de-sovereignization process, as governance comes to rely less and less on total, exclusive forms of authority, but that this process remains ongoing, deeply contested, and critically incomplete. I have characterized this process as a limited sympoiesis. Just like natural ecosystems, each component part shapes the others and is shaped by them in complex, dynamic, and asymmetrical ways.

An Overview of the Relationship between
First Nations and Settler Authorities

The relationship between First Nations and settler authorities features a set of practices which are in many ways quite similar, and in other ways quite distinct. While it, too, is marked by ongoing contestation birthing interpenetrating institutions, codecision mechanisms, and conditional forms of authority, these practices have declined, rather than accelerated, over time. Initially, pluralist practice on that part of Turtle Island sometimes called Canada was quite sophisticated in the political, legal, and economic realms. Over time, however, a series of military, commercial, and demographic developments decreased mutual need between First Nations and settler authorities. At the same time, settler conceptions of authority became more total and exclusive. As a result, settler authorities have sought to absorb First Nations structures into their own, thereby attempting to transform a landscape of plurality and multilateralism to one defined by their own total, exclusive authority. First Nations have resisted these shifts and have, to varying degrees, preserved space for multilateral engagement even in a context of profound power asymmetry.

In the political sphere, for example, treaties were initially a commitment to share authority. The treaty relationship was characterized by continuing, ad hoc multilateralism, built on forms of interpenetration, codecision, and conditional authority between independent authorities. This system allowed actors to coordinate and contest their relationships over time without recourse to an ultimate authority. As imperial competition on the continent ended and demographic balances shifted, however, settler authorities worked to gradually reconceptualize treaties not as agreements to share authority, but as agreements to cede authority entirely. Thus, settlers repositioned themselves as having total, exclusive authority. Most First Nations have consistently enacted their own independent authority beyond the settler state and defended a view of treaty as ongoing multilateralism. This contestation has forced a degree of continued multilateralism, leaving settler authorities forever reaching violently toward, but never quite achieving, total and exclusive forms of authority.

The legal sphere displays a similar logic. Settler and First Nations authorities initially engaged in hybrid legal structures and negotiated jurisdictional arrangements. Bit by bit, however, settler authorities worked to incorporate these structures into their own institutions, re-expressing First Nations as a sub-component of the settler state, rather than an independent and external source of authority. Thus, settler thought slid from a view of First Nations as foreign entities to autonomous but subordinate components of settler empires to components of the local colonial legality to bearers of domestic constitutional rights. With each step, settler authorities moved to re-imagine First Nations authority as something delegated from the state, rather than an expression of their independent legal status. In so doing, they seek to make the persistence of First Nations compatible with their own claims to total, exclusive authority. First Nations have both availed themselves of settler law and persisted in giving their laws independent life. This has forced a continued degree of multilateralism, but against interlocutors who increasingly understood their own power as sovereign.

The economic sphere is not an exception to this pattern. Relations between First Nations and settler economies were initially characterized by a sort of mutual incorporation, as each system incorporated inputs from the other into its own economic organization. This period was characterized by a high degree of plurality, autonomy, and mutual (if asymmetrical) benefit. As the basis of economic production shifted away from the fur trade and toward agriculture and wage labour, however, settlers increasingly began dispossessing First Nations' lands and resources while at the same time reconceptualizing them as private property subject to the total, exclusive authority of the property owner. Thus, economic authority became more and more centralized in settler hands. First Nations have participated in and resisted the settler economy pragmatically, as well as persisting in their own distinct economic practices. Here too, contestation has preserved some limited forms of multilateralism, but these take place against a backdrop of profound power asymmetry.

In all three spheres, then, we see an initial state of mutual need and multilateralism where no actor exercised total or exclusive authority. Instead, various actors coordinated and contested their competing authority claims through interpenetrating authority structures, codecision mechanisms, and practices of conditional authority. Over time, however, military, demographic, and economic shifts worked to reduce mutual need between the parties. As mutual need declined, settler authorities pursued increasingly unilateral relations and increasingly total, exclusive forms of authority. First Nations have both made use of opportunities within the settler system and also persisted in enacting sources of legal, political, and economic organization independent of the settler system. In both ways, First Nations have worked to preserve a degree of multilateralism even in the face of deeply asymmetrical power relations. The end result is a system that is not quite sovereign, yet a long way from genuine pluralism. Overall, we might characterize this process as a deeply contested, ongoing, and only partially successful sovereignization process. I have characterized this process as a sort of symbiogenesis – a deep interaction between asymmetrically arranged but interdependent actors, where one attempts to absorb the other, which in turn resists its incorporation and seeks spaces of autonomy within a hostile but shared environment.

Comparison – Apples to Apples after All?

Comparing these two settings is inherently challenging. Indeed, I deliberately chose an apples-to-oranges comparison, placing a deeply colonial, coercive, and profoundly intercultural relationship between the state and older, so-called sub-state or non-state actors alongside a non-colonial, consensual, and intracultural relationship involving state and newer supra-state actors. The relationship between settler and First Nations authorities began from a place of non-state, largely non-capitalist pluralism and progressed gradually toward these institutional forms. Conversely, European pluralism began from a place of sovereign states and capitalist markets and has progressed gradually and unevenly toward different institutional arrangements. In other words, these two cases were chosen so as to be as different as possible.

It is all the more instructive, then, that there are startling similarities between the two cases. In both settings, the sites and periods which most closely resemble sovereign unilateralism are those where transsystemic relations are the most strained, the most violent, and the most oppressive. Similarly, in both settings, where multiple sites of authority coexist, society has not descended into destructive competition or chaos. Instead, actors have developed remarkably similar practices of interpenetration, codecision, and mutual conditionality which allow them to navigate their pluralist environment, contesting and coordinating their respective claims without recourse to an overarching authority.

Sovereignty's Claims

When one looks for sovereignty in these cases, something surprising emerges. To put it simply, power was never as unitary, coherent, and ordered as sovereign conceptions of authority suggest. Rather, power is always multilateral, contested, negotiated, assented to, resisted, made partial, and subjected to spaces and categories of exception. In short, the power of the "sovereign" always works through, and in relation to, the subject.[11] Agency is inherently distributed. Seen in this light, the so-called sovereign is just another of many actors struggling to shape their world. It is negotiation and contestation which are the bedrock of social order and this is true whether there is an actor calling itself the sovereign or not.

Given that power is always partial, contested, and distributed, a charitable reconstruction of the sovereignty myth might look something like this: although multilateralism is inescapable, order is most secure where multilateralism most closely resembles unilateralism. This version of sovereignty rephrases sovereignty as an aspirational ideal, rather than a descriptive reality. According to this ideal, order should function best where it most approximates sovereignty; in other words, where authority is most exclusive and total. Recall sovereignty's justification – that, absent a sovereign, competition between authority sites would create violence, chaos, and oppression. If this claim is true, the periods and sites which most approximate sovereignty should be the least violent and oppressive, while the periods and sites most marked by pluralism should be chaotic, competitive, and oppressive.

Interestingly, my two cases suggest just the opposite. In Canada, the earliest stages of encounter – where no actor enjoyed total or exclusive authority – are generally seen as the golden age of settler–First Nations relations. Practices of mutual aid and mutually, if asymmetrically, beneficial trade predominated. European diseases did cause an immense loss of life, and wars and even massacres did take place. Violence was certainly not uncommon, but it did not constitute a systematic assault on First Nations lifeways as such. As settler institutions began to impose more exclusive and total conceptions of power onto the relationship, violence became institutionalized and systemic,[12] entrenched in multifaceted policies of physical and cultural extermination.[13] Indeed, a great many of the most prominent practices of the North American genocide – residential schools, forced relocations, confinement to reservations, the destruction of traditional food sources and economies, germ warfare, forced sterilization, the suppression of traditional languages, the criminalization of traditional governance – all peaked during the zenith of the sovereignization process. Some, like the denial of adequate services, the lack of clean drinking water, over-incarceration, over-representation in child welfare, the disproportionate rates of Missing and Murdered Indigenous Women (MMIW), and many others, continue to this day. Nevertheless, to the limited extent that recent decades have seen a retreat from sovereignization, they have also seen some mitigation of the ongoing genocide against First Nations. Sovereignization processes in Canada are therefore bound up with a genocidal project that is also ongoing, contested, and incomplete. Sovereignization facilitates this project, even as the decimation of First Nations populations and polities facilitates sovereignization in turn.

In Europe, practices of sovereignty were, to an extent, deliberately abandoned precisely because they had produced centuries of ceaseless and ever more destructive wars,[14] fed global imperialism,[15] and facilitated the rise of fascism – which is, after all, the logic of sovereignty taken to the extreme.[16] As Europe has cultivated practices of pluralism, war between member states has gradually become unthinkable. Even seismic geopolitical shifts like Brexit now occur without open violence. Serious democratic challenges remain and some member states have shown particularly troubling authoritarian tendencies in recent years. In some ways, the integration process may help prop up such regimes, but it also acts as a constraint on their authoritarian tendencies and, in particular, on the open deployment of political violence by the state.[17] Neocolonialism remains as well, but it too is characterized less by overt force than it once was.[18] It would be naïve to say that European societies have transcended their reliance on violence and oppression entirely or achieved some sort of pluralist utopia, yet it is undeniable that Europe is noticeably less violent, chaotic, and oppressive than it was before the de-sovereignization process began. Erstwhile enemies now cooperate closely, and, where they compete, they do so in less destructive ways. The relationship between constitutional courts, for example, is filled with contestation yet almost never involves direct conflict. Qualified majority voting in the council and the proportional allocation of seats in the European parliament may provide a mechanism for large, rich countries to disproportionately influence smaller, poorer ones; but they also work to constrain a relationship of outright domination. Indeed, those places where authority most resembles sovereignty, as in technocratic institutions, play outsized roles driving the continent's increasingly volatile populism. Pluralism has not been a panacea, but it has not led to chaos and strife – indeed, just the opposite.

Thus, in both cases, sovereignty fails to deliver on its claims. The times and places that most approximate sovereignty have been the most violent, the most oppressive, and the most competitive, while those periods that most closely approach pluralism have seen the development of cooperative institutions which actually appear to decrease the presence of coercion in public life. Sovereignty, then, is not only a poor description of how the world *does* work, but also a poor ideal for how it *should* work. Indeed, the primary effect of sovereignty seems to be that it serves to legitimize and perpetuate arbitrary hierarchies, the myriad inequalities they produce, and the ceaseless violence necessary to maintain them.

Practices of Pluralism

In both contexts, then, the practice of sovereignty has failed to deliver on its promise to minimize violence and oppression. Likewise, where multiple sites of authority coexist, we have not seen an outbreak of competitive violence. Rather, we see three very similar sets of practices emerging – interpenetrating authority structures, codecision mechanisms, and mutually conditional authority claims. Together, these practices help actors to navigate their interactions, contesting and coordinating their respective claims over time without recourse to an overarching sovereign.

Codecision Mechanisms and Interpenetrating Authority Structures

One prominent pluralist practice has been the development of shared institutional spaces. Sometimes, actors have created new, shared institutions to exercise authority jointly – for example, the comanagement bodies on Haida Gwaii or the consociational arrangements in Ireland. These institutions allow actors to pool their authority together quite directly. In other cases, codecision or double-majority systems play a similar role. The ordinary (or codecision) procedure in the EU's legislative process, for example, requires majorities in both the supranational Parliament and the inter-governmental Council. Once again, authority is exercised jointly. By taking away the capacity for unilateral action, at least in their limited jurisdictions, such spaces create the conditions for compromise. I have been calling these formally shared spaces codecision mechanisms.

These codecision mechanisms can be comprehensive. Often, however, they are deliberately limited in scope such that each party retains spaces of autonomy alongside spaces of codecision. Thus, codecision mechanisms tend to complement, rather than replace the institutions of each participant. They do not erase the parties as independent entities or merge them into a totally shared institutional space, creating a new sovereign. Instead, they allow parties to share authority in targeted ways.

In other cases, actors choose to draw one another into their own pre-existing institutional spaces, as when settler authorities assumed names in First Nations' kin systems, or where heads of state act in the European Council. In this way, distinct institutions can interpenetrate one another such that the personnel comprising the two systems are not entirely discreet. The practice of offering national minorities or

Indigenous people guaranteed seats in national legislatures can be thought of this way as well. Compared with codecision mechanisms, these practices of interpenetration do less to prevent the parties from acting unilaterally, and thus do less to force compromise. Instead, they ensure that the concerns of each party are factored into the decisions of the others. In some cases, interpenetration takes place at the level of rules or principles, rather than personnel. For example, EU law is based in the constitutional traditions of its member states such that the rules and principles that underpin the two orders are not totally discrete. Likewise, aspects of Indigenous law are seen as continuing at common law. Again, each system of law remains distinct and autonomous, but their internal processes have been made responsive to the concerns of others. In all these ways, the boundaries between systems can become blurred, the systems themselves intertwined, in ways that facilitate coordination.

Codecision mechanisms and practices of interpenetration therefore constitute closely linked, but distinct pluralist practices. Both work to create shared institutional space. Still, we might imagine a spectrum ranging from mandatory compromise to mere coordination. Codecision mechanisms fall closer to the compromise end of the spectrum, while interpenetration facilitates coordination. Another way to put the same point would be that codecision mechanisms tend to be symmetrical, in that each party wields formally equal power. Where institutions interpenetrate, each party tends to retain a definitive majority in its own institutions. Forms of interpenetration, like guaranteed legislative representation, should not therefore be confused with codecision. Regardless, sharing institutional space has helped actors in both Europe and Canada to coordinate and contest their claims over time without creating a new sovereign to reign over them.

Both these practices can also coexist. The state of deep, ad hoc multilateralism which White famously called the "Middle Ground," for example, was one of interpenetration between settler and First Nations political, legal, and economic systems. Settler leaders were given names and titles that placed them within local kin structures, settler nations were brought into treaty alliances and confederacies, and a new class of imperial officials arose which White actually terms "French (and later English) chiefs" because they wielded authority not only within the imperial system but also within the kin system.[19] Similarly, First Nations leaders were offered uniforms and medals – the hallmarks of authority within the settler system[20] – and were drawn into European diplomacy. Settlers and First Nations authorities also developed codecision mechanisms like joint treaty councils, where officials drawn from both systems would participate in joint decision-making processes. Over time, these shared processes generated thin intercommunal norms, such that the principles, rules, and procedures of the two systems were not entirely distinct.[21] These intercommunal norms stood alongside, rather than replacing, the distinct normative structures of the parties. Similarly, criminal matters were often the subject of codecision, with chiefs serving as juries, English trials ending in an exchange of gifts, or settler and First Nations leaders meeting together in council to render a verdict.[22] First Nations and settler authorities thus participated in one another's structures and also developed shared structures. These practices did not replace, but rather complemented, their respective institutions. Each party was autonomous and retained the capacity for independent thought and action yet each also shared institutional space.

Contemporary visions of the relationship between settler and First Nations authorities are remarkably similar in this regard. Henderson's "treaty federalism," for example, envisions an interpenetration of Canadian and First Nations political institutions, with nations acting as constitutional units within a federation[23] with guaranteed legislative representation, judicial representation, and a seat at the constitutional negotiating table.[24] Indigenous law would also play a role in Canadian courts. In each case, settlers would presumably retain a definitive majority, such that settler institutions would be responsive to, but not meaningfully constrained by, First Nations concerns. In other cases, comanagement bodies might provide for formal codecision. Henderson is clear, however, that First Nations legal and political systems are not derivative of the settler constitutional structure and that First Nations political agency should not be exhausted by participation in settler institutions.[25] Rather, Henderson argues that initial treaties created areas of shared responsibility while also reserving some areas to each community.[26] First Nations therefore appear as independent polities with their own authority claims and their own authoritative institutions beyond the settler authority structure, while at the same time participating in limited shared institutions, norms, and forms of interpenetration. In this sense, treaty federalism is not neatly reducible to traditional federalism.[27] While both feature multiple independent authorities, traditional federalism focuses more on dividing powers into compartments, such that each actor moves unilaterally in its own sphere. The addition of codecision and interpenetration practices allows actors to not only divide authority, but also share it where appropriate.

The similarities to Europe are striking. The EU's legislative process, for example, deals with some issues under a "codecision procedure" that requires the consent of both the Parliament and the Council, while other issues are subject only to a "consultation procedure" where the Parliament can offer input, but the Council acts autonomously. Institutional space is shared to different degrees for different issues, and both the Commission and the national governments retain areas of autonomous action as well. Similarly, the personnel and principles of the two systems tend to blur together. Council members are drawn from national governments and continue to play roles in domestic government. Likewise, members of the European Parliament are often from national parties. Domestic courts enforce EU law and domestic governments carry out EU policies and programs, while the Commission advises on national budgets. Thus, personnel from national institutions participate directly in EU decision-making and vice versa, even while both maintain their own autonomous spheres of action and their own authority claims. Similarly, the ECJ draws on the constitutional traditions of its member states and the jurisprudence of the ECtHR, such that the rules and principles underlying the three systems are not totally discrete. Reference questions also allow the ECJ to participate directly in cases being heard at the national level, albeit in limited ways. In all these ways, it can be difficult, and fruitless, to try to tell exactly where one system ends and the other begins.[28] By creating different degrees of shared institutional space without erasing the autonomy of each actor, practices like these allow actors to coordinate without any of them exercising total or exclusive authority.

Both codecision mechanisms and interpenetrating authority structures therefore work to create shared institutional space. Simply because space is shared, however, does not mean that it is shared equally. Comanagement practices in Canada, for example, typically occur within the confines of the settler constitution, with interpretation and enforcement done unilaterally by settler courts.[29] Most comanagement structures are also advisory in nature, leaving ultimate authority with the relevant settler cabinet minister,[30] and governments often undermine or ignore them when political pressure is not sustained.[31] Even when they function well, comanagement structures tend to be established only when they can facilitate settler authorities' goals.[32] In all these ways, contemporary comanagement structures can sometimes be a technology of rule whereby Indigenous peoples are offered a limited voice in exchange for affirming the legitimacy of a fundamentally colonial system.[33] Similarly, activists in Spain's radically participatory 15M movement and politicians from allied political parties like Podemos have been experimenting with shared institutional spaces. While 15M retains its own autonomous public assemblies, many also support Podemos and allied parties in local, national, and European elections. Sometimes politicians report back to or receive instruction from local assemblies or use digital tools to consult 15M members.[34] In this sense, 15M participants are drawn into representative power structures. They have "one foot in and one foot out" of traditional institutions.[35] As a result, the two systems begin to blur together. However, many in 15M feel that elected leaders make the real decisions behind closed doors in a top-down manner and bring these decisions to local assemblies as a means of generating electoral support without genuinely listening to 15M input.[36] In these ways, Podemos can be accused of coopting, rather than cooperating with, 15M. Clearly, comanagement and other forms of interpenetration can sometimes work to reinforce hierarchy, offering limited forms of participation to subaltern partners in ways that allow dominant partners to coopt competing authority claims for their own ends.

Regardless, we can see that actors in both Europe and Canada have developed ways of sharing institutional space. In myriad ways, the personnel, rules, or principles of different systems are not entirely discrete. Sometimes, each party participates directly in the pre-existing institutions of its partner, such that the two systems interpenetrate. Sometimes they create new institutions based on codecision, where both parties exercise authority jointly. Sometimes both these practices cooccur. Typically, both partners retain the capacity for autonomous decision-making and action and both parties retain their own authority claims; yet each actor also exceeds the boundaries of its own social systems, influencing those of its partners. In return, each party accepts the influence of its partners as well. These flows of mutual influence are not always balanced. Sometimes they can work to challenge hierarchies, at other times to reinforce them. Still, to varying degrees, they eschew total and exclusive conceptions of authority, allowing actors to coordinate their respective systems without combining them completely nor subordinating them to an overarching sovereign.

Conditional Authority

While codecision mechanisms and interpenetrating institutions have played an important role in pluralist practice, actors in both Canada and Europe have also developed ways of exercising mutual influence without creating shared institutional spaces. In particular, actors in both settings have developed condition-setting practices. In essence, various actors recognize one another as independent authorities, but only subject to certain conditions. Because each actor has an incentive to secure the recognition of the others, each has an incentive to act within these conditions. Because the effective authority of each actor is maintained, in part, through the support of its peers, authority is not exclusive. Because each authority is subject to limits, authority is not total. Instead, practices of conditional authority allow actors to coordinate decisions without recourse to sovereignty.

While shared institutional spaces allow actors to share authority, they also require actors to come to more or less explicit agreements about how and where sharing will occur. They must agree on how shared spaces will be structured as well, both ontologically and procedurally. Similarly, shared spaces require actors to formally forego autonomous action, at least in certain areas. Conversely, condition-setting practices require no such agreements. Each actor can hold different, even contradictory, understandings of where authority does and should lie. Each can maintain its own distinct ontologies and decision-making practices, and each can retain, at least formally, full capacity for autonomous action. As long as each actor has an incentive to court the support of its peers, each will exercise its autonomy in ways that are acceptable to those peers. By allowing each party to explicitly spell out its own redlines, condition-setting practices help actors manage conflict. Indeed, the very process of engaging in inter-institutional dialogue about what does and doesn't cross those lines can help actors to find mutually acceptable solutions over time.

Forms of conditional authority are common in Europe, and they are diverse. For example, the Union operates through subsidiarity – the principle that program delivery ought to occur through the smallest competent government.[37] National and regional governments police the principle and can object to EU programs they feel they could deliver themselves. Thus, outside of its exclusive competences, the Union can make valid authority claims only where lower orders of government have abstained from competing claims. The Union's authority in these areas is, in that sense, subject to conditions. Likewise, Eurozone states are subject to the European Stability and Growth Pact and the European Fiscal Compact, which set limits on the size of budget deficits and national debts.[38] If countries violate these criteria they risk fines and sanctions and intrusive budgetary oversights.[39] In this sense, national spending authority is conditional upon meeting certain externally determined macroeconomic outcomes. Where states fail to meet these conditions, their authority is to that extent called into question by other actors. Loans to indebted countries are another prominent mechanism of conditionality, as credit is typically dependent on a package of policy reforms.[40] Indebted government's continuing ability to govern is – in a very real, financial way – conditioned upon meeting certain externally imposed policy outcomes.[41] In each of these cases, authority is not unfettered or exclusive. Rather, authority is contingent upon the support of other actors, and this support is tied to conditions. As a result, the condition-receiver must satisfy multiple standards – their own internal standards, as well as those of the condition-setter.[42]

In perhaps the most advanced example of this practice in Europe, the European Court of Justice has moved to place conditions on national law-making by proclaiming the supremacy of EU law over conflicting national legislation,[43] and even over national constitutions.[44] As a result, national legislators and courts are constrained to exercise their authority within the parameters of EU law. National courts, however, have contested the ECJ's claims of supremacy.[45] As we have seen, national courts have largely embraced what has been euphemistically referred to as the so-long-as approach – so long as the EU does not systematically violate core national principles, it will be considered supreme. In effect, the Court of Justice must comply with minimal standards set by each member state or else risk serious challenges to its own legitimacy. Because each actor needs other courts to accommodate its claims, each has an incentive to accommodate the claims of others. The courts therefore engage in dialogue, signalling concerns to one another until a mutually acceptable outcome is reached. This creates a system of autonomous but closely coordinated action, as each court manoeuvres to make claims that are true to its own internal body of law while also acceptable to their peers.[46] As a result, the system gradually generates a body of transnational precedent which is constructed and revised multilaterally.

Forms of conditional authority are also common in Canada. Early treaties, for example, often allowed for settler presence on the condition that First Nations lifeways not be disrupted. In something of a role reversal, Modern Treaties often feature equivalence provisions allowing First Nations to legislate freely in certain areas, but only provided that they not conflict with federal and provincial standards.[47] Even in areas where First Nations jurisdiction is paramount, it must operate within the confines of the Canadian Charter.[48] In all these ways, the authority that Modern Treaties grant is premised on certain conditions. Where those conditions are not met, settler courts will withhold their recognition, to that degree calling First Nations' authority into question. Funding for First Nations governments is also often subject to conditions set by the federal government.[49] Much like the conditional loans of the IMF and ECB, these conditional funding arrangements make *de facto* governing ability contingent upon meeting the standards of the funder. In these latter cases, condition-setting functions unilaterally – settler authorities set conditions and First Nations receive them – such that conditions act as a form of neocolonialism which allow settler authorities to control outcomes in First Nations communities indirectly.

In an illuminating study of the north-west coast potlatch system, Trosper observes a similarly conditional logic.[50] However, in this case conditions are set multilaterally, such that each party is both a condition-setter and a condition-receiver. According to Trosper, Indigenous governance on the north-west coast is conducted through linked groups of houses. Each house has its own territory and its own title-holding leadership. Each house selects its own leadership, but leadership claims have to be validated through potlatches. That is, in order to claim a title the contender must host a ritual feast, inviting the titleholders of neighbouring houses.[51] Once assembled, these neighbouring dignitaries observe rites designed to demonstrate that the claimant is qualified. They also receive gifts, which serve both as a recognition of their title and as proof that the claimant is able to manage the claimed territory well and produce wealth from it. If they are satisfied, they affirm the claimant's title. If they refuse, new claimants may manoeuvre to hold potlatches of their own. In this sense, one's claim to authority is contingent on the support of other titleholders. Once installed, both authority and title to land remained contingent on several duties, notably a duty to take care of the claimed land and preserve its productive capacity for future generations, and a duty to redistribute a portion of the wealth generated within the territory to other houses. Trosper calls this system "contingent proprietorship" because valid title claims are contingent upon meeting certain conditions. Importantly, this system is multilateral and does not depend on a hierarchy of titleholders. Rather, each titleholder both places conditions on others, and is subject to the conditions of others.

Contemporary activism on the north-west coast has also extended this logic in interesting ways. For example, Wet'suwet'en hereditary leaders have established broad protocols for their allies – conditions which solidarity actions must meet. Allies are empowered to act under the authority of the Wet'suwet'en, but only subject to conditions. Where those conditions are violated, the authority to act is to that extent called into question. In this case, condition-setting practices are more or less unidirectional. The Wet'suwet'en place conditions on their allies, and allies accept these conditions not as a deliberate means to upset prevailing power imbalances.

All these cases involve conditional forms of authority – forms where the authority of an actor is contingent on validation by other actors. The bearer of conditional authority must therefore satisfy multiple standards at once – their own internal standards and those of the condition-setter(s). Often, conditional forms of authority arise in contexts of profound power asymmetry, where dominant actors impose conditions on subaltern actors unilaterally. These relationships are inherently asymmetrical – the condition-setter is entirely autonomous and also enjoys the power to impose conditions. The condition-receiver enjoys only a constrained form of autonomy and has only a severely limited ability to influence the condition-setter. However, conditional forms of authority can also be used to deliberately upset pronounced power imbalances. Careful attention to power dynamics is therefore key – conditional authority can both express and undermine oppressive relations, in complex and con-text-dependent ways. Perhaps the most interesting forms of conditional authority are those where conditions are mutual, such that each actor is both a condition-receiver and a condition-setter at the same time. In the potlatch system or the relationship between European courts, each actor must meet several different standards of legitimacy simultaneously.[52]

Both in Europe and in Canada, then, actors have consistently employed condition-setting practices. These practices allow actors to coordinate, manage conflicts, and engage in dialogue even in the absence of (or alongside) shared institutional spaces. This practice does not depend on formal compromise or joint decision-making, nor does it depend on watertight compartments that make each actor sovereign in their own domains. Each actor retains the capacity for autonomous action accord-ing to its own internal processes, but each also has an incentive to wield its authority in ways that are acceptable to its peers. As a result, condi-tion-setting allows actors to exercise authority which is independent but not total or exclusive. This allows actors to coordinate and contest their relationship without recourse to sovereignty. As with codecision mecha-nisms and interpenetrating authority structures, condition-setting prac-tices can mask forms of top-down rule that closely resemble sovereignty. However, they can also create genuinely multilateral, heterarchical envi-ronments that model decidedly non-sovereign forms of authority.

Theorizing Pluralism: Contestation and Need as Conditions of Pluralist Practice

So it appears that sovereignty, for all its popular cachet, does not live up to its claims in either Europe or Canada. Multilateralism does not necessarily cause chaos and competition, and unilateralism does not necessarily minimize violence and coercion. Rather, multilateralism can occasion the development of interpenetrating institutions, codecision mechanisms, and conditional forms of authority which actually enable actors to coordinate, cooperate, and manage conflict remarkably effectively. However, as we have seen, each of these practices can be a tool of oppression, as well as a means of genuine multilateralism, depending on the context. This section uses agonist theory to explore the conditions that lead to multilateralism, furnishing some rough criteria we might use to assess, develop, and refine our practices of pluralism.

Briefly, agonists see differences of opinion as an inevitable and irresolvable part of human existence, such that any given political arrangement necessarily reflects the dominance of some views over others.[53] For agonists like Mouffe and Connolly, contestation allows a community to revisit and revise contentious issues over time. Conflict is, in this sense, creative and generative, allowing society to respond to shifting interests, ideologies, and relationships.[54] Agonists therefore see the ability to contest social norms as a key feature of a healthy regime.[55] Indeed, Ivison argues that it is contestability that ultimately legitimizes authority.[56] Liberal understandings of democracy, based on the idea of a social contract, legitimize governance through appeals to the consent of the governed – but this is obviously counterfactual. We are all born into social relations we did not explicitly consent to. The key question for Ivison is how easily we are able to remake inherited social relations to suit present needs, interests, and conceptions of justice.[57] Thus, it is contestation and not consent that grounds legitimacy. Institutions are oppressive to the extent that they are closed to effective contestation.

If contestation is one key to a healthy society, then the degree of contestability is one criterion by which social structures can be assessed. For Wiener, access to contestation is therefore a key concern – the issue is not simply the degree of contestability, but its distribution between actors.[58] Wiener therefore argues for regularized channels of contestation designed to involve all affected as a means of generating legitimate social decisions.[59]

The extent and distribution of access to contestation provides a helpful criterion for assessing the practices of interpenetration and conditional authority we have observed. Where interpenetrating institutions are shaped by meta-norms and goals that are not subject to contestation, they can often be technologies of oppression. In some comanagement structures in Canada, for example, critics complain that the development goals of the settler authorities are not open to discussion, reducing the First Nations' role to one of merely shaping how development will occur.[60] Likewise, European economic practices create forms of conditional authority, but those conditions are insulated from popular control by embedded structures that prevent effective institutional contestation. In effect, the ability to contest the European economic structure is confined to a very small group of powerful technocratic actors. Practices like these constitute forms of oppression because access to contestation is so limited, and because the distribution of access to contestation is so one-sided. Conversely, Maduro suggests that the relationship between European courts has been successful precisely because the conditional forms of authority it generates can be meaningfully contested by any actor at any time.[61] In these ways, an agonist focus on contestation helps us understand and assess many of the observed tendencies in the two contexts explored by this book.

Canonical agonists like Mouffe and Connolly also devote a great deal of attention to cultivating the conditions under which contestation is socially productive, differentiating properly political contestation from divisive and potentially dangerous conflicts.[62] Crucially, participants must understand one another not as Schmittian "enemies" but as adversaries, opponents who are nonetheless worthy of respect and care.[63] When political struggles display this ethical quality, conflict can be generative, positive, and democratic. The ethical disposition of social actors is therefore a paramount concern for many agonists.

My reading of the cases studied here, however, does not square well with an ethics-focused conception of agonism. Indeed, the early encounter between First Nations and settlers in Canada would be difficult to characterize as based on mutual respect. Settler authorities, by and large, viewed themselves as superior and foresaw the eventual assimilation, subjugation, or outright extinction of their "savage" interlocutors. For most colonial officials, the Middle Ground was never an ideal situation – it was a temporary accommodation on the road to eventual settler dominance. While First Nations were often treated with respect, this respect appears to my eye to have little to do with an ethical appreciation of the other. Rather, settler authorities engaged in multilateralism because they had to. Economically, militarily, politically, and legally, settler authorities *needed* their First Nations interlocutors. It was need, rather than an ethic of mutual respect, which drove pluralism.

Likewise, when the integration project first began to take hold of the European imagination and political landscape, the countries involved harboured deep, centuries-old antagonisms toward one another. To say that the EU was possible because the Germans and the French had come to respect each other as adversaries rather than enemies is, in my mind, too simple. Rather, erstwhile enemies – their economies ravaged, their overseas empires collapsing, their citizens hungry for durable peace, their eastern borders menaced by the Red Army, and their collective influence eclipsed by the United States – found themselves in a context of *mutual need*. It was the promise of security, global influence, and prosperity that pulled European countries together, not an abiding mutual respect or a sudden disappearance of age-old antagonisms. If the EU today is characterized by an agonist respect between the participants, I submit that this has been a result of, rather than a precondition for, the integration process.

All of this tentatively suggests that agonist *behaviour* is not necessarily so dependent on an agonist *ethic*. If anything, the ethic seems to flow from the behaviour, rather than the other way around. Indeed, Webber argues that pragmatic concerns often lead parties to accommodate one another and that the resulting institutions and shared expectations can gradually develop normative force after the fact.[64] What was once a mere matter of prudence over time becomes a matter of principle as both sides attach normative value to regularized patterns of interaction. Gradually, a shared normative grammar emerges, but this is as often as not a result, rather than a precondition, of community.[65] Webber's analysis suggests that the conditions which allow contestation to be generative, rather than destructive, have less to do with the ethical disposition of the participants and more to do with the presence of pragmatic reasons for mutual accommodation. In other words, agonist behaviour seems to spring, at least in part, from a context of mutual need.

The founders of the EU seemed to understand this point. They worked to erect a machinery of shared governance and a context of economic interdependence gradually, and largely behind the scenes, precisely because they worried that the public at large did not share an agonist ethic and would not consent to such cooperation if it was presented all at once.[66] Rather, they preferred a piecemeal approach, believing that the incremental accumulation of shared institutions and shared interests would gradually generate the necessary ethical commitments and group identities. White's influential account of the Middle Ground in central Canada also provides support. Throughout, White emphasizes that the Middle Ground depends on a suitable "infrastructure," a dense network of lived connections, mutual endeavours, and mutual need.[67] When new governors arrived from France, they typically brought continental arrogance with them and began their tenures by attempting unilateralism. Over time, each successive governor came to an awareness of mutual need and, with it, came to accept multilateral negotiations.[68] Agonist behaviour, in other words, often appears to flow from mutual need and shared endeavours, producing rather than resulting from agonist ethics.

Just as institutional structures can create and distribute access to contestation, they can also create and distribute need. This suggests that the distribution of need between actors is another key criterion that can be used to assess interpenetrating institutions and conditional forms of authority. For example, Canadian law requires that settler governments consult First Nations regarding development projects on their lands but does not generally require that they actually obtain First Nations consent.[69] This purely consultative approach works to limit the extent to which settler governments are in need of their First Nations partners. At the end of the day, settler needs can often be met even over First Nations objections. To the extent that legal decisions, protests, direct actions, and shifting political winds have put settlers in need, multilateral institutions have begun to emerge. First Nations have long argued for a pocket veto over development projects on their lands. This would place First Nations, corporations, and settler governments in a context of greater mutual need. If the patterns observed in this book are any guide, we might expect such mutual need to give rise to more shared institutions and practices of mutual influence. In other words, it would enable order. Just as importantly, it would provide a way past the all-or-nothing contests that currently characterize resource development; and it would do so in a manner that does not require the parties to come to the table as friends, but rather provides them with the means to build friendships over time. This example is not intended as a panacea, but rather to show how legal, political, and economic structures work to distribute need within our society, and how the distribution of need is one key criterion that can be used to differentiate forms of conditionality, codecision, and interpenetration that are oppressive from forms which are genuinely multilateral.

The growing, but still inadequate, role of the European Parliament can be understood in a similar manner. Initially, European elites could count on a broad "permissive consensus" and did not need to actively cultivate popular support. As integration became politicized, however, the need for input legitimacy feed a series of reforms which successively empowered the Parliament, regularized referenda, facilitated civil society consultation and even created limited forms direct democracy. European elites did not develop a new respect for popular opinion, rather than found themselves in a new position of need. Once again, the distribution of need between actors provides a valuable way to assess how multilateral their relationship really is.

Applying agonist theory to the cases studied here therefore suggests at least two useful criteria that we can use to assess codecision, interpenetration, and condition-setting practices. Where institutional arrangements can be used to foster mutual need and widespread contestability, this will allow actors to develop practices which are genuinely heterarchical. Where need and contestability are distributed in lopsided ways, these practices are more likely to support hierarchies and systems of oppression. We might therefore cultivate, assess, and revise our practices of pluralism with an eye to how they distribute both need and contestability.

Toward a Non-Sovereign Pluralism

The preceding sections suggest that sovereignty is a poor response to the presence of multiple authority sites. Sovereignty works to justify and legitimize violent hierarchy based on the claim that this is the only way to avoid destabilizing conflicts and ensure order. In the absence of sovereignty, however, the cases studied here have not descended into violent chaos. Instead, they have both shown the development of interpenetrating institutions, codecision mechanisms, and practices of conditionality which allow actors to coordinate and manage conflict without recourse to a sovereign.

Upon analysis, such practices are rooted in mutual need and shaped by the way they distribute access to contestation. This suggests that, where multiple authority sites coexist, the cultivation of mutual need and contestability ought to be of primary concern. Sovereignty falls short as a response to pluralism precisely because it cannot cultivate these characteristics. A sovereign aspires not to mutual need, but to unilateralism. It envisions not contestation, but obedience. Indeed, a sovereign's power is, by definition, exclusive. If a sovereign were in need of another, this other would have power and the sovereign would, to that extent, no longer be sovereign at all. More than this, reliance on others is presented as a threat to social order. Sovereignty is therefore fearful of need and contestation, working actively to suppress their development.

Fostering practices of pluralism therefore requires reconceptualizing authority. What we need, as Foucault says, "is a political philosophy that isn't erected around the problem of sovereignty ... We need to cut off the King's head: in political theory that has still to be done."[70] "We must abandon the juridical model of sovereignty ... [R]ather than looking for the single point from which all forms of power derive ... we must begin to let them operate in their multiplicity, their differences, their specificity, and their reversibility; we must therefore study them as relations of force that intersect, refer to one another, converge, or, on the contrary, come into conflict and strive to negate one another."[71] Many Indigenous scholars also advocate abandoning the concept of sovereignty as a conceptual dead end that only obscures the more interesting variety of concepts Indigenous theory has to offer.[72] As Alfred says, we need "mode[s] of social organisation in which there is no absolute authority."[73] In ridding ourselves of the expectation of sovereignty, we open ourselves to an infinitely wider variety of possible relationships, outcomes, and structures. At the same time, we expose those outcomes, whatever they may be, as the contingent result of shifting power relations, thereby opening them to assessment, critique, and revision. By "cutting off the King's head," in other words, we bring into focus the actual practice of pluralism.

To excise sovereignty from our theories is not enough. We must also move away from institutional forms that rely on the logic of sovereignty. The modern state, for example, is literally defined by its ability to monopolize power.[74] Yet when we seek pluralism, we almost always do so in reference to the state. We speak about the relationship between a state and a group within it. We ask whether the group warrants its own state, such that it too can enjoy unilateral authority. If we conclude it does not, we seek forms of accommodation which preserve the total authority of the state, and thus create deeply asymmetrical practices that are pluralist in only the thinnest sense. Alternatively, we turn to federal structures that divide sovereignty, offering each party unilateral power in their own specified jurisdictions. Such practices focus on the division of unilateral authority, they do not give us occasion to share authority, to cooperate and contest and coordinate with one another. There may be a place for practices of federalism, but alone they do not cultivate mutual need or facilitate contestation. Instead, we remain "captives of sovereignty"[75] – continually trying to shoehorn pluralism into a set of institutions that are fundamentally hostile to its preconditions.

Private property is based on a similar logic. Just as there is one sovereign per polity, there is one owner per property. A person's house is, as the saying goes, their castle. In other words, a person stands in relation to their house as a king stands in relation to their country, a wielder of total and exclusive authority. Indeed, some theories define ownership precisely as the ability to exclude.[76] Discussions of pluralism, however, typically take the inviolability of private property as a given.[77] Often, discussions of pluralism do not involve questions of ownership at all. When they do, we seek to divide property, but rarely to share it. Again, we find ourselves working to realize pluralism using institutional forms that are inherently hostile to mutual need and contestation.

Both private property and the sovereign state therefore participate in a conceptual schema which minimizes the need for interdependence and contestation, stifling the conditions that lead to pluralism. As a result, pluralism takes one of two forms – either we divide authority, leaving each party sovereign in their own domains, or else we create forms of pluralism consistent with sovereignty, offering accommodations that are so fundamentally one-sided that they represent little more than a means of legitimizing domination. The three practices offered here expand the toolset we can bring to bear on these questions, letting us share, as well as divide, authority.

If we want to "cut off the King's head" and foster genuine pluralism, we need to experiment with ways to share authority. When opportunities arise to do just that, however, many react with trepidation. In Europe, there is constant anxiety over the loss, modification, or diminishment of state sovereignty at the hands of the EU. This fear both fuels Euroscepticism and shapes the growth of the Union, as actors seek to realize the clear benefits of cooperation without losing the conceptual security sovereignty supposedly provides. Likewise, in Canada, treaty negotiations are constantly haunted by the spectre of sovereignty. The Hul'qumi'num Treaty Group (HTG), for example, came to the negotiating table seeking forms of comanagement, revenue sharing, and shared decision-making, particularly regarding land-use decisions and land taxes.[78] The group also sought a measure of non-exclusive cultural and property rights on privately owned lands within their territories. Like the Tsleil-Waututh,[79] Stó:lō,[80] and many others, HTG sought forms of shared authority that challenge the total, exclusive nature of sovereign governments and property owners. Settler negotiators, however, invariably take the position that pluralism can only occur within the logic of sovereignty, with clear-cut boundaries and established hierarchies to provide the long sought after, and much elusive, certainty that settler authorities crave.[81] As a result, proposals like HTG's are routinely rejected, contributing to the breakdown of treaty processes across the country, frustrating change, and ultimately feeding conflict.

In both cases, stubbornly clinging to sovereign forms of authority makes genuine pluralism impossible. It is time to accept that sovereignty has never brought us peace, justice, or order – and it never will. All sovereignty has done, all it will ever do, is work to justify the status quo and the violence necessary to maintain it. When opportunities arise to seek forms of pluralism that challenge sovereignty, to embrace practices that do not rely on absolutism, we should jump at the chance. We should do this knowing that we can rely on a set of practices – practices which are tested and proven in diverse contexts new and old, near and far – practices that prove a simple truth sovereignty has long worked to deny – pluralism works, if we let it.

Conclusions – A Bridge over Troubled Water

Having explored two deeply different pluralist contexts, mulled their similarities and differences, and reflected on the nature of pluralism as lived praxis, I am, perhaps, finally in a position to return to the questions that drove this inquiry. When I began, I was moved by the experience of watching as Tsleil-Waututh and Canadian law clashed over the Trans Mountain Pipeline. I saw how the drive toward sovereignty worked to create a coercive, competitive relationship defined by oppression and resistance, one with little room for cooperation or coexistence. I found myself asking how far, and in what ways, it might be possible to think differently[82] about authority in pluralist contexts.

Studying the actual practice of pluralism revealed that it is not only possible to *think* differently about authority, it's possible to *act* differently too.[83] In particular, my cases suggest at least three persistent mechanisms that actors in pluralist settings have used to manage conflict, facilitate cooperation, and coordinate claims without recourse to sovereign forms of authority. Both in Canada and in Europe, interpenetrating institutions, shared decision-making structures, and condition-setting practices have allowed actors to coordinate in a context of persistent pluralism. When these practices work to cultivate mutual need between parties over time, and when they distribute access to contestation widely and inclusively, they can allow diverse actors to navigate fundamental disagreements without recourse to violent hierarchies. Compared to traditional federalism, these practices allow us to share as well as divide authority, thus expanding the toolkit we can bring to bear on questions of pluralism.

I have therefore argued that institutions which presuppose sovereignty, like the sovereign state and private property, are conceptually counterproductive. By starting from political, legal, and economic forms which idealize total, exclusive authority, such institutions are resistant to power sharing, artificially limiting our responses to pluralism. This either stifles the development of pluralism or else mis-shapes pluralist practice, encouraging actors to distribute need and access to contestation so asymmetrically that pluralism simply masks and legitimizes hegemonic control. Institutions which presuppose sovereignty thus lead us to impoverished forms of pluralist practice. We should be ready to leave such institutional forms behind and embrace a wider array of pluralist practice.

It is not always easy to trust that practices of pluralism can really work. We have been taught that only hierarchy can ensure order. We have been taught that plurality can only bring chaos. We have been deeply conditioned into political, legal, and economic structures which not only allocate exclusive power to some – but also endeavour to leave others with nothing. This leaves opponents with little choice but to respond with unilateral assertions of their own, as both the Tsleil-Wau-tuth and Wet'suwet'en have done. Cycles of conflict inevitably ensue, and it is invariably oppressed, racialized, and colonized populations who bear most of the costs. We have been taught that this is simply the price of social order. If the process of writing this book has convinced me of anything, it is that these cycles of conflict are not inescapable. In fact, we are much better at managing conflict and much more capable of complex cooperation than sovereignty gives us credit for. By bringing to light real, existing practices – not just hypotheticals – I hope to reveal the very real possibility of a functioning, efficacious social order based on multiple sources of authority with no overarching sovereign to rule over them. We have the tools to respond differently to pluralism. These tools are tried and tested, they have been proven effective in a number of diverse settings. We can use them, if we choose to.

Notes

Law(s) and Order(s): Pluralism, Sovereignty, and the Rule of Law

1 I am a cis-het, white, settler male from L'nu (Mi'Kmaq) territories, subject to the Peace and Friendship Treaties of 1726, 1749, 1752, 1760, 1778, and 1779. I currently write and live on Lekwungen and W̱SÁNEĆ territories, subject to the Doulas Treaties of 1850 and 1852 respectively. I acknowledge the ongoing authority of the L'nu, Lekwungen, and W̱SÁNEĆ peoples pursuant to the spirit and intent of those treaties, and I recognize that continued disregard for treaty terms makes settler governance an act of ongoing colonization. I would like to acknowledge the generous financial support of the residents of Canada through their Social Sciences and Humanities Research Council, the Irving K. Barber Society, the Center for International Governance Innovation (CIGI), the Killam Foundation, the Center for Global Studies at the University of Victoria, and the Center for Constitutional Studies at the University of Alberta, without whom this book would not have been possible.

2 Protect the Inlet, "Kwekwecnewtxw," accessed 12 November 2019, https://protecttheinlet.ca/structure/.

3 I paraphrase based on my own best recollection.

4 For a classic account of state sovereignty see Albert Dicey, *Introduction to the Study of the Law of the Constitution*, 3rd ed. (London: MacMillan & Co., 1889), especially at 38–9. For discussion see Jonathan Havercroft, *Captives of Sovereignty* (Cambridge: Cambridge University Press, 2011).

5 Authority, as opposed to plain force, is an exercise of power which makes a claim to being justified. That is, authorities tell a story about why their power is legitimate. The police officer from the cartoons of my youth doesn't simply yell "stop" – they yell, "stop, in the name of the law!" This is precisely what makes law different from the command of an armed robber. The robber exercises power, but they do not tell us a story about

why their power is justified. Authority is more than the order of a gunman because it is an order paired with a legitimacy-generating narrative. Lon Fuller, "Positivism and Fidelity to Law: A Reply to Professor Hart," *Harvard Law Review* 71, no. 4 (1958).

6 Havercroft, *Captives of Sovereignty*, 4.

7 Thomas Hobbes, *Leviathan* (Cambridge: Cambridge University Press, 1904).

8 "[S]overeignty means neither more nor less than this, namely ... the right to make or unmake any law whatever; and, further, that no person or body is recognized ... as having a right to override or set aside the legislation." Dicey, *Constitution*, 38. Quoting Blackstone with approval, Dicey refers to sovereign power as "absolute despotic power" and "omnipotence" (39) and further stresses "the absence of any competing power" (48). This does not necessarily mean that power is totally unitary – sovereign states are often divided into multiple branches of government (executive, legislative, judicial) as well as into territorial units, as in federations. Because each of these units is sovereign within its own spheres, however, the spectre of pluralism does not arise. Pluralism, in the sense used in this book, arises when authority claims are not only multiple, but overlapping and conflicting, with no clear arbiter to settle disputes.

9 Stephen Krasner, "Westphalia and All That," in *Ideas and Foreign Policy: Beliefs, Institutions, and Political Change*, eds. Judith Goldstein and Robert Keohane (Ithaca, NY: Cornell University Press, 1993).

10 Robert Cover, "Nomos and Narrative," in *Narrative, Violence and the Law*, eds. Martha Minnow, Mark Ryan, and Austin Sarat (Ann Arbor: University of Michigan Press, 1995), 110.

11 James Tully, "Lineages of Contemporary Imperialism," in *Lineages of Empire: The Historical Roots of British Imperial Thought*, ed. Duncan Kelly (Oxford: Oxford University Press, 2009).

12 Boaventura de Sousa Santos, *Epistemologies of the South: Justice against Epistemicide* (Boulder, CO: Paradigm, 2014), especially 92, 153, 209, 238. Santos has recently been accused of gendered misconduct and sexual assault. I stand in solidarity with anyone who has been harmed. To erase such authors from our citations, however, would invisiblize the presence of patriarchy and gendered oppression in progressive academia, creating the convenient illusion that our intellectual influences (and by extension ourselves) are unsullied and uncomplicated. Writing in relation to racism, Ibram X. Kendi argues that we must recognize, rather than deny, the inevitable ways systems of oppression manifest in our communities and in our selves. I therefore prefer to foreground the allegations as a reminder of the pervasive effects of patriarchy, and of our own duties to continually name and confront it. Ibram X. Kendi, *How to Be an Antiracist* (New York: One World, 2019).

13 Cover, "Nomos and Narrative," especially 139–41, 155–63.

14 Michel Foucault, *The History of Sexuality, Vol. 2: The Use of Pleasure*, trans. Robert Hurley (New York: Random House, 1990), 8–10.

15 In Neil Walker's excellent collection *Sovereignty in Transition* (Portland: Hart Publishing, 2003), for example, Walker, Hans Lindahl, Richard Bellamy, Michael Keating, Miriam Aziz, Bruno de Witte, Cesary Mik, Anneli Albi, and Miguel Maduro all discuss terms like these in their contributions.

16 James Tully, *Public Philosophy in a New Key: Volume 1* (Cambridge: Cambridge University Press, 2009), especially chapter 1: Public Philosophy as a Critical Activity.

17 Boaventura de Sousa Santos, "A Non-Occidentalist West? Learned Ignorance and Ecology of Knowledge," *Theory, Culture & Society* 26, no. 8 (2009), 109.

18 Tully, *Public Philosophy*, 3.

19 For reasons of scope, my project will not meaningfully analyse the Metis or Inuit relationships to settlers. See the section on the Scope of the Inquiry below.

20 For a discussion of the institutional forms associated with sovereignty see Jeremy Webber, "We Are Still in the Age of Encounter: Section 35 and a Canada Beyond Sovereignty," in *From Recognition to Reconciliation: Essays on the Constitutional Entrenchment of Aboriginal and Treaty Rights*, eds. Patrick Macklem and Douglas Sanderson (Toronto: University of Toronto Press, 2016), 82. For a discussion of how Indigenous political organization challenges sovereignty see Taiaiake Alfred, "Sovereignty," in *Sovereignty Matters: Locations of Contestation and Possibility in Indigenous Struggles for Self-Determination*, ed. Joanne Barker (Lincoln: University of Nebraska Press, 2005), 33–50; Note that Alfred resigned from the University of Victoria after an investigation into gendered misconduct. The details are not public. I continue to cite his work for the reasons explained in supra note 12. Patricia Monture, "Notes on Sovereignty," in *Justice for Natives: Searching for Common Ground*, eds. Andrea P. Morrison and Irwin Cotler (Montreal: McGill-Queens University Press, 1997). Regarding the EU, "Jacques Delors, Formerly France's Minister of Finance and President of the European Commission, is said to have once called the European Union 'un objet politique non identifie'" (Thibaud 1991:47; Marks, Scharpf, et al. 1996:1). Many scholars appear to agree, characterizing the European Union as "sui generis," "unique," "new," "exceptional," "hybrid," and differing from ("more than," "less than") both federal states and international organizations – or even "a continuously changing 'in between order'" (Risse-Kappen 1996:56; see also Risse in Puchala 1972:269–70, 277; Burley [Slaughter] and Mattli 1993:41; Hix 1994:1; Laffan 1998:236; Moravcsik 1998:1, 79; Schmidt, Tsebelis, et al. 1999; Wallace 1999:203, 1983:403; Koslowski 2001:48; Wind 2001:103)." William Phelan, "What Is Sui Generis about the European Union? Costly International Cooperation in a Self-Contained Regime," *International Studies Review* 14, no. 3 (2012): 367; see also Katarina Peročević, "EU as Sui Generis – A Platypus-like Society," *Intereulaweast* 4, no. 2 (2017).

I would also like to acknowledge that I cite Taiaiake Alfred several times in this book. Alfred has recently resigned from the University of Victoria for presiding over a toxic and patriarchal environment, and has faced numerous criticisms regarding his relationship with women in particular. It would be wrong to cite his work without acknowledging his problematic behaviour and making clear that I in no way condone his actions. I stand in solidarity with all the students and others who have experienced harm, and I strive never to recreate such harms in my own life or work. Alfred has since taken some steps to accept accountability. Judging the adequacy of these steps is not my place. To ignore Alfred's undeniable contributions to the field or refuse to cite his work would, however, erase not only Alfred, but also the people he has harmed and the work they have done to create visibility and accountability around his actions. Instead, I prefer to foreground the conflict. See, for example, Anna Dodd, "Founding Director of UVic's Indigenous Governance Program Says He 'Embodied toxic Masculinity'," *The Martlet*, 7 March 2019, accessed 10 October 2021, https://www.martlet.ca/professor-taiaiake-alfred-resigns-from-uvic/.

21 This is not to say that the differences between European cultures are not significant. However, European peoples have interacted and shared ideas for millennia and have, as a result, developed a shared ontological, normative, and philosophical grammar the likes of which does not exist between Indigenous and settler peoples. On normative grammars see Jeremy Webber, "The Grammar of Customary Law," *McGill Law Journal* 54, no. 4 (2009). On the gradual development of such a grammar between settlers and First Nations see Jeremy Webber, "Relations of Force and Relations of Justice: The Emergence of Normative Community between Colonists and Aboriginal Peoples," *Osgoode Hall Law Journal* 33, no. 4 (1995).

22 For discussion see Thomas Hueglin, "Treaty Federalism as a Model of Policy Making: Comparing Canada and the European Union," *Canadian Public Administration* 56, no. 2 (2013).

23 There are limited exceptions, like Papillon's work on First Nations using the European concept of "multi-level governance." Martin Papillon, "Canadian Federalism and the Emerging Mosaic of Aboriginal Multilevel Governance," in *Canadian Federalism: Performance, Effectiveness, and Legitimacy*, eds. Herman Bakvis and Grace Skogstad, 3rd ed. (Oxford: Oxford University Press, 2012).

24 I do not engage with municipal governments because municipalities are not traditionally understood as making sovereignty claims. Their authority is delegated and not independent. Thus, relations between Indigenous peoples and municipalities involve somewhat different conceptual issues. For a discussion of municipal relations with First Nations see, for example, Christopher Alcantara and Jen Nelles, *A Quiet Evolution: The Emergence of Indigenous-Local Intergovernmental Partnerships in Canada* (Toronto: University of Toronto Press, 2016); Papillon, "Aboriginal Multilevel Governance."

25 Cover, "Nomos and Narrative," especially 106–12.

26 Alan Hunt, "Law as a Constitutive Mode of Regulation," in *Explorations in Law and Society: Toward a Constitutive Theory of Law* (New York: Routledge, 1993), 326. See also Alan Hunt, "Encounters with Juridical Assemblages: Reflections on Foucault, Law and the Juridical," in *Re-Reading Foucault: On Law, Power and Rights*, ed. Ben Golder (New York: Routledge, 2012).

27 Hunt, "Juridical Assemblages," 71.

28 See especially Yann Allard-Tremblay, "Braiding Liberation Discourses: Dialectical, Civic and Disjunctive Views about Resistance and Violence," *Canadian Journal of Political Science* 55, no. 2 (2022); Oonagh Fitzgerald and Risa Schwartz, "Introduction," in *UNDRIP Implementation Braiding International, Domestic and Indigenous Laws* (Waterloo, ON: Centre for International Governance Innovation, 2017). See also John Borrows et al., eds., *Braiding Legal Orders: Implementing the United Nations Declaration on the Rights of Indigenous Peoples* (Waterloo, ON: Centre for International Governance Innovation, 2019); Robin Wall Kimmerer, *Braiding Sweetgrass: Indigenous Wisdom, Scientific Knowledge and the Teachings of Plants* (Minneapolis: Milkweed Editions, 2013).

29 Readers may wonder why I choose to treat the economic, political, and legal dimensions of each relationship in separate chapters, when these subjects are so closely interrelated. My reasoning is this: there are countless stories that could be told about these relationships from countless different lenses. Each story reveals some aspect of a larger understanding, but no story captures everything comprehensively. Thus, the partiality of each story is important – it reminds us that whatever we have understood from any given account, there is always more to the story. The idea of a single comprehensive account is, in fact, a dangerous illusion that lends itself to hubris and erases whatever it omits. By treating the economic, legal, and political dimensions of this work separately, I hope to performatively enact that this book offers a variety of particular perspectives but does not, indeed cannot, offer a comprehensive account.

1. Political Practices

1 As the Royal Commission on Aboriginal Peoples puts it: "Relations between the British colonies and aboriginal peoples were complex and diverse, with strong elements of contradiction and paradox that often defy understanding even today," Canada, Georges Erasmus, and René Dussault, *Report of the Royal Commission on Aboriginal Peoples – Volume 1: Looking Forward, Looking Back* (Ottawa: Royal Commission on Aboriginal Peoples, 1996), 107.

2 J.R. Miller's influential division uses four phases: commercial compacts, peace and friendship treaties, territorial treaties, and modern treaties. The seminal Royal Commission on Aboriginal Peoples (RCAP) also uses four phases: Separate Worlds, Contact and Co-operation, Displacement and Assimilation, and Negotiation and Renewal. These map fairly well onto

Miller's divisions. See J.R. Miller, *Skyscrapers Hide the Heavens* (Toronto: University of Toronto Press, 1989); Canada, *Royal Commission*.

3 For complementary discussions of this transition see, for example, John Borrows, "Canada's Colonial Constitution," in *The Right Relationship: Reimagining the Implementation of Historical Treaties*, eds. John Borrows and Michael Coyle (Toronto: University of Toronto Press, 2017); Joshua Nichols, *A Reconciliation without Recollection?: An Investigation of the Foundations of Aboriginal Law in Canada* (Toronto: University of Toronto Press, 2019).

4 See Mary Louise Pratt, *Imperial Eyes: Travel Writing and Transculturation* (London: Routledge, 1992), especially 4.

5 I recognize that using the term "Canada" is problematic, in that it implicitly naturalizes and foregrounds the settler state rather than Indigenous nations. Some use the term "Turtle Island," drawn from the occurrence of the turtle in many Indigenous creation stories. Gary Snyder, "The Rediscovery of Turtle Island," in *Deep Ecology for the 21st Century*, ed. George Sessions (Boulder, CO: Shambhala, 1995), 9–16. However, Turtle Island refers to the whole of North America, and thus includes substantial areas that are not covered in this book. Of course, First Nations have words for their own territories, but to my knowledge there is no widely used term that refers to the whole geographic area that is sometimes called "Canada." Thus, for lack of an alternative way to accurately refer to the area covered in this book, Canada is the term I will use.

6 The phrase is borrowed from Richard White's influential account in *The Middle Ground: Indians, Empires, and Republics in the Great Lakes Region, 1650–1815* (Cambridge: Cambridge University Press, 2010).

7 The period runs roughly until the fall of New France, when the balance of power tilted definitively towards the British. However, the actual timing of British dominance varies substantially, occurring earlier in areas closer to British settlement and later areas that were farther away, more remote, or of less economic and geopolitical importance.

8 See Mattias Åhrén, *Indigenous Peoples' Status in the International Legal System* (Oxford: Oxford University Press, 2016), especially Part 1; Antony Anghie, *Imperialism, Sovereignty and the Making of International Law* (New York: Cambridge University Press, 2005), especially chapter 1.

9 Harald Prins, *Storm Clouds over Wabanakiak: Confederacy Diplomacy until Dummer's Treaty (1727)* (Amherst: The Atlantic Policy Congress of First Nations Chiefs, 1999), 6.

10 Robert Nichols, *Theft Is Property! Dispossession and Critical Theory* (Durham, NC: Duke University Press, 2019), especially chapter 3.

11 Miller, *Skyscrapers*, 51.

12 Canada, *Royal Commission*, 120.

13 See, for example, Miller, *Skyscrapers*, 37.

14 White, *Middle Ground*, 179.

15 White, *Middle Ground,* especially the Introduction.

16 See especially James Tully, "On the Expression 'Sharing the Land' in Treaty Making," in *Just Relations: Kinship, Law and Politics,* eds. Rob Wishart and Sarah Moritz (Edmonton: University of Alberta Press, forthcoming); White, *Middle Ground*; Peter Cook, Neil Vallance, John Lutz, Graham Brazier, and Hamar Foster, eds., *To Share, Not Surrender Indigenous and Settler Visions of Treaty-Making in the Colonies of Vancouver Island and British Columbia* (Vancouver: University of British Columbia Press, 2021); J.R. Miller, *Compact, Contract, Covenant: Aboriginal-Treaty-Making in Canada* (Toronto: University of Toronto Press, 2009); Canada, *Royal Commission,* vol. 1.

17 Jon Parmenter, "The Meaning of Kaswentha and the Two Row Wampum Belt in Haudenosaunee (Iroquois) History: Can Indigenous Oral Tradition Be Reconciled with the Documentary Record?" *Journal of Early American History* 3, no. 1 (2013).

18 Michael Asch, *On Being Here to Stay: Treaties and Aboriginal Rights in Canada* (Toronto: University of Toronto Press, 2014), 131.

19 See, for example, Prins, *Storm Clouds,* 12; or, more generally, Canada, *Royal Commission,* Part 1, chapter 5 – Contact and Cooperation.

20 Kent McNeil, "Shared Indigenous and Crown Sovereignty: Modifying the State Model," *Osgoode Legal Studies Research Paper* 2815 (2020); David E. Wilkins and Tsianina Lomawaima, *Uneven Ground: American Indian Sovereignty and Federal Law* (Norman: University of Oklahoma Press, 2002), especially 19–63.

21 Prins, *Storm Clouds,* 7.

22 Prins, *Storm Clouds,* 13.

23 The title comes from Alan Taylor's influential book of the same name. Alan Taylor, *The Divided Ground: Indians, Settlers and the Northern Borderland of the American Revolution* (New York: Knopf, 2006).

24 This range runs roughly from the fall of New France to the last of the Numbered Treaties.

25 To the British, differences between nations became less salient. Rather than dealing with First Nations one on one or in their self-organized confederacies, for example, the British began identifying parcels of land they desired, and then gathering all affected nations and insisting on treating with them collectively, even when this cut across traditional diplomatic lines. Indeed, the Royal Proclamation asserted British sovereignty even over those nations with whom it had never treated. Sebastien Grammond, *Terms of Coexistence: Indigenous Peoples and Canadian Law* (Toronto: Carswell, 2013), 358–60.

26 Robert Hamilton, *Sovereignty, Terra Nullius, Crown Lands, and Indian Reserves* (PhD diss., University of Victoria, 2016), 81.

27 For discussion see Taylor, *Divided Ground,* 40–1.

28 Canada, *Royal Commission,* Part 1, chapter 6: Displacement and Assimilation.

29 John Borrows, "Wampum at Niagara: The Royal Proclamation, Canadian Legal History, and Self Government," in *Aboriginal and Treaty Rights in Canada: Essays on Law, Equity, and Respect for Difference*, ed. Michael Asch (Vancouver: University of British Columbia Press, 1997), 4.

30 In part, the proclamation represents a solidification of existing colonial ambiguities, reflecting both the international status of First Nations, here cast in the European mould of territorially discrete units, and also their supposed pre-sovereign status, captured by their presumed subordination even within those territories and their inability to alienate said territory to anyone but the Crown. For a complementary discussion see Borrows, "Wampum," 4.

31 Promislow explains: "In the 17th and 18th centuries, when the law of nations had not yet settled into its later fixations on the state and territorial sovereignty, Indian nations in North America were generally conceived as having some status and rights amongst nations, albeit not the same status and rights as Christian nations ... As settler pressures grew in the 19th century, and as the law of nations and British imperialism shifted under the influence of the emerging positivism, so did judicial treatments of treaties. Tribes lost their status on the international stage and were no longer recognized as having the capacity to enter into international treaties. Further, the rights of the European discoverer shifted from achieving only territorial claims against other European powers – claims that had to be completed through war or treaties of cession – to achieving full territorial rights upon which the property rights of prior inhabitants persisted only by the goodwill of the Crown. This shift rendered treaties a matter of pragmatics and policy rather than law." Janna Promislow, "Treaties in History and Law," *U.B.C. Law Review* 47, no. 3 (2014): 1143.

32 See, for example, James Daschuk, *Clearing the Plains: Disease, Politics of Starvation, and the Loss of Aboriginal Life* (Regina, SK: University of Regina Press, 2013).

33 Jon William Parmenter, "Pontiac's War: Forging New Links in the Anglo-Iroquois Covenant Chain, 1758–1766," *Ethnohistory* 44, no. 4 (1997), 633.

34 Taylor, *Divided Ground*, 8.

35 Heidi Kiiwetinepinesiik Stark, "Marked by Fire: Anishinaabe Articulations of Nationhood in Treaty-Making with the United States and Canada," *American Indian Quarterly* 36, no. 2 (2012).

36 Borrows, "Wampum"; see also Aaron Mills and Kaitlin McNabb, "To All My Relations: Contemporary Colonialism, and Treaty Citizenship Today," *Rabble*, 12 August 2014.

37 Such pragmatism knew no bounds. In treaty negotiations between the French and British, for example, the British came to argue that the French had obtained sovereignty over all of Acadia without any treaty to that effect. This position clashed with Britain's own treaty-based approach, but permitted them to exaggerate the authority they gained from the French surrender. France, in turn, pointed to the lack of treaties to argue that they could not cede sovereignty because they had never acquired it, despite a long-standing practice of claiming sovereignty without treaties. Alain Beaulieu, "The Acquisition of Aboriginal Land in Canada: The Genealogy of an Ambivalent System (1600–1867)," in *Empire by Treaty: Negotiating European Expansion 1600–1900*, ed. Saliha Belmessous (Oxford: Oxford University Press, 2015) 107–14.

38 This period runs roughly from the Robinson-Huron Treaties to 1969, the White Paper on Indian Policy.

39 Miller, *Skyscrapers*, 93. For an excellent discussion of how this line between international and domestic subject has been policed and blurred in practice, see Joshua Nichols, "Sui Generis Sovereignties: The Relationship between Treaty Interpretation and Canadian Sovereignty," *in Reflections on Canada's Past, Present and Future in International Law*, eds. Oonagh E. Fitzgerald, Valerie Hughes, and Mark Jewett (Waterloo, ON: CIGI, 2018).

40 Miller, *Skyscrapers*, 193.

41 For discussion see Hamar Foster, "'We Want a Strong Promise': The Opposition to Indian Treaties in British Columbia, 1850–1990," *Native Studies Review* 18, no. 1 (2009).

42 Asch, *Being Here to Stay*, 8, 80, 161.

43 Miller, *Skyscrapers*, 110–14.

44 Miller, *Skyscrapers*, 188.

45 Miller, *Skyscrapers*, 192.

46 Promislow, "Treaties," 1146.

47 Nichols calls the relationship one of "administrative despotism." Joshua Nichols, *Reconciliation and the Foundations of Aboriginal Law in Canada* (PhD diss., University of Victoria, 2016), for discussion see especially note 88.

48 Promislow, "Treaties," 1146–7.

49 John Borrows and Leonard Rotman, *Aboriginal Legal Issues – Cases, Materials and Commentary*, 4th ed. (New York: LexisNexis, 2012), 36.

50 For discussion of the events leading up to the formation of Manitoba see John Borrows, *Freedom and Indigenous Constitutionalism* (Toronto: University of Toronto Press, 2016), 109.

51 John Lutz, *Makuk* (Vancouver: University of British Columbia Press, 2009), especially chapter 5. For an excellent example see Robert Galois, "The History of the Upper Skeena," *Native Studies Review* 9, no. 2 (1993).

52 The Laurier Memorial sent to Sir Wilfred Laurier, Premier of the Dominion of Canada from the Chiefs of the Shuswap, Okanagan, and Couteau Tribes of British Columbia, Chief John Tetlenitsa (Nlaka'pamux), Chief Petit Louis (Secwepemc), and Chief John Chilahitsa (Syilx), presented at Kamloops, BC, 25 August 1910. On 10 May 1911, a similar memorial was sent to Frank Oliver, Minister of the Interior and signed by chiefs from the Secwepemc, T'silqot'in, St'lat'limc, Okanagan, Carrier, Thompson (N'lkapmc), Tahltan, and Sto:lo Nations. Quoted in Tully, "'Sharing the Land' in Treaty Making." See also the extended discussion in James Tully, "Two Ways of Being Colonial: Guest and Settler," paper presented to the *Workshop on Colonization and Decolonization* (Vancouver: University of British Columbia, 12 April 2017).

53 For extended discussion see Harold Cardinal, *The Unjust Society* (Vancouver: Douglas & McIntyre, 1969).

54 During this era, Canada, and much of the colonial world, was in the final stages of transition from old, polyarchic empires where colonial and imperial officials exercised layered authority, to independent nation-states which enjoyed total sovereignty. The proposed elimination of First Nations as political communities can be understood as participating in the same logic, seeking to wipe away the multilateralism of earlier eras in favour of total and exclusive conceptions of political authority.

55 Borrows, *Freedom and Indigenous Constitutionalism*, 115–29.

56 Borrows, *Freedom and Indigenous Constitutionalism*, 124.

57 Borrows, *Freedom and Indigenous Constitutionalism*, 63.

58 Ben Isitt, *Patterns of Protest: Property, Social Movements, and the Law in British Columbia* (PhD diss., University of Victoria, 2018), 67, 207.

59 Borrows, *Freedom and Indigenous Constitutionalism*, 77.

60 In 2008, the settler state agreed to settle a massive civil suit brought by survivors of residential schools by, among other things, establishing a Truth and Reconciliation Commission (TRC) that would become a major touchstone in the discourse of reconciliation. Truth and Reconciliation Commission of Canada, *Truth and Reconciliation Commission of Canada: Calls to Action* (Winnipeg: TRC, 2015). Its focus on residential schools and their effects, however, mean that the TRC is not squarely focused on questions of sovereignty or authority, and thus is not central to my discussion. In fact, Coulthard has argued that the TRC actually works to naturalize and legitimize settler sovereignty: "the TRC temporally situates the harms of settler-colonialism in the past and focuses the bulk of its reconciliatory efforts on repairing the injurious legacy left in the wake of this history." As a result, "Indigenous subjects are the primary

object of repair, not the colonial relationship." Glen Coulthard, *Red Skin, White Masks* (Minneapolis: University of Minnesota Press, 2014), 127. For discussion see also Matt James, "A Carnival of Truth? Knowledge, Ignorance and the Canadian Truth and Reconciliation Commission," *International Journal of Transitional Justice* 6, no. 2 (2012); Dale Turner, "On the Idea of Reconciliation in Contemporary Aboriginal Politics," in *Reconciling Canada: Critical Perspectives on the Culture of Redress*, eds. Jennifer Henderson and Paulinem Wakeham (Toronto: University of Toronto Press, 2013); Matt James, "The Structural Injustice Turn, the Historical Justice Dilemma and Assigning Responsibility with the Canadian TRC Report," *Canadian Journal of Political Science* 54, no. 2 (2021); Audra Simpson, "Reconciliation and Its Discontents: Settler Governance in an Age of Sorrow," *Public Lecture*, 22 March 2016. University of Saskatchewan. https://www.youtube.com/watch?v=vGl9HkzQsGg; Dian Million, *Therapeutic Nations Healing in an Age of Indigenous Human Rights* (Tucson: University of Arizona Press, 2013).

61 For extended discussion see the discussion of practices in the following section of this chapter.

62 For extended discussion see the discussion of practices in the following section of this chapter.

63 Taiaiake Alfred, *Peace, Power, Righteousness: An Indigenous Manifesto* (Oxford: Oxford University Press, 2008), 154.

64 Coulthard, *Red Skin*.

65 Johnny Mack, "Hoquotist: Reorienting through Storied Practice," in *Storied Communities: Narratives of Contact and Arrival in the Constitution of Political Community*, eds. Hester Lessard, Rebecca Johnson, and Jeremy Webber (Vancouver: University of British Columbia Press, 2010), 298.

66 Andrew Woolford, "Transition and Transposition: Genocide, Land and the British Columbia Treaty Process," *Journal of Marxism and Interdisciplinary Inquiry* 4, no. 2 (2011): 70.

67 Stó:lō Nation, "Integrated Cultural Assessment for the Proposed Transmountain Expansion Pipeline Project 2014," in *NEB Application and Environmental Impact Assessment, Kinder Morgan Canada* (Calgary: National Energy Board, 2014), especially chapter 18.

68 Tsleil-Waututh, *Submission to the Expert Panel on National Energy Board Modernization (March 30th, 2017)*, 4, 6.

69 Shiri Pasternak, *Grounded Authority: The Algonquins of Barriere Lake against the State* (Minneapolis: Minnesota University Press, 2017), 150. At 269, Pasternak describes the BLA conception of sovereignty as "the right to be properly entangled."

70 Paul Rynard, "'Welcome in, but Check Your Rights at the Door': The James Bay and Nisga'a Agreements in Canada," *Canadian Journal of Political Science* 33, no. 2 (2000), 216; Andrew Woolford, "Negotiating Affirmative Repair: Symbolic Violence in the British Columbia Treaty Process," *Canadian Journal of Sociology* 29, no. 1 (2004): 112.

71 Originally the Crown insisted that aboriginal rights be "extinguished" or "surrendered" as a consequence of any modern treaty. Indigenous peoples resisted, and the Crown changed strategy. Now, existing rights are "released" or "modified" into new, tightly defined treaty rights. The effect is, however, largely the same. Even the government's own reports note this. See, for example, Douglas Eyford, *A New Direction: Advancing Aboriginal and Treaty Rights* (Ottawa: Indigenous and Northern Affairs Canada, 2015).

72 Hamar Foster, Heather Raven, and Jeremy Webber, eds., *Let Right Be Done: Aboriginal Title, the Calder Case, and the Future of Indigenous Rights* (Vancouver: University of British Columbia Press, 2007), 17.

73 It is interesting to note that territories are creatures of federal statute, exercising autonomous but delegated powers. In this sense, territories stand in relation to the federal government in much the same way that municipalities stand in relation to provincial governments – as autonomous but subordinate organs of a higher power. Conceptually, territories are something akin to federal municipalities, making similarly derivative authority claims. In practice, however, the range of powers exercised by territories is much broader than that possessed by municipalities, more closely resembling the authority of a province.

74 To take an illustrative range, *The Nisga'a Final Agreement* (Sections 48, 62), *The Sahtu Dene and Metis Comprehensive Land Claim Agreement* (Sections 19.1.2, 23.2.1), and the *Tsawwassen Final Agreement* (Section 14) all use the term "fee simple." *The James Bay Northern Quebec Agreement* does not, though Quebec is a civil law jurisdiction and fee simple is a common law concept. Instead, Quebec retains "bare ownership" of Category 1A lands, which are "set aside for the exclusive use and benefit of respective James Bay Cree Bands" (Section 5.1.2). For Category 1B lands "The ownership of such lands, under provincial jurisdiction, will vest in such Cree corporations outright, provided that the lands can only be sold or ceded to Quebec" (Section 5.1.3). See Grand Council of the Crees of Quebec, Northern Quebec Inuit Association, Hyrdo Quebec, Quebec, and Canada, *The James Bay and Northern Québec Agreement* (Ottawa: Indian and Northern Affairs, 1976), accessed 11 November 2019, http://www.naskapi.ca/documents/documents/JBNQA.pdf; Sahtu Dene and Métis Nations, *The Northwest Territories, Canada, Sahtu Dene and Metis Comprehensive Land Claim Agreement* (Ottawa: Indian and Northern Affairs, 1993), accessed 11

November 2019, https://www.eia.gov.nt.ca/sites/eia/files/sahtu_dene
_and_metis_comprehensive_land_claim_agreement_0.pdf; Nisga'a Nation,
British Columbia, and Canada, *Nisga'a Final Agreement* (Ottawa: Federal
Treaty Negotiation Office, 1999), accessed 11 November 2019, https://
www.nnkn.ca/files/u28/nis-eng.pdf; Tsawwassen First Nation, British
Columbia, and Canada, *Tsawwassen Final Agreement* (Ottawa: Aboriginal
Affairs and Northern Development Canada, 2007), accessed 11 November
2019, https://www.aadnc-aandc.gc.ca/DAM/DAM-INTER-BC/STAGING
/texte-text/tfnfa_1100100022707_eng.pdf.

75 For example, the *James Bay Northern Quebec Agreement* (Section 5.2),
    Sahtu Dene and Metis (Section 13.4.10), and *Nisga'a* (Section 9.1)
    agreements all make provisions for parcels of Crown land where
    the Nations enjoy special hunting, fishing, and harvesting rights.
    Tsawwassen territory is now an urban area, and as such the Tsawwassen
    agreement does not include hunting rights over settlement lands. It
    does, however, include a category of land in which the nation enjoys a
    right of first refusal (Section 35). It also includes a Tsawwassen Fishing
    Area, chapter 9.

76 *The James Bay Northern Quebec Agreement* includes provisions dealing
    with health and social services, education, administration of justice,
    police, environmental protection, land use, hunting and fishing, and local
    taxation. *The Nisga'a Final Agreement* provides jurisdiction over Nisga'a
    governments, citizenship, culture, and language; Nisga'a property, lands,
    and assets; public order and safety; buildings, structures, and public
    works; traffic and transportation; marriages, social services, health
    services, child and family services, education, gambling, intoxicants,
    and cultural property. *The Tsawwassen Agreement* provides jurisdiction
    over Tsawwassen lands, land management, land access, forest resources,
    fisheries, wildlife, migratory birds, national and provincial parks, culture
    and heritage, environmental management, Tsawwassen governance,
    and local taxation. *The Sahtu Dene Metis Agreement* does not deal with
    self-government, but a subsequent Agreement in Principle on self-
    government includes citizenship, language, culture and spirituality,
    traditional healing, education, adoption, income support, social housing,
    solemnization of marriage, settlement lands, gaming and gambling,
    liquor, administration of justice, taxation of citizens, and local services.
    See Crown-Indigenous Relations and Northern Affairs Canada, "Self-
    Government Agreement-in-Principle for the Sahtu Dene and Metis of
    Norman Wells," accessed 11 November 2019, https://www.canada.ca
    /en/crown-indigenous-relations-northern-affairs/news/2019/01/self
    -government-agreement-in-principle-for-the-sahtu-dene-and-metis-of
    -norman-wells.html.

77 Brian Thom, "Disagreement-in-Principle: Negotiating the Right to Practice Coast Salish Culture in Treaty Talks on Vancouver Island, BC," *Journal of Marxism and Interdisciplinary Inquiry* 2, no. 1 (2008): 27.

78 Thom, "Disagreement-in-Principle," 28.

79 Brian Crane, Robert Mainville, and Martin Mason, *First Nations Governance Law* (New York: LexisNexis, 2008), 99.

80 Michael Murphy, ed., *Canada: The State of the Federation: Reconfiguring Aboriginal-State Relations* (Kingston, ON: Institute of Intergovernmental Relations, 2005), 135.

81 M.A. Smith, "Natural Resource Co-Management with Aboriginal Peoples in Canada: Coexistence or Assimilation," in *Aboriginal Peoples and Forest Lands in Canada*, eds. D.B. Tindall, Ronald Trosper, and Pamela Perreault (Vancouver: University of British Columbia Press, 2013), 95.

82 Woolford, "Negotiating Affirmative Repair" 115–35. See also Andrew Woolford, "Transition and Transposition: Genocide, Land and the British Columbia Treaty Process," *Journal of Marxism and Interdisciplinary Inquiry*, no. 2 (2001).

83 Dwight Newman and Levi Graham, "Indigenous-Industry Agreements, Legal Uncertainty, and Risk Allocations," in *Indigenous-Industry Agreements, Natural Resources, and the Law*, eds. Ibironke Odumosu-Ayanu and Dwight Newman (London: Routledge, 2020), 49.

84 Shiri Pasternak, "Wet'suwet'en: Why Are Indigenous Rights Being Defined by an Energy Corporation?" *Yellowhead Institute Briefs* 7 (2020), 2.

85 Ayanu and Newman, "Introduction," 7, 9. See also Ciaran O'Faircheallaigh, *Negotiations in the Indigenous World: Aboriginal Peoples and the Extractive Industry in Australia and Canada* (London: Routledge, 2015).

86 *Haida Nation v. British Columbia*, 2004 SCC 73 [2004] 3 SCR 511.

87 *Tsleil-Waututh Nation v. Canada*, 2018 FCA 153 [2019] 2 FCR 3.

88 *Tsilhqot'in*; *Delgamuukw v. British Columbia*, [1997] 3 SCR 1010.

89 Murphy, *State of the Federation*, 135.

90 Smith, "Co-Management," 95.

91 Tyler McCreary and Vanessa Lamb, "A Political Ecology of Sovereignty in Practice and on the Map: The Technicalities of Law, Participatory Mapping, and Environmental Governance," *Leiden Journal of International Law* 27, no. 3 (2014): 606.

92 For a detailed discussion of these acts and their eventual consolidation see Canada, *Royal Commission*, chapter 9.

93 Miller, *Skyscrapers*, 105.

94 Some modifications have been made over the years, notably in 1952, but Miller contends that the fundamental structure of domination continues. Miller, *Skyscrapers*, 222.

95 Miller, *Skyscrapers*, 192.

96 Canada, *Royal Commission*, 250.

97 Truth and Reconciliation Commission of Canada, *Final Report of the Truth and Reconciliation Commission of Canada* (Winnipeg: Truth and Reconciliation Commission of Canada, 2015).

98 For a contemporary account of settler interference with traditional governance through the band council system, see Shiri Pasternak, *Grounded Authority*.

99 Canada, *Royal Commission*, 253.

100 Nichols, *Reconciliation without Recollection*, especially 111–81.

101 Christopher Bracken, *The Potlatch Papers: A Colonial Case History* (Chicago: University of Chicago Press, 1997), 228.

102 Unist'ot'en Camp. "About," accessed 11 November 2019, http://unistoten .camp/about/.

103 Donald Bourgeois, "The Six Nations: A Neglected Aspect of Canadian Legal History," *The Canadian Journal of Native Studies* 6, no. 2 (1986): 255.

104 Leanne Simpson and Kiera Ladner, *This Is an Honour Song: Twenty Years Since the Blockades* (Winnipeg: Arbeiter Ring, 2011).

105 Laura Alice DeVires, *What's at Stake on (un)Common Ground? The Grand River Haudenosaunee and Canada in Caledonia, Ontario* (MA diss., University of British Columbia, 2009).

106 Dania Igdoura, "An Examination of Settler Colonialism in Canada's Legal Institutions: 1492 Land Back Lane," *Aletheia* 1, no. 1 (2021).

107 Pasternak, *Grounded Authority*.

108 Hanna Petersen, "Premier John Horgan Talks Salmon Farms in Alert Bay," *North Island Gazette*, 12 October 2017, accessed 11 November 2019, https://www.northislandgazette.com/news/premier-john-horgan -visits-alert-bay-to-talk-salmon-farms/; Office of the Premier, "Premier John Horgan's Statement on His Visit to 'Namgis First Nation in Alert Bay'," accessed 11 November 2019, https://news.gov.bc.ca/releases /2017PREM0096-001713.

109 Ryan Newell, "Only One Law: First Nations Land Disputes and the Contested Nature of the Rule of Law," *First Nations Law Journal* 41, no. 1 (2012): 51.

110 For discussion see Newell, "Only One Law"; Rachel Ariss and John Cutfeet, "Kitchenuhmaykoosib Inninuwug First Nation: Mining, Consultation, Reconciliation and Law," *Indigenous Law Journal* 10, no. 1 (2011).

111 For discussion see, for example, James Tully, Michael Asch, and John Borrows, eds., *Resurgence and Reconciliation* (Toronto: University of Toronto Press, 2018).

112 See, for example, Leanne Simpson, Audra Simpson, Glen Coulthard, Taiaiake Alfred, and Jeff Corntassel.

113 Aaron Mills, "The Lifeworlds of Law: On Revitalizing Indigenous Legal Orders Today," *McGill Law Journal* 61, no. 4 (2016), 854.

114 For a discussion of "the turn away" see Coulthard, *Red Skin*, 154–5.

115 Leanne Simpson, *Dancing on Our Turtles Back* (Winnipeg: Arbeiter Ring, 2011), 17.
116 For example, Taiaiake Alfred, *Wasáse* (Peterborough: Broadview, 2009), 85, 275.
117 For a basic timeline see, for example, Shreya Shah, "Wet'suwet'en Explained," *The Indigenous Foundation*, accessed 1 November 2022, https://www.theindigenousfoundation.org/articles/wetsuweten-explained.
118 For a basic timeline see, for example, Stefan Sinclair-Fortin, "How Did It Get to This? A Recent Timeline of Indigenous Lobster-Fishing Rights," *The Coast*, 15 November 2020, accessed 1 November 2022, https://www.thecoast.ca/halifax/how-did-it-get-to-this-a-recent-timeline-of-indigenous-lobster-fishing-rights/Content?oid=25091418. Read more at: https://www.thecoast.ca/halifax/how-did-it-get-to-this-a-recent-timeline-of-indigenous-lobster-fishing-rights/Content?oid=25091418.
119 John Borrows, *Freedom and Indigenous Constitutionalism* (Toronto: University of Toronto Press, 2016), especially chapter 2.
120 Borrows, *Freedom and Indigenous Constitutionalism*, 56–61.
121 Borrows, *Freedom and Indigenous Constitutionalism*, 55–8.
122 Brian Egan, "Towards Shared Ownership: Property, Geography, and Treaty Making in British Columbia," *Geografiska Annaler* 95, no. 1 (2013), 45.
123 Haida Nation and Her Majesty the Queen in Right of the Province of British Columbia, "Kunst'aa Guu – Kunst'aayah Reconciliation Protocol," accessed 10 November 2019, http://www.llbc.leg.bc.ca/public/pubdocs/bcdocs2010/462194/haida_reconciliation_protocol.pdf. See also the preamble to Heiltsuk First Nation and the Government of B.C., "Strategic Land Use Planning Agreement," accessed 10 November 2019, http://archive.ilmb.gov.bc.ca/slrp/lrmp/nanaimo/central_north_coast/docs/Heiltsuk_FN_Signed_SLUPA.pdf.
124 Webber, "Age of Encounter," especially 53–4.

2. Legal Practices

1 In this chapter, I will use the terms "law" and "legality." Law refers to a set of rules, while legality captures not only the rules themselves but also the institutions, stories, and world views from which they spring. To borrow from Aaron Mills, laws are the leaves of the tree, while institutions, stories, and world views constitute the branches, trunk, and roots. "Legality" refers to the entire tree, while "law" refers to only the leaves (positive rules). See Aaron Mills, "Miinigowiziwin: All That Has Been Given for Living Well Together," *One Vision of Anishinaabe Constitutionalism* (PhD diss., University of Victoria, 2019)," 38–49. I am primarily interested in the status of First Nations' legalities, not laws. This chapter therefore focuses on the changing recognition of First Nations legal institutions, rather than the reception of specific laws into the common law.

2 Mills, "Miinigowiziwin" especially 35–7.

3 The term is inspired by Audra Simpson's concept of the "politics of refusal." In contrast to a politics of recognition, which seeks validation from a status-bestowing other, refusal constitutes an independent act of self-affirmation which rejects the implied hierarchy between recognition-giver and recognition-receiver. In so doing, a politics of refusal positions Indigenous peoples as independent political, and in this case legal, jurisdictions, rather than cultural units within the settler state. Audra Simpson, *Mohawk Interruptus: Political Life across the Borders of Settler States* (Durham, NC: Duke University Press, 2014), generally, but especially 11–12, 19–23.

4 Webber, "Age of Encounter," especially 55–6.

5 This period runs roughly from contact until the Royal Proclamation.

6 *Inter se* means "between or among themselves," such that an *inter se* offence involves either two settlers or two Indigenous persons. Offences involving members of both communities would be intercommunal rather than *inter se*.

7 Jan Grabowski, "French Criminal Justice and Indians in Montreal, 1670–1760," *Ethnohistory* 43, no. 3 (1996): 413.

8 See, for example, Katherine Hermes, "'Justice Will Be Done Us' Algonquian Demands for Reciprocity in the Courts of European Settlers," in *Many Legalities of Early America*, eds. Christopher Tomlins and Bruce Mann (Chapel Hill: University of North Carolina Press, 2001), 134.

9 Grabowski, "French Criminal Justice," 419.

10 Yasu Kawashima, "Jurisdiction of the Colonial Courts over the Indians in Massachusetts, 1689–1763," *The New England Quarterly* 42, no. 4 (1969): 540.

11 The Mutiny Act (1765) confirmed this variable territorial schema. It provided that disputes arising "within his Majesty's Dominions in *America*, which are not within the Limits or Jurisdiction of any Civil Government" were to be tried by the courts of the "next adjoining Province." However, the Act seems to have been applied only among settlers inter se. Inter se offences in First Nations communities were not prosecuted, and officials were instructed to resolve intercommunal offences with First Nations according to "their own Customs and Ceremonies." Mark Walters, *The Continuity of Aboriginal Customs and Government under British Imperial Constitutional Law as Applied in Colonial Canada, 1760–1860* (PhD diss., University of Oxford, 1995), 147–8.

12 Kawashima, "Jurisdiction of the Colonial Courts," 54.

13 Kawashima, "Jurisdiction of the Colonial Courts," 532.

14 Kawashima, "Jurisdiction of the Colonial Courts," 541.

15 For a series of discussions of the complex relationship between consent and coercion see Jeremy Webber and Colin Macleod, eds., *Between*

Consenting Peoples: Political Community and the Meaning of Consent (Vancouver: University of British Columbia Press, 2010).

16 Webber, "Age of Encounter," especially 56.

17 This period runs roughly from the fall of New France and the Royal Proclamation until the confederation of Canada.

18 Walters, *Continuity of Aboriginal Customs*, 72.

19 Walters, *Continuity of Aboriginal Customs*, 251.

20 Walters, *Continuity of Aboriginal Customs*, 253. One additional case sheds light on the jurisprudence indirectly. In *Cameron (1835)*, imperial courts held that colonies were not sovereign *ex proper vigore*, but rather possessed only such powers as were delegated from the imperial sovereign. Legislation that affects First Nations could not therefore extinguish Aboriginal rights unless that authority had been explicitly delegated, which it had not. This again suggests that First Nations were considered subject to imperial, but not local colonial, law. Bruce Clark, *Native Liberty, Crown Sovereignty: The Existing Aboriginal Right of Self-Government in Canada* (Kingston: McGill-Queen's University Press, 1990), 39.

21 Asch, *On Being Here to Stay*, 40.

22 When the British moved to interfere with Mohawk relations to the Mississauga, for example, the Mohawk protested that they were "a free people," and the Indian department so affirmed – despite regular use of imperial tribunals and other mediated fora. Mark Walters, "According to the Old Customs of Our Nation: Aboriginal Self-Government on the Credit River Mississauga Reserve, 1826–1847," *Ottawa Law Review* 30, no. 1 (1998): 17.

23 Administrator Peter Russell referred to Indian lands as "extra-judicial" because they were beyond the pale of English justice – sentiments echoed by Chief Justice Robinson in *Regina v. McCormick (1859)*. Mark Walters, "The Extension of Colonial Criminal Jurisdiction over the Aboriginal Peoples of Upper Canada: Reconsidering the Shawanakiskie Case (1822–26)," *University of Toronto Law Journal* 46, no. 2 (1996): 286.

24 In 1803 the imperial parliament passed legislation extending criminal and limited civil jurisdiction to unceded Indian lands. However, it appears that, in practice, First Nations were not subject to the legislation unless associated with European fur traders. For an influential discussion see Clark, *Native Liberty, Crown Sovereignty*. Foster argues that Clark's thesis is mistaken, insofar as he presents the legislation as extending criminal but not civil jurisdiction. Foster argues that the statutes provide for elements of both. He agrees, however, that the legislation was not understood to apply to Indigenous people unless employed by the HBC, and potentially not even then. See Hamar Foster, "Forgotten Arguments: Aboriginal Title and Sovereignty in Canada *Jurisdiction Act Cases*," *Manitoba Law Journal* 21, no. 1 (1992).

25 This period runs roughly from the confederation of Canada to the reconsideration of Aboriginal rights in the modern period.

26 See Walters, *Continuity of Aboriginal Customs*, 39.

27 Sidney Harring, *White Man's Law: Native People in Nineteenth-Century Canadian Jurisprudence* (Toronto: University of Toronto Press, 1998), 68.

28 This construction, however, never gained the salience of its American counterpart, perhaps because even Robinson failed to apply it consistently. *Sheldon v. Ramsay (1852)* confirmed that the Haldimand deed was not binding, but reversed *Wilkes* in finding that the deed would have been deficient anyway, for lack of a grantee. In *R v. McCormick (1859)*, Robinson equivocated further, finding that Indian groups have some collective capacity, but not that of a corporation and certainly not that of a nation. Thus, a single judge reached three different positions, each of which denied First Nations legalities an independent existence for different reasons. Harring, *White Man's Law*, 76.

29 *A.-G. Can. v. A.-G. Ont., A.-G. Que. v. A.-G. Ont.* [1897] AC 199 [1896] CR 11 AC 308, 213; See also *R. v. Syliboy* [1929] 1 DLR. 307, 50 CCC. 389, finding that First Nations had no capacity to make treaties and that existing treaties were void ab initio. The treaty of 1752, the court held, "[was] not a treaty at all … it [was] at best a mere agreement made by the Governor and council with a handful of Indians. In *Logan v. Styres* [1959] 20 DLR. (2d) 416, 5 CNLC 261 (Ont. HC), the court returned to this logic, ruling that, by accepting a treaty, the Six Nations had become subjects of the Crown, and therefore subject to the Crown's total sovereignty – including, it seems, its ability to ignore the very treaty by which sovereignty was gained.

30 Official letter to Robert Wilmot Horton, Under-Secretary of State for War and the Colonies, 14 March 1824. Cited in Bruce, *Native Liberty, Crown Sovereignty*, 23.

31 Cayuga Indians (*Can. v. U.S.*) [1926] 173 R. Int'l Arb. Awards 309. For discussion see Russell Lawrence Barsh, "Indigenous North America and Contemporary International Law," *Oregon Law Review* 62, no. 1 (1983): 74.

32 *R. v. Commanda* [1939] DLR 635 [1939] 72 CCC 246 (Ont. H.C.).

33 Convictions were, however, inconsistent and often ineffective. For discussion see Constance Blackhouse, *Colour-Coded: A Legal History of Racism in Canada, 1900–1950* (Toronto: University of Toronto Press, 1999), especially chapter 3 "'Bedecked in Gaudy Feathers': The Legal Prohibition of Aboriginal Dance"; Bracken, *Potlatch Papers*, 60.

34 For discussion see Bourgeois, "The Six Nations," 296.

35 To list just a few illustrative examples, in 1859, Nahnebahwequay, a Mississauga woman, travelled to London to petition the Crown directly to protest treaty abuses by the colonial government. D.B. Smith, "Nahnebahwequay (1824–1865): 'Upright Woman'," *Canadian Methodist*

Historical Society Papers 13, no. 1 (2001). In 1860, Cree leaders placed their concerns directly before Prince Albert on a royal visit. Likewise, in 1890, the Haudenosaunee wrote to the governor general requesting negotiations and insisted on the terms of the Covenant Chain treaty. Because the treaty was with the Crown, the Haudenosaunee would not negotiate with Canada. English courts rejected the claim, reasoning that the Crown was a divided entity. As recently as 1976, however, the Queen received several First Nations delegations at Buckingham Palace. Beverly Jacobs, *International Law/The Great Law of Peace* (MA diss., University of Saskatchewan, 2000), 46.

36 For example, when a First Nations man employed by a man named Youmans drowned on the job and Youmans refused to follow local laws requiring restitution to relatives, Youmans was put to death. When settler police complained, they were told that Youmans knew the law of the territory and that his death had been in accordance with legal procedure. Ultimately, in an executive nod to the continued independence of First Nations law, the killer's sentence was commuted. Galois, "History of the Upper Skeena," 134–6.

37 Indeed, where settler law was deemed inappropriate, many First Nations communities chose to simply ignore it, rather than contesting it. Harring, *White Man's Law*, 99. For example, some Anishinaabe continued formal supervision of their fisheries long after settler governments began doing the same. John Borrows, "A Genealogy of Law: Inherent Sovereignty and First Nations Self-Government," *Osgoode Hall Law Journal* 30, no. 2 (1992): 50.

38 First Nations also continued to make creative use of settler institutions to apply their own laws. In her analysis of the introduction of criminal law on the plains, for example, Gavigan finds that the number of cases involving First Nations was initially rather low, and that most cases involved First Nations chiefs as complainants or informants, even in *inter se* offences. It seems some Plains Cree may have understood treaty as giving them a right to call on the North West Mounted Police and the courts to maintain order in their communities. Shelley Gavigan, "Prisoner Never Gave Me Anything for What He Done: Aboriginal Voices in the Criminal Court," *Socio-Legal Review* 3 (2007), especially 79, 81, 85.

39 See, for example, Gord Hill, *500 Years of Indigenous Resistance* (Oakland, CA: PM Press, 2010). For a thoughtful discussion in Borrows, *Indigenous Constitutionalism*, chapter 3.

40 Settlers responded by pairing their sweeping assertions of *de jure* jurisdiction with considerable *de facto* accommodation. For example, in 1839, Powlis was tried and convicted of murder inter se, but pardoned

on the grounds that his crime had been in accordance with First Nations custom. Harring, *White Man's Law*, 158. In 1861, a BC court convicted Dick of killing a Squamish man, but asked the governor for a commutation on the grounds that the act was in keeping with Squamish law. Tina Loo, "Savage Mercy: Native Culture and the Modification of Capital Punishment in Nineteenth-Century British Columbia," in *Qualities of Mercy: Justice, Punishment, and Discretion*, ed. Carolyn Strange (Vancouver: University of British Columbia Press, 1996), 112.

41 For extended discussion see Loo, "Savage Mercy."

42 Promislow, "Treaties," 1123.

43 This period begins with the reconsideration of Aboriginal rights and title in *R. v. White and Bob* (1964), 50 D.L.R. (2d) 613, 52 W.W.R. 193 (B.C.C.A.) and *Calder et al. v. Attorney-General of British Columbia* [1973] SCR 313 [1973] 4 WWR 1.

44 *Mikisew Cree First Nation v. Canada* [2005] 3 SCR 388, 2005 SCC 69 at 51–2.

45 For example, *Haida*, 25.

46 *Van der Peet*, 45–6.

47 *R. v. Bernard*, 2005 SCC 43 [2005] 2 SCR 220 at 51.

48 See, for example, *Sparrow*, 1114–15; *R v. Gladstone* [1996] 2 SCR 723 [1996] 137 DLR (4th) 648 at 62–5, and *Delgamuukw v. British Columbia* [1997] 3 SCR 1010 at 160–9.

49 *Gladstone*, 73.

50 See *supra* note 23.

51 *R. v. Fournier* [2004] OTC 260 [2004] CanLII 66288 (ON SC) at 2.

52 *Francis* at 4; *R. v. Yellowhorn*, 2006 ABQB 307 [2006] 399 AR 144 at 29.

53 Discussed in Barsh, "Indigenous North America," 94–7.

54 Kitchenuhmaykoosib Inninuwug First Nation and the Algonquins of Barriere Lake, "Joint Submission by the KI and the Algonquins of Barriere Lake, United Nations Economic and Social Council Permanent Forum on First Nations Issues, 7th Session, New York, April 21–May 2, 2008," accessed 10 November 2019, www.barrierelakesolidarity.org/2008/04 /canada-quebec-condemned-before-un.html; Algonquins of Barriere Lake, "Submission by the Algonquins of Barriere Lake, United Nations Economic and Social Council Permanent Forum on First Nations Issues, 1st Session, New York, May 13–24, 2002," accessed 10 November 2019, http://www.turtleisland.org/news/news-algonquin3.htm.

55 Beaulieu, "Acquisition," 105.

56 Walters, "According to the Old Customs," 17.

57 Peter Russell and Roger Jones, "Aboriginal Peoples and Constitutional Reform," paper prepared for the *Royal Commission on Aboriginal Peoples* (Ottawa: Royal Commission on Aboriginal Peoples, 1995), 9.

58 This makes the confused nature of settler thought on the topic somewhat more understandable. Because many First Nations appeared to occupy multiple spots on the spectrum at once, settler authorities were likely able to interpret First Nations as having whatever status settlers were inclined to ascribe them. Whatever rung on the ladder settler authorities chose, they could find at least partial support for their interpretation in First Nations practice and discourse.

59 *Restoule v. Canada (Attorney General)*, 2018 ONSC 7701 [2019] CNLR 1 (Plaintiffs' Memorandum of Argument, 4 May 2018).

60 Stó:lō Nation, "Integrated Cultural Assessment for the Proposed Transmountain Expansion Pipeline Project 2014," in *NEB Application and Environmental Impact Assessment*, ed. Kinder Morgan Canada (Calgary: National Energy Board, 2014), especially sections 12, 14.

61 *Haida Nation v. British Columbia (Minister of Forests)* [2004] 3 SCR 511 at 25, "Put simply, Canada's Aboriginal peoples were here when Europeans came, and were never conquered."

62 *Tsilhqot'in Nation v. British Columbia* [2014] 2 SCR 257 at 69, "The doctrine of terra nullius (that no one owned the land prior to European assertion of sovereignty) never applied in Canada."

63 For discussion see, for example, Asch, *On Being Here to Stay*; John Borrows, "Wampum at Niagara: The Royal Proclamation, Canadian Legal History, and Self Government," in *Aboriginal and Treaty Rights in Canada: Essays on Law, Equity, and Respect for Difference*, ed. Michael Asch (Vancouver: University of British Columbia Press, 1997); Aaron Mills and Kaitlin McNabb, "To All My Relations: Contemporary Colonialism, and Treaty Citizenship Today," *Rabble*, 12 August 2014, www.rabble.ca/Indigenous /to-all-my-relations-contemporary-colonialism-and-treaty-citizenship -today/.

64 See especially *R. v. Yellowhorn* [2006] 399 AR 144 at 45–8; see more generally *R. v. Sparrow* [1990] 1 SCR 1075 at 1103.

65 Keith Cherry, "'The Kids Don't Want Reconciliation, They Want Land Back': Thinking about Decolonization and Settler Solidarity after the Death of Reconciliation" *Contemporary Political Theory* (2024), 4–6. For discussion see John Borrows, "Sovereignty's Alchemy: An Analysis of Delgamuukw v. British Columbia," *Osgoode Hall Law Journal* 37, no. 3 (1999).

66 Beaulieu, "Acquisition of Aboriginal Land" 107–14.

67 Kent McNeil, "The Onus of Proof of Aboriginal Title," *Osgoode Hall Law Journal* 37, no. 4 (1999) 777–82.

68 Ryan Beaton, "De facto and de jure Crown Sovereignty: Reconciliation and Legitimation at the Supreme Court of Canada," *Constitutional Forum* 27, no. 1 (2018), 26–7; McNeil, "Doctrine of Discovery," 727.

69 Kent McNeil, "First Nations Sovereignty and the Legality of Crown Sovereignty: An Unresolved Constitutional Conundrum," *Osgoode Digital Commons* 320 (2017): 2, 1.

70 *Thomas and Saik'uz First Nation v. Rio Tinto Alcan Inc.*, 2022 BCSC 15 at 198.

71 Harring, *White Man's Law*, 123; Walters, *Continuity*, 52; Foster, *Forgotten Arguments*, 345.

72 Cited in Clark, *Native Liberty*, 19.

73 *Syliboy*, 313.

74 *Sparrow*, 1103.

75 Loo, "Savage Mercy."

76 White, *Middle Ground*, 79.

77 Harring, *White Man's Law*, 184.

78 Both statues explicitly extended criminal, and some civil, jurisdiction over Indian lands. The statutes were used to try settlers for offences committed on Indian lands, but their provisions were not seen to apply to Indians or even Métis unless they were in the direct employment of the HBC. In this sense, the statutes extended jurisdiction over Indian *lands*, but not necessarily Indian *subjects*. See Harring, *White Man's Law*, 270. HBC testimony before an imperial committee confirms this interpretation, as does the case law, though both show that there was some confusion around the issue. For discussion see Hamar Foster, "British Columbia: Legal Institutions in the Far West, from Contact to 1871," *Manitoba Law Journal* 23, no. 1 (1995): especially 65.

79 Tina Loo, "Savage Mercy."

80 A Gladue report is a type of pre-sentencing report that a Canadian court can request when sentencing an offender of Aboriginal background under Section 718.2(e) of the Criminal Code. Note that this occurs after culpability has been determined. See Native Women's Association of Canada, "What Is Gladue?" accessed 10 November 2019, https://www.nwac.ca/wp-content/uploads/2015/05/What-Is-Gladue.pdf.

81 Conceptually, this mechanism also helps settler authorities to transmute First Nations law from something truly legal to mere custom or tradition. Typically, discretion is offered at the arrest and sentencing stages, before or after the law has been spoken. Thus, the trial itself, where the law is considered, is insulated from any consideration of First Nations legalities. These factor in only as a means of explaining behaviour, not as a source of law *per se*. Rachel Ariss and John Cutfeet, *Keeping the Land: Kitchenuhmaykoosib Inninuwug, Reconciliation and Canadian Law* (Black Point, NS: Fernwood Publishing, 2012), 43.

82 Harring, *White Man's Law*, 158.

83 Harring, *White Man's Law*, 243.

84 Sidney Harring, "'There Seemed to Be No Recognized Law': Canadian Law and the Prairie First Nations," in *Laws and Societies in the Canadian Prairie West 1670–1940*, eds. Jonathan Swainger and Louis Knafla (Vancouver: University of British Columbia Press, 2005), 96–101.

85 Harring, *White Man's Law*, 243.

86 Deborah Rose Peña, "The Power to Punish: Conflicts of Authority in the Case of Jack Fiddler," *Hypocrite Reader* 2 (2011): 3.

87 Mark Walters, "Mohegan Indians v. Connecticut (1705–1773) and the Legal Status of Aboriginal Customary Laws and Government in British North America," *Osgoode Hall Law Journal* 33, no. 4 (1995): 806.

88 Barsh, "Indigenous North America," 78.

89 Barsh, "Indigenous North America," 96–8; Grace Li Xiu Woo, "Canada's Forgotten Founders: The Modern Significance of the Haudenosaunee (Iroquois) Application for Membership in the League of Nations," *Law, Social Justice and Global Development Journal* 1 (2003).

90 Barsh, "Indigenous North America," 97.

91 Discussed in Barsh, "Indigenous North America," 94–7.

92 See Anghie, *Imperialism*; Siba N'Zatioula Grovogui, *Sovereigns, Quasisovereigns, and Africans: Race and Self-Determination in International Law* (Minneapolis: University of Minnesota, 1996).

93 Xavier Scott, "Repairing Broken Relations by Repairing Broken Treaties: Theorizing Post-Colonial States in Settler Colonies," *Studies in Social Justice* 12, no. 2 (2018): 392–3.

94 See Patrick Macklem, "First Nations Self-Government and the Borders of the Canadian Legal Imagination," *McGill Law Review* 36 (1991): 1 generally and especially 392, 399, 412, 454.

95 Martti Koskenniemi, *The Gentle Civilizer of Nations* (Cambridge: Cambridge University Press, 2001), 127–31.

96 Adom Getachew, *Worldmaking after Empire* (Princeton, NJ: Princeton University Press, 2019), 20.

97 Hamar Foster, "We Are Not O'Meara's Children: Law, Lawyers and the First Campaign for Aboriginal Title in British Columbia, 1908–1928," in *Let Right Be Done: Aboriginal Title, the Calder Case, and the Future of Indigenous Rights*, eds. Hamar Foster, Heather Raven, and Jeremy Webber (Vancouver: University of British Columbia Press, 2007), 4.

98 Douglas Sanders, "The Indian Lobby," in *And No One Cheered: Federalism, Democracy, and the Constitution Act*, eds. Keith Banting and Richard Simeon (Toronto: Taylor & Francis, 1983), 303.

99 CBC News, "Attawapiskat Chief Won't Attend PM Meeting in GG's Absence," accessed 10 November 2019, http://www.cbc.ca/news/politics/attawapiskat-chief-won-t-attend-pm-meeting-in-gg-s-absence-1.1369435.

100 *Lovelace v. Canada*, UNHRC Communication No.24/1977: Canada
    30/07/81 [1977] UN Doc. CCPR/C/13/D/24/1977.
101 Michael Asch, "UNDRIP, Treaty Federalism, and Self-Determination,"
    Review of Constitutional Studies 24, no. 1 (2019): 3. For extended discussion
    see Barsh, "First Nations."
102 Prins, *Storm Clouds*, 5.
103 Walters, "Old Customs," 17.
104 "Treaty Alliance against Tar Sands Expansion," accessed 10 November
    2019, www.treatyalliance.org/wp-content/uploads/2016/12/Treatyand
    AdditionalInformation-20161216-OL.pdf.
105 Aboriginal title, being a form of property, is addressed in chapter 3.
106 *Calder et al. v. Attorney-General of British Columbia [1973] SCR 313, [1973] 4
    WWR 1* at 314–16.
107 "[T]he court must examine the pre-sovereignty aboriginal practice
    and translate that practice into a modern right. The process begins
    by examining the nature and extent of the pre-sovereignty aboriginal
    practice in question. It goes on to seek a corresponding common law
    right" *Marshall and Bernard*, 51.
108 See, for example, *Sparrow* at 1114–15; *R v. Gladstone* [1996] 2 SCR 723
    [1996] 137 DLR (4th) 648 at 62–5, and *Delgamuukw* at 160–9.
109 "[A]boriginal interests and customary laws … were absorbed into
    the common law as rights, unless (1) they were incompatible with the
    Crown's assertion of sovereignty, (2) they were surrendered voluntarily
    via the treaty process, or (3) the government extinguished them,"
    Mitchell, 10.
110 Mills, *Miinigowiziwin*, especially chapters 3, 7.
111 John Borrows, *Canada's Indigenous Constitution* (Toronto: University of
    Toronto Press, 2010); John Borrows, *Recovering Canada: The Resurgence of
    Indigenous Law* (Toronto: University of Toronto Press, 2002).
112 James (Sákéj) Youngblood Henderson, "Empowering Treaty Federalism,"
    Saskatchewan Law Review 58, no. 1 (1994).
113 Mills, *Miinigowiziwin*, especially 200.
114 Mills, *Miinigowiziwin*, especially 215.
115 The treaty is captured in the Three-Figure-Wampum, featuring figures
    representing each of three parties joining hands beside a Christian cross,
    signifying the sacred nature of the agreement. Pasternak, *Grounded
    Authority*, 78.
116 Pasternak, *Grounded Authority*, 4.
117 Pasternak, *Grounded Authority*, 140–9.
118 Pasternak, *Grounded Authority*, especially 162–204.
119 Pasternak, *Grounded Authority*, 171.
120 See a list of direct actions at http://www.barrierelakesolidarity.org/.

121 See, for example, Kitchenuhmaykoosib Inninuwug First Nation and the Algonquins of Barriere Lake, "Joint Submission"; Algonquins of Barriere Lake, "Submission."

122 See Shiri Pasternak, *On Jurisdiction and Settler Colonialism: The Algonquins of Barriere Lake against the Federal Land Claims Policy* (PhD diss., University of Toronto, 2014), especially 1–31.

3. Economic Practices

1 For discussion of their relation see Morris Cohen, "Property and Sovereignty" *Cornell Law Review* 13, no. 8 (1927): 13.

2 "Dispossession combines two different processes normally thought distinct from one another: the transformation of non-proprietary relations into proprietary ones alongside systematic divestment," Nichols, *Theft Is Property!,*. 86.

3 Indeed, Trosper refers to it as the "sovereign model of property ownership," Ronald Trosper, *Resilience, Reciprocity and Ecological Economics: Northwest Coast Sustainability* (New York: Routledge, 2011), 78.

4 Lutz terms the mixture of First Nations and capitalist productive forms a "moditional" economy, to capture that it has both traditional and modern components which First Nations can draw on variably to suit changing needs and circumstances; see *Makuk*, 23. I am greatly indebted to this insight. However, I feel the words "traditional" and "modern" imply that only wage labour is truly suitable to the present, while non-wage activity is a relic of the past. This is not the thrust of Lutz's work, but it is, I believe, an unfortunate implication of his semantic choice. I prefer "multi-modal" economy because it conveys the idea that many First Nations people draw on multiple economic forms in flexible ways while steering clear of any allusion to modernist narratives.

5 This period extends until about 1725, roughly when the French fur trade began to collapse and the English agricultural model began to surge (see White, *Middle Ground*, 121–7).

6 Alan Greer, *Property and Dispossession: Natives, Empires and Land in Early Modern North America* (Cambridge: Cambridge University Press, 2018), 196 regarding New England, 75 regarding New France.

7 Greer, *Property and Dispossession*, 157.

8 For discussion of the parallels between state and company see Edward Cavanagh, "A Company with Sovereignty and Subjects of Its Own? The Case of the Hudson's Bay Company, 1670–1763," *Canadian Journal of Law and Society* 26, no. 1 (2011).

9 Indeed, they have been called "company-states," Cavanagh, "A Company with Sovereignty," 27.

10 White, *Middle Ground*, 118.

11 See Cavanagh, "A Company with Sovereignty"; Philip Stern, "'A Politie of Civill & Military Power': Political Thought and the Late Seventeenth-Century Foundations of the East India Company-State," *Journal of British Studies* 47 (2008).

12 Trosper, *Reciprocity*, 14.

13 Greer, *Property and Dispossession*, 41.

14 Greer, *Property and Dispossession*, 91, 206.

15 Greer, *Property and Dispossession*, 90.

16 Lutz, *Makuk*, especially the Introduction.

17 White, *Middle Ground*, 132.

18 Geopolitically, however, new-world trade began improving the relative position of colonizers in the manoeuvres of European states while simultaneously shifting power balances within those states by lining the pockets of a newly ascendant merchant class in each of them. As in Europe, trade was also increasing the relative domestic standing of trading chiefs within their communities, as well as shifting the geopolitical balance of power between those groups with access to the trade and those without. P.J. Cain and A.G. Hopkins, "Gentlemanly Capitalism and British Expansion Overseas I. The Old Colonial System, 1688–1850," *The Economic History Review* 39, no. 4 (1986); P.J. Cain and A.G. Hopkins, "Gentlemanly Capitalism and British Expansion Overseas II: New Imperialism 1850–1945," *South African Journal of Economic History* 7, no. 1 (1992); Thomas Wien, "Selling Beaver Skins in North America and Europe, 1720–1760: The Uses of Fur-Trade Imperialism," *Journal of the Canadian Historical Association* 1, no. 1 (1990): 307.

19 White, *Middle Ground*, 112.

20 White, *Middle Ground*, 95, 119, 480.

21 White, *Middle Ground*, 119.

22 Onur Ulas Ince, "Primitive Accumulation, New Enclosures, and Global Land Grabs: A Theoretical Intervention," *Rural Sociology* 79, no. 1 (2014): 118.

23 This period begins around 1725 as the French fur trade began to collapse and the English agricultural model began to surge (see White, *Middle Ground*, 121–7), and extends until the canal and railroad building booms around 1840 began a new era of wage labour. See Allan Greer and Ian Radforth, eds., *Colonial Leviathan: State Formation in Mid-nineteenth-century Canada* (Toronto: University of Toronto Press, 1992), 6. Of course, all date ranges are approximate and subject to local variation. For example, the transition to agricultural and resource development in British Columbia did not occur until considerably later, with gold rushes and agricultural pre-emption only beginning in earnest in the 1850s.

24 White, *Middle Ground*, 485.
25 Miller, *Skyscrapers*, 69, 70, 77.
26 E.P. Thompson, *The Making of the English Working Class* (London: Penguin, 1991), 217.
27 Karl Polanyi, *The Great Transformation: The Political and Economic Origins of Our Time* (Boston: Beacon Press, 2001), 70–81.
28 See, for example, E.P. Thompson, *Whigs and Hunters: The Origin of the Black Act* (New York: Pantheon Books, 1975).
29 Cain and Hopkins, "Gentlemanly Capitalism 1688–1850," 515. See also Cain and Hopkins, "Gentlemanly Capitalism 1850–1945."
30 Continental wars were becoming increasingly expensive. Money could be raised in one of three ways: tax land, tax goods, or tax trade. Taxing land meant taxing the ruling class and risking losing their support, taxing goods meant hardship for the peasant class and risked social unrest, but taxing trade could be done without destabilizing the mother country. Cain and Hopkins, "Gentlemanly Capitalism 1688–1850."
31 David Harvey, "The 'New' Imperialism: Accumulation by Dispossession," *Socialist Register* 40 (2004): 82; Cain and Hopkins, "Gentlemanly Capitalism 1688–1850," 523.
32 However, the British appear to have asserted some overarching rights and radical title to even the First Nations zones. See chapter 1.
33 Greer, *Property and Dispossession*, 233.
34 Taylor, *Divided Ground*, 8. Cole Harris, *Making Native Space: Colonialism, Resistance, and Reserves in British Columbia* (Vancouver: University of British Columbia Press, 2003), 266; Wendy Brown, *Walled States, Waning Sovereignty* (New York: Zone, 2010).
35 See Lutz, *Makuk*, chapters 4 and 5 comparing the Lekwungen and Tsilhqot'in responses, respectively.
36 Taylor, *Divided Ground*, 8.
37 Taylor, *Divided Ground*, 10.
38 See, for example, Joseph Bauerkemper and Heidi Kiiwetinepinesiik Stark, "The Trans/National Terrain of Anishinaabe Law and Diplomacy," *Journal of Transnational American Studies* 4, no. 1 (2012).
39 Allan Greer, "Commons and Enclosure in the Colonization of North America," *The American Historical Review* 117, no. 2 (2012): 377.
40 Taylor, *Divided Ground*, 73.
41 Miller, *Skyscrapers*, 68.
42 Miller, *Skyscrapers*, 70, 77.
43 French tenure continued under the terms of surrender, as a sort of civil-law reserve in a common-law sea. Indigenous title in New France, however, was assumed to have been transferred along with French title, despite the fact that France had never purchased said title as British custom required.

In essence, French tenure was creatively reimagined as total and exclusive, despite all evidence to the contrary. Even this incorporation of difference, then, worked to render property more exclusive and unitary. Greer, *Property and Dispossession*, 403.

44 Significant as they are, these shifts should not be exaggerated. Huge tracts of land had (and have to this day) virtually no settler presence.

45 Tully, "Guest and Settler."

46 This period begins around 1840 as canal and railroad building booms created a new labour market (See Greer and Radforth, *Colonial Leviathan*, 6) and continues until the rise of neoliberalism around the economic crises of the 1970s.

47 Cain and Hopkins, "Gentlemanly Capitalism 1688–1850," 394.

48 Polanyi, *Great Transformation*, 70–81.

49 Greer and Radforth, *Colonial Leviathan*, 6, 7.

50 Allan Greer, "Wage Labour and the Transition to Capitalism," *Labour* 15 (1985): 7, 19.

51 The state's monopoly on land purchases from First Nations also allowed the state to buy land cheaply, while its policy of selling dear to settlers lined state coffers even as it created a labouring class and an investing class. Dean Neu and Richard Therrien, *Accounting for Genocide: Canada's Bureaucratic Assault on Aboriginal People* (Black Point, NS: Fernwood Publishing, 2003), 41.

52 Neu and Therrien, *Accounting for Genocide*, 109, 125.

53 Neu and Therrien, *Accounting for Genocide*, 129; Bruce Curtis, "Representation and State Formation in the Canadas, 1790–1850," *Studies in Political Economy* 28, no. 1 (1989): 62.

54 For examples see Donna Feir, Rob Gillezeau, and Maggie Jones, "The Slaughter of the Bison and Reversal of Fortunes on the Great Plains," *Center for Indian Country Development*, Working Paper 2019-01 (2019); Lutz, *Makuk*, 186–200.

55 First Nations commodities were also increasingly captured by industrial processes, as traditional staples like the salmon, cod, eel, and bison were all aggressively monopolized and overexploited by wage-based productive forms.

56 Ince, "New Enclosures," 118.

57 See Lutz, *Makuk*, chapters 5 and 4 respectively.

58 Lutz, *Makuk*, 201.

59 Lutz, *Makuk*, 200.

60 Steven High, "Native Wage Labour and Independent Production During the 'Era of Irrelevance'," *Labour* 37 (1996): 244.

61 Of course, there are significant spatial variations. In some places, like the prairies, it is probably true that First Nations labour had limited

economic importance. In others, as in the north-west coast canneries or the resource extraction zones of northern and western Ontario, First Nations labour was central to capitalist development. Variation was also temporal. When labour was in short supply, especially in times of war, First Nations participation in wage labour was high, but when the troops returned home, so did First Nations marginality. Thus, First Nations continued to act as something of a reserve labour force, meaningfully independent of the market but involved opportunistically. Rolf Knight, *Indians at Work: An Informal History of Native Labour in British Columbia, 1858–1930* (Vancouver: New Star, 1996), especially 201, 203, 204, 208.

62 Lutz, *Makuk*, 217. See also High, "Native Wage Labour"; Stuart Jamieson, "Native Indians and the Trade Union Movement in British Columbia," *Human Organization* 20, no. 4 (1962). Jamieson's work is based on the west coast, but he argues that "the general picture that emerges is, perhaps, fairly typical of Indians in several areas of this continent that have been undergoing rapid industrial expansion and union growth," 219.

63 Jamieson, "Trade Union Movement," 220.

64 The Canadian component of this class is, of course, predominantly settler. Ownership of Canadian production, however, continues to be largely foreign, and the productive model continues to be based on resource extraction for foreign profit. See Leo Panitch, "Class and Power in Canada," *Monthly Review* 36, no. 11 (1985). Within this dependency, Coulthard argues that processes of "primitive accumulation" are ongoing, as settler authorities commoditize Indigenous lands and resources. Coulthard, *Red Skin*, especially the Introduction and chapter 2. We might therefore say that the modern Canadian economy expresses a dual core-periphery relation – Canada is peripheral to the centres of global finance, and First Nations economies are peripheral to that settler-dominated periphery.

65 This impacted First Nations workers in particular, as increased competition largely marginalized First Nations in labour unions, leaving First Nations workers even more vulnerable than their settler counterparts. High, "Native Wage Labour," 252; Jamieson, "Trade Union Movement," 222.

66 Onur Ulas Ince, "Primitive Accumulation, New Enclosures, and Global Land Grabs: A Theoretical Intervention," *Rural Sociology* 79, no. 1 (2014), 120.

67 Tully, "Lineages," 4.

68 For an extensive discussion see Andrew Woolford and R.S. Ratner, "A Measured Sovereignty: The Politics of Nation-Making in British Columbia," *Canadian Journal of Native Studies* 24, no. 2 (2004).

69 See, for example, Lutz on the "moditional" economy. Lutz, *Makuk*, 23.

70 Jeff Corntassel, "Re-envisioning Resurgence: First Nations Pathways to Decolonization and Sustainable Self-Determination," *Decolonization: Indigeneity, Education & Society* 1, no. 1 (2012).

71 Polanyi, *Great Transformation*.

72 Asch, *On Being Here to Stay*, 139.

73 For an excellent discussion focusing on the BC treaty process see Andrew Woolford, *Between Justice and Certainty: Treaty Making in British Columbia* (Vancouver: University of British Columbia Press, 2006).

74 Woolford, "Transition and Transposition," 70.

75 James Tully, *A Discourse on Property: John Locke and His Adversaries* (Cambridge: Cambridge University Press, 1982); James Tully, "Rediscovering America: The Two Treatises and Aboriginal Rights," in *Rediscovering America: The Two Treatises and Aboriginal Rights*, ed. An Approach to Political Philosophy: Locke in Contexts (Cambridge: Cambridge University Press, 1993).

76 Tully, "Rediscovering America."

77 *St. Catherine's Milling* described Crown title as "a substantial and paramount interest upon which the Aboriginal title was a mere burden," characterizing Aboriginal title as "a personal and usufructuary right, dependent upon the good will of the sovereign." *St. Catherine's Milling and Lumber Co. v. The Queen* (1888), 14 App. Cas. 46 at 54.

78 *Delgamuukw*, 111;*Tsilhqot'in*, 74.

79 McNeil, "Aboriginal Title," 66.

80 *Delgamuukw*, 165. See also per J. La Forest, 202.

81 *Delgamuukw*, 113, *Tsilhqot'in*, 74.

82 While the test was detailed in *Sparrow*, its application to Aboriginal title as well as Aboriginal rights was made clear in *Gladstone*, 73 and reaffirmed in *Tsilhqot'in*, 77–88.

83 *Delgamuukw*, 168, *Tsilhqot'in*, 71.

84 *Haida v. British Columbia*, 27.

85 Indeed, the fact that title land can only be sold to the Crown has historically allowed the government to buy land at well below market rates and fund its own expansion by redistributing the land to settlers at a profit. When title was re-affirmed at law in *Calder* after decades of disuse, settler governments immediately initiated a Comprehensive Land Claims Process and later a Modern treaty Process, both of which were largely designed to facilitate state purchase of any lands where title might be asserted. Andrew Woolford, "Negotiating Affirmative Repair: Symbolic Violence in the British Columbia Treaty Process," *Canadian Journal of Sociology* 29, no. 1 (2004), 112.

86 The Tsilhqot'in.

87 Tonina Simeone, *Federal-Provincial Jurisdiction and Aboriginal Peoples* (Ottawa: Parliamentary Information and Research Service, 2001).
88 For a critical discussion of this push see Shiri Pasternak, "How Capitalism Will Save Colonialism: The Privatization of Reserve Lands in Canada," *Antipode* 47, no. 1 (2015).
89 *Guerin*, 336.
90 Greer, "Commons and Enclosure," 376.
91 High, "Native Wage Labour," 256.
92 Indeed, the effects of staple collapse have been dramatic and enduring: formerly bison-dependent societies had between 20 and 40 per cent less income per capita in 2000 than the average Native American nation, and this effect is strongest among the least historically diverse economies. Feir, Gillezeau, and Jones, "Slaughter of the Bison."
93 Blanca Tovias, "Navigating the Cultural Encounter: Blackfoot Religious Resistance in Canada," in *Empire, Colony, Genocide: Conquest, Occupation, and Subaltern Resistance in World History*, ed. Dirk Moses (New York: Berghahn Books, 2008), 271.
94 The construction of the Coastal Gas Link Pipeline, for example, recently caused the destruction of active trap lines in Unist'ot'en Yintah. Unist'ot'en Camp, "Coastal Gas Link Bulldozes Unist'ot'en Trapline," accessed 10 November 2019, https://unistoten.camp/cgl-bulldozes -trapline/.
95 James Davey concludes that "colonialism occurs both through forest harvesting and park designation." James Davey, *A Bridge to Nowhere: British Columbia's Capitalist Nature and the Carmanah Walbran War in the Woods (1988–1994)* (MA diss., University of Victoria, 2019), especially chapter 2: *The Carmanah War in the Woods: Falldown and Sitka Spruce Wilderness (1967–1990)*. For extended discussion see Brydon Kramer, *Entangled with/in Empire: Indigenous Nations, Settler Preservations, and the Return of Buffalo to Banff National Park* (MA diss., University of Victoria, 2020). However, some conservation efforts have embraced comanagement mechanisms, which are in some ways reminiscent of the layered property claims of earlier eras. For an example and discussion see Saul Brown, "Indigenous Marine Response Centre Breathing Life into Reconciliation," *National Observer*, 6 April 2018.
96 Asch, *On Being Here to Stay*, 139; Neu and Therrien, *Accounting for Genocide*, 62.
97 Sarah Carter, *Lost Harvests: Prairie Indian Reserve Farmers and Government Policy* (Kingston: McGill-Queens University Press, 1993), see, for example, 164, 219, 253; Daschuk, *Clearing the Plains*, 149.
98 High, "Native Wage Labour," 258.
99 Neu and Therrien, *Accounting for Genocide*, 82.

100 "[T]reaty rights are limited to securing 'necessaries' (which I construe in the modern context, as equivalent to a moderate livelihood), and do not extend to the open-ended accumulation of wealth," *Marshall*, 7; *Gladstone* recognized a commercial right to fish, but limited it to providing "the basics of food, clothing and housing, supplemented by a few amenities," 41.

101 Tim Schouls, "Between Colonialism and Independence: Analyzing British Columbia Treaty Politics from a Pluralist Perspective," paper presented to the *Canadian Political Science Association Annual Meeting* (London, 3 June 2005), 14.

102 See, for example, Corntassel, "Re-envisioning Resurgence."

103 Lutz, *Makuk.*

104 Harold Demsetz, "Toward a Theory of Property Rights," *American Economic Review* 57, no. 1 (1967).

105 Saul Levmore, "Two Stories about the Evolution of Property Rights," *Journal of Legal Studies* 31, no. 2 (2002).

106 Which he refers to using the now outdated name "Montagnais."

107 Stuart Banner, "Transitions between Property Regimes," *Journal of Legal Studies* 31, no. 2 (2002): 359.

108 Of course, every one of these assumptions is questionable. Many First Nations clearly have not adopted western ownership norms or have combined these creatively with Indigenous norms. Where conversion has occurred, it was not spontaneous or in the absence of coercion and state interference. It is therefore highly debatable whether the shifts Demsetz describes actually occurred as he describes them.

109 Banner, "Transitions," 368.

110 Levmore, "Two Stories," 424.

111 Levmore notes that transitions between common and private ownership continue to occur in both directions, to suit different needs and circumstances. Levmore, "Two Stories," 429.

112 Banner, "Transitions," 369.

113 Levmore, "Two Stories," 430; Cain and Hopkins, "Gentlemanly Capitalism 1850–1945," 515.

114 For example, Maquinna, a Nuu-chah-nulth chief, rose to a prominence formerly unknown in his society through his centrality in the trade. Similarly, the Tsimshian, under a series of newly ascendant trading chiefs named Legaic, moved to monopolize trade routes for geopolitical and domestic advantage. Others, like the Cree and Assiniboine, imposed themselves as tithe-extracting middlemen instead. Robin Fisher, *Contact and Conflict: Indian-European Relations in British Columbia, 1774–1890* (Vancouver: University of British Columbia Press, 1992), 18, 32; Susan Marsden and Robert Galois, "The Tsimshian, the Hudson's Bay Company, and the Geopolitics of the Northwest Coast Fur Trade,

1787–1840," *Canadian Geographer* 39, no. 2 (1995); Wien, "Selling Beaver," 297.

115 Trosper, *Resilience and Reciprocity*, 14.

116 Excluding earlier Viking visits and possible fishing voyages which, although forms of contact, did not involve lasting settlement.

117 Cavanagh, "A Company with Sovereignty," 32; Chris Magoc and David Bernstein, eds., *Imperialism and Expansionism in American History: A Social, Political, and Cultural Encyclopedia and Document Collection* (Santa Barbara: ABC-CLIO, 2015), 31.

118 Cavanagh, "Company with Sovereignty," especially 28–47.

119 See, for example, Stern, "Company-State," 253–83, 257. See also Philip Stern, "Politics and Ideology in the Early East India Company-State: The Case of St Helena, 1673–1709," *Journal of Imperial and Commonwealth History* 35, no. 1 (2007): 1–23.

120 Promislow, "Treaties," 1117–20.

121 In fact, the presence of HBC forts was often advantageous for local Nations geopolitically, and many proactively sought the establishment of forts in their territories. See, for example, Marsden and Galois, "Geopolitics of The Northwest Coast Fur Trade."

122 "The use of the Made Beaver (MB) to value trade goods and Native produce (furs, hides and provisions) permitted an application of exchange value to a barter system … In effect, the HBC had monetarized a barter system of trade; the Made Beaver standard could be converted easily into English pound sterling currency" such that "a European mercantile company adapted to a barter situation, [and] Indians adjusted to the market system," Frank Tough, "Indian Economic Behaviour, Exchange and Profits in Northern Manitoba During the Decline of Monopoly, 1870–1930," *Journal of Historical Geography* 16, no. 4 (1990): 388–9.

123 Tough, "Indian Economic Behaviour," 399.

124 Cavanagh, "A Company with Sovereignty," 43.

125 John Galbraith, "Land Policies of the Hudson's Bay Company, 1870–1913," *The Canadian Historical Review* 32, no. 1 (1951): 1.

126 Galbraith, "Land Policies of the Hudson's Bay Company," 2.

127 Tough, "Indian Economic Behaviour," 396.

128 Tough, "Indian Economic Behaviour," 396.

129 Tough, "Indian Economic Behaviour," 392–7.

130 Galbraith, "Land Policies of the Hudson's Bay Company."

131 David Monteyne, "Constructing Buildings and Histories: Hudson's Bay Company Department Stores, 1910–1930," *Bulletin: The Journal of the Society for the Study of Architecture in Canada* 20, no. 4 (1995): 97.

132 Galbraith, "Land Policies of the Hudson's Bay Company," 20.

133 John Selwood, "An Early Example of Globalisation: The Hudson's Bay Company's Interlocking Directorships," *Prairie Perspectives* 3 (2000): 9; Galbraith, "Land Policies of the Hudson's Bay Company," 20.
134 Robert Paine, "The Path to Welfare Colonialism," in *The White Arctic: Anthropological Essays on Tutelage and Ethnicity*, ed. Robert Paine (St. John's: Memorial University of Newfoundland, 1997).
135 Greer, *Property and Dispossession*, 426.
136 Greer, *Property and Dispossession*, 202, 218.
137 Onur Ulas Ince, "Between Equal Rights: Primitive Accumulation and Capital's Violence," *Political Theory* 46, no. 6 (2018): 17.
138 Greer, "Land, Property," 11.

4. Pluralism and Sovereignty in Canada

1 Richard Day, "Who Is This We That Gives the Gift? Native American Political Theory and the Western Tradition," *Critical Horizons* 2, no. 2 (2001): 195.
2 Anghie, *Imperialism*.
3 Tully, "Rediscovering America."
4 James Tully, "Modern Constitutional Democracy and Imperialism," *Osgoode Hall Law Journal* 46, no. 3 (2008): especially 483–7; Veracini, *Settler Colonialism*.
5 Cain and Hopkins, "Gentlemanly Capitalism 1688–1850."
6 Cain and Hopkins, "Gentlemanly Capitalism 1688–1850."
7 *Worcester v. Georgia* [1832] 31 U.S. (6 Pet.) 515 [1832] 31 USR 63 at 520.
8 Alan Cairns, *Citizens Plus: Aboriginal Peoples and the Canadian State* (Vancouver: University of British Columbia Press, 2000). For discussion see Gordon Christie, Book Review: Citizens Plus: Aboriginal Peoples and the Canadian State, by Alan C. Cairns; First Nations? "Second Thoughts, by Tom Flanagan; A People's Dream: Aboriginal Self-Government in Canada, by Dan Russell," *Osgoode Law Journal* 40, no. 2 (2002).
9 Donna Haraway, *Staying with the Trouble: Making Kin in the Chthulucene* (Durham, NC: Duke University Press, 2016), especially chapter 3.
10 See Scott Gilbert, Jan Sapp, and Alfred Tauber, "A Symbiotic View of Life: We Have Never Been Individuals," *Quarterly Review of Biology* 87, no. 4 (2012); Donna Haraway, "Staying with the Trouble: Anthropocene, Capitalocene, Chthulucene," in *Anthropocene or Capitalocene? Nature, History, and the Crisis of Capitalism*, ed. Jason Moore (Cambridge, MA: MIT Press, 2016), especially note 16.
11 Lynn Margulis, "Symbiogenesis and Symbionticism," in *Symbiosis as a Source of Evolutionary Innovation: Speciation and Morphogenesis*, ed. Lynn Margulis (Cambridge, MA: MIT Press, 1991). See also S.R. Bordenstein and KR. Theis, "Host Biology in Light of the Microbiome: Ten Principles of Holobionts and Hologenomes," *PLoS Biology* 13, no. 8 (2015).

12 Anghie, *Imperialism*; John Breuilly, "Modern Empires and Nation-States," *Thesis Eleven* 139, no. 1 (2017): 11–29.
13 Mack, "Hoquotist."
14 Or, as Haraway puts it: "symbiotic assemblages, at whatever scale of space or time, which are more like knots of diverse intra-active relatings in dynamic complex systems, than like the entities of a biology made up of preexisting bounded units (genes, cells, organisms, etc.) in interactions that can only be conceived as competitive or cooperative … Holobionts require models tuned to an expandable number of quasi-collective/quasi-individual partners in constitutive relatings; these relationalities are the objects of study," Haraway, *Trouble*, 63.
15 Haraway notes that symbiogenesis allows us to think relationships which transcend the dichotomy between competition and cooperation, showing how actors are involved in both dynamics at once. Haraway, *Trouble*, 60.

5. Political Practices

1 Emmanuel Brunet-Jailly, Achim Hurrelmann, and Amy Verdun, eds., *European Union Governance and Policy Making: A Canadian Perspective* (Toronto: University of Toronto Press, 2017), especially the Introduction.
2 Richard Bellamy, "A European Republic of Sovereign States: Sovereignty, Republicanism and the European Union," *European Journal of Political Theory* 16, no. 2 (2017): 198.
3 Paul Craig and Grainne de Burca, *EU Law: Text, Cases, and Materials*, 5th ed. (Oxford: Oxford University Press, 2011), 4–5.
4 For discussion see Antje Wiener and Thomas Diez, *European Integration Theory* (Oxford: Oxford University Press, 2009), 25–66.
5 The locus classicus of the functionalist argument is Ernst Haas, *Beyond the Nation State* (Stanford, CA: Stanford University Press, 1964).
6 For discussion see Wiener and Diez, *Integration Theory*, 67–87.
7 See, for example, Andrew Moravcsik, "Preferences and Power in the European Community: A Liberal Intergovernmental Approach," *Journal of Common Market Studies* 31, no. 4 (1993); Andrew Moravcsik, *The Choice for Europe* (Berkeley: University of California Press, 1999).
8 Craig and de Burca, *EU Law*, 7.
9 Jacques Delors, "Speech by Jacques Delors (9 September 1985)," in *Bulletin of the European Union No. 9* (Luxembourg: Office for Official Publications of the European Communities, 1985).

10 Giuliano Amato, Enzo Moavero-Milanesi, and Gianfranco Pasquino, eds., *The History of the European Union: Constructing Utopia* (Oxford: Bloomsbury, 2019), chapters 6 and 7.

11 Craig and de Burca, *EU Law*, 6.

12 Amato et al., *Constructing Utopia*, chapter 7.

13 A qualified majority consists of 55 per cent of member states (at least sixteen) containing a super-majority of population (65 per cent). Certain policy areas, including membership of the Union, the finances of the Union, harmonization in the field of social policy; most aspects of the common security and defence policy, citizenship, and most institutional changes require unanimous approval by the Council. See European Council, "European Council – Voting System," accessed 10 November 2019, www.consilium.europa.eu/en/council-eu/voting-system/.

14 Desmond Dinan, *Europe Recast: A History of the European Union*, 2nd ed. (Boulder, CO: Lynne Reinner, 2014), 104–7.

15 Craig and de Burca, *EU Law*, 13.

16 Amato et al., *Constructing Utopia*, 145–82.

17 Dinan, *Europe Recast*, 273; Amato et al., *Constructing Utopia*, 215–18.

18 Dinan, *Europe Recast*, 231–51; Craig and de Burca, *EU Law*, 14.

19 Craig and de Burca, *EU Law*, 24–8.

20 Amato et al., *Constructing Utopia*, 139; Dinan, *Europe Recast*, 307–16.

21 Craig and de Burca, *EU Law*, 28.

22 Kalypso Nicolaidis, *Exodus, Reckoning, Sacrifice: Three Meanings of Brexit* (London: Unbound, 2019).

23 Nicolaidis, *Exodus, Reckoning, Sacrifice*.

24 Cormac Mac Amhlaigh, "Back to a Sovereign Future?: Constitutional Pluralism after Brexit," *Cambridge Yearbook of European Legal Studies* 21 (2019).

25 European Parliament, "About the European Parliament – Legislative Powers," accessed 10 November 2019, http://www.europarl.europa.eu /aboutparliament/en/20150201PVL00004/Legislative-powers.

26 National parliaments also play a role through their position in EU committees and through subsidiarity, leading some to describe them as a virtual third chamber. See, for example, Ian Cooper, "Comment: Will National Parliaments Use Their New Powers?," *EU Observer*, 16 October 2009, accessed 11 November 2019, https://euobserver.com /opinion/28839.

27 These areas include internal market exemptions and competition law. See "Legislative Powers."

28 These areas include the admission of members, methods of withdrawal, and combating discrimination. See "Legislative Powers."

29 These areas include the Common External Tariff Policy and the Common Commercial Policy. European Union, *Consolidated Version of the Treaty on the Functioning of the European Union*, accessed 10 November 2019, http://data.europa.eu/eli/treaty/tfeu_2012/oj, especially Article 31 and Article 207.

30 Ulrike Liebert, "Postnational Constitutionalisation in the Enlarged Europe," in *Democracy Beyond the State: Assessing European Constitutionalisation*, eds. U. Liebert, J. Falke, and A. Maurer (Baden-Baden, Germany: Nomos, 2005), 12.

31 See Fritz Scharpf, *Governing in Europe: Effective and Democratic?* (Oxford: Oxford University Press, 1999), especially chapter 1; Fritz Scharpf, "Problem Solving Effectiveness and Democratic Accountability in the EU," *IHS Political Science Series* no. 107 (2006): especially 1–4.

32 Varoufakis says technocracy is in the EU's genes, see Yanis Varoufakis, *And the Weak Suffer What They Must? Europe's Crisis and America's Economic Future* (New York: Nation Books, 2016), 111, 237; McGiffen and Streeck both call the democratic deficit "structural"; Steve McGiffen, "Bloodless Coup d'Etat: The European Union's Response to the Eurozone Crisis," *Socialism and Democracy* 25, no. 2 (2011): 26; Wolfgang Streeck, "Peoples and Markets: Democratic Capitalism and European Integration," *New Left Review* 73, no. 1 (2012): 26. Isikel argues that "the EU's so-called democratic deficit—the purported dearth of democratic mechanisms of control, accountability, and responsiveness commensurate to its powers—is a systemic feature, not a bug," going on to call technocratic management "the guiding objective of the European Union" and "the broader philosophy of European integration," Turkuler Isiksel, *Europe's Functional Constitution: A Theory of Constitutionalism Beyond the State* (Oxford: Oxford University Press, 2016), especially chapter 2.

33 Thomas Biebricher, "Europe and the Political Philosophy of Neo-Liberalism," *Contemporary Political Theory* 1, no. 38 (2013): 5; Wolf Sauter, "The Economic Constitution of the European Union," *Columbia Journal of European Law* 4, no. 27 (1998): 48.

34 Lord and Magnette argue that a sort of hierarchy exists between different claims to legitimacy in the EU, with indirect vectors featuring more prominently than directly democratic vectors. Christopher Lord and Paul Magnette, "E Pluribus Unum? Creative Disagreement about Legitimacy in the EU," *Journal of Common Market Studies* 42, no. 1 (2004): 191.

35 See, for example, Pieter de Wilde, "Politicisation of European Integration: Bringing the Process into Focus," *University of Oslo ARENA Working Papers*, no. 18 (2007): 7.

36 See Richard Haesly, "Euroskeptics, Europhiles and Instrumental Europeans: European Attachment in Scotland and Wales," *European Union Politics* 2, no. 1 (2001).

37 Maarten Hillebrandt, "Rejection by Referendum: A New Expression of Discontent in the EU," *Reinvention* 1, no. 2 (2008).

38 Mark Franklin, Michael Marsh, and Lauren McLaren, "Uncorking the Bottle: Popular Opposition to European Unification in the Wake of Maastricht," *Journal of Common Market Studies* 32, no. 4 (1994): 468.

39 Protest votes against national governments accounted for 18 per cent of the "no" vote in France and 14 per cent in the Netherlands. Taggart, "Questions of Europe," 16–19. In both cases, reasons for opposing the Constitution were highly heterogeneous, with opposition from the left and the right for an enormous variety of reasons. In this sense "the constitutional treaty appears to have become the vehicle for popular venting of any number of discreet grievances, most unconnected with the actual contents of the treaty," Robin Niblett, "Shock Therapy," *Euro-Focus* 11, no. 2 (2005): 1.

40 Thomas Jensen, "The Democratic Deficit of the European Union," *Living Reviews in Democracy* 1 (2009).

41 Craig and de Burca, *EU Law*, chapter 1.

42 Sabine Saurugger, "The Social Construction of the Participatory Turn: The Emergence of a Norm in the European Union," *European Journal of Political Research* 49, no. 4 (2009); Barbara Finke, "Civil Society Participation in EU Governance," *Living Review of European Governance* 2, no. 2 (2007).

43 Donatella Della Porta and Manuela Caiani, *Social Movements and Europeanization* (Oxford: Oxford University Press, 2009), 90.

44 European Council, "Laeken Declaration on the Future of the European Union (15 December 2001)," in *Bulletin of the European Union No. 12* (Luxembourg: Office for Official Publications of the European Communities, 2001). For discussion, Emanuela Lombardo, "The Participation of Civil Society in the European Constitution-Making Process," paper presented to the *CIDEL Workshop Constitution Making and Democratic Legitimacy in the EU* (London, 10 November 2004). Lombardo notes that "Giscard D'Estaing, opened the first substantive debate of the Convention, claiming that "the citizens of Europe felt that their voice was not being heard on the future of Europe and that the first phase of the Convention should therefore be a listening phase," 8.

45 This provision was eventually realized in the Lisbon Treaty. Organizers must gather at least one million signatures, meeting a threshold of 750 signatures per member of the European Parliament in at least seven member states.

46 Paul Taggart, "Questions of Europe – The Domestic Politics of the 2005 French and Dutch Referendums and Their Challenge for the Study of European Integration," *Journal of Common Market Studies* 44, no. 1 (2006): 12.

47 See, for example, Commission of the European Communities, *European Governance White Paper COM 428* (Brussels: CEC, 2001), 3, 4, 7, 8, 11, 16; Erik Eirksen, "Deliberative Supranationalism in the EU," in *Democracy in the European Union: Integration Through Deliberation?*, eds. Erik Eirksen and John Fossum (New York: Routledge, 2000), 47–55.

48 John Fitzgibbon, "Citizens against Europe? Civil Society and Eurosceptic Protest in Ireland, the United Kingdom and Denmark," *Journal of Common Market Studies* 51, no. 1 (2013): especially 110–11; Della Porta and Caiani, *Social Movements*, 95.

49 Della Porta argues that the participatory turn is better understood as "a rhetorical device to gain legitimacy rather than a genuine move towards a more pluralistic EU democracy," Della Porta and Caiani, *Social Movements*, 95.

50 Giandomenico Majone, "The Common Sense of European Integration," *Journal of European Public* 13, no. 5 (2006): 616.

51 David Khabaz, "Framing Brexit: The Role, and the Impact, of the National Newspapers on the EU Referendum," *Newspaper Research Journal* 39, no. 4 (2018).

52 Cas Mudde, "The Populist Zeitgeist," *Government & Opposition* 39, no. 3 (2004).

53 Chantal Mouffe, *For a Left Populism* (London: Verso, 2018), chapter 1.

54 Mudde, "Populist Zeitgeist." This line can be drawn in a variety of ways, from nationalistic and xenophobic populism on the right to progressive, egalitarian, and radically participatory populism on the left. One of the particular features of this discourse is that it makes no necessary distinction between elites at the national level and those at the European level. Some populists focus their ire on one or the other according to local political currents, but both are subject to the populist critique. What all of these clusters of populism share is a pronounced distrust of traditional politics as overly elite-driven and technocratic – a feeling that ordinary people have been marginalized and disenfranchised in favour of a shadowy elite, and a strong sense that current political structures prevent a genuinely democratic decision-making process. Mouffe, *Left Populism*, 4. For a discussion of the distinction in the context of European political parties and movements see Gilles Ivaldi, Maria Elisabetta, and Lanzone Woods, "Varieties of Populism across a Left-Right Spectrum: The Case of the Front National, the Northern League, Podemos and Five Star Movement," *Swiss Political Science Review* 23, no. 4 (2017). See also Mary Kaldora and Sabine Selchow, "The 'Bubbling Up' of Subterranean Politics in Europe," *Journal of Civil Society* 9, no. 1 (2013): 84.

55 Wiener and Diez, *Integration Theory*, 37.

56 European Council, *Intergovernmental Committee on European Integration, The Brussels Report on the General Common Market* (Luxemburg: Information Service, High Authority of the European Coal and Steel Community, 1956).

57 For discussion of this asymmetry see Stephan Leibfried and Paul Pierson, "Prospects for Social Europe," *Politics and Society* 20, no. 3 (1992).

58 See, for example, Emmanuel Mourlon-Druol, "The Making of a Lopsided Union: Debates about Economic Adjustment in Europe before the Euro," *West European Politics* 37, no. 6 (2014).

59 European Commission, *Humanitarian Aid and Civil Protection: Syria Crisis Factsheet* (Brussels: ECHO, 2016); European Commission, *Managing the Refugee Crisis: EU Support to Lebanon and Jordan Since the Onset of Syria Crisis* (Brussels: ECHO, 2016).

60 "Migrant Crisis: EU-Turkey Deal Comes into Effect," *BBC News*, 20 March 2016, accessed 10 November 2019, https://www.bbc.com/news/world-europe-35854413.

61 Vasudevan Sridharan, "EU to Triple Funding for 'Operation Triton' to Tackle Mediterranean Migrant Crisis," *International Business Times*, 24 April 2015, accessed 10 November 2019, https://www.ibtimes.co.uk/eu-triple-funding-operation-triton-tackle-mediterranean-migrant-crisis-1498100.

62 Nick Gutteridge, "EU Migrant Relocation Plan 'DEAD' as Poland REFUSES to Take in Thousands of Asylum Seekers," *Sunday Express*, 15 April 2016, accessed 10 November 2019, https://www.express.co.uk/news/politics/661166/EU-migrant-relocation-plan-dead-Poland-refuse-take-in-asylum-seekers.

63 For a historical discussion see Françoise de La Serre and Helen Wallace, "Flexibility and Enhanced Cooperation in the European Union: Placebo Rather than Panacea?" *Notre Europe: Research and Policy Papers* 2 (1997); for an updated discussion see Carlo Maria Cantore, "We're One, But We're Not the Same: Enhanced Cooperation and the Tension between Unity and Asymmetry in the EU," *Perspectives on Federalism* 3, no. 3 (2011).

64 Bulgaria, Croatia, Cyprus, Ireland, and Romania are also EU states outside of the Schengen Area.

65 In fact, nine countries (Bulgaria, Croatia, Czech Republic, Denmark, Hungary, Poland, Romania, Sweden, and the United Kingdom) are EU members but do not use the euro.

66 This is also the case in San Marino, Vatican City, and Andorra. Kosovo and Montenegro also use the euro as a *de facto* domestic currency. European Commission, "Euro Area," accessed 10 November 2019, http://ec.europa.eu/economy_finance/euro/world/outside_euro_area/index_en.htm.

67 Iceland, Norway, and Liechtenstein are also non-EU states within the Schengen Area.

68 La Serre and Wallace, "Enhanced Cooperation," 6.

69 La Serre and Wallace, "Enhanced Cooperation," 9.
70 La Serre and Wallace, "Enhanced Cooperation," 8.
71 Examples include agreements on divorce law and unitary European patents. For discussion see Cantore, "We're One, But We're Not the Same," 10–14.
72 La Serre and Wallace, "Flexibility and Enhanced Cooperation," 6.
73 Cantore, "We're One, But We're Not the Same," 9.
74 For a discussion of national variations in social policy, for example, see Egidijus Barcevičius, Timo Weishaupt, and Jonathan Zeitlin, eds., *Assessing the Open Method of Coordination: Institutional Design and National Influence of EU Social Policy Coordination* (London: Palgrave Macmillan, 2014), especially chapter 9, Timo Weishaupt, "The Social OMC's at Work: Identifying and Explaining Variations in National Use and Influence."
75 For a discussion of how subsidiarity has facilitated a highly variable approach to energy policy, for example, see Roberto Serralles, "Electric Energy Restructuring in the European Union: Integration, Subsidiarity and the Challenge of Harmonization," *Energy Policy* 34 (2006): 2546–50.
76 For discussion see Udo Bullmann, "The Politics of the Third Level," *Regional & Federal Studies* 6, no. 2 (1996).
77 For discussion see Leon Lindberg and Stuart Scheingold, *Europe's Would-be Polity: Patterns of Change in the European Community* (Englewood, CO: Prentice-Hall, 1970).
78 Sabine Saurugger, "The Social Construction of the Participatory Turn: The Emergence of a Norm in the European Union," *European Journal of Political Research* 49, no. 4 (2009), 6–13. See also Eirk O. Eirksen, "Deliberative Supranationalism in the EU," in *Democracy in the European Union: Integration Through Deliberation?*, eds. Erik Eriksen and John Fossum (New York: Routledge, 2000).
79 See Turkuler Isiksel, *Functional Constitution*, generally and especially chapter 1.
80 Government of the U.K., *Why the Government Believes That Voting to Remain in the European Union Is the Best Decision for the UK* (London: Cabinet Office Publishing Service, 2016), accessed 10 November 2019, https://www.gov.uk/government/uploads/system/uploads/attachment_data/file/515068/why-the-government-believes-that-voting-to-remain-in-the-european-union-is-the-best-decision-for-the-uk.pdf.
81 See, for example, Anne-Marie Slaughter, "Disaggregated Sovereignty: Towards the Public Accountability of Global Government Network," *Government and Opposition* 39, no. 2 (2014); Bruno de Witte, "Sovereignty and European Integration: The Weight of Legal Tradition," in *The European Courts and National Courts: Doctrine and Jurisprudence*, eds. Anne-Marie

Slaughter, Alec Stone Sweet, and J.H.H. Weiler (Portland: Hart Publishing, 1998), 171.

82 Gráinne De Burca, "Sovereignty and the Supremacy Doctrine of the European Court of Justice," in *Sovereignty in Transition*, ed. Neil Walker (Portland: Hart Publishing, 2003), 459.

83 In Neil Walker's excellent collection "Sovereignty in Transition" (Portland: Hart Publishing, 2003), for example, Walker, Hans Lindahl, Richard Bellamy, Miriam Aziz, Bruno de Witte, Cesary Mik, Anneli Albi, and Miguel Maduro all discuss terms likes these in their contributions.

84 Lord and Magnette, "E Pluribus Unum?"

85 Lord and Magnette, "E Pluribus Unum?," especially 184.

86 Nicolaïdis, "Demoi-cracy," 77. Church and Phinnemore also discuss "dual legitimacy." Church and Phinnemore, *European Constitution*, 131.

87 Indeed, Bellamy stresses how estates were able to balance different classes of society. In this regard, it is noteworthy that the European Union, although balancing many different actors, does not in fact make any deliberate attempt to balance social classes.

88 See Richard Bellamy, "Sovereignty, Post-Sovereignty and Pre-Sovereignty: Three Models of the State, Democracy and Rights within the EU," in *Sovereignty in Transition*, ed. Neil Walker (Portland: Hart Publishing, 2003), especially 170–2.

89 Bellamy, "Sovereignty, Post-Sovereignty and Pre-Sovereignty" 171, 186.

90 Richard Bellamy, *Liberalism and Pluralism* (New York: Routledge, 1999), 220; Richard Bellamy, *Rethinking Liberalism* (London: Continuum, 2005), 237.

91 Bellamy, *Liberalism and Pluralism*, 212; Bellamy, *Rethinking Liberalism*, 251.

92 Seminal statements include Markus Jachtenfuchs, "Theoretical Perspectives on European Governance," *European Law Journal* 1, no. 2 (1995); Liesbet Hooghe and Gary Marks, *Multi-Level Governance and European Integration* (Lanham, MD: Rowman & Littlefield, 2001); Scharpf, *Governing in Europe*.

93 For a brief discussion see Hans Lindahl, "Sovereignty and Representation in the European Union," in *Sovereignty in Transition*, ed. Neil Walker (Portland: Hart Publishing, 2003), 90.

94 Mark Pollack, "Theorizing the European Union: International Organization, Domestic Polity, or Experiment in New Governance?" *Annual Review of Political Science* 8, no. 1 (2005): 383.

95 Pollack, "Theorizing the European Union," 380.

96 Neil Walker, "Late Sovereignty in the European Union," in *Sovereignty in Transition*, ed. Neil Walker (Portland: Hart Publishing, 2003), especially 19.

97 Walker, "Late Sovereignty," 20.

98 Craig and de Burca, *EU Law*, 33.

99 Kalypso Nicolaïdis, "The New Constitution as European 'Demoi-cracy'?" *Critical Review of International Social and Political Philosophy* 7, no. 1 (2004): 80.

100 Clive Church and David Phinnemore, *Understanding the European Constitution* (London: Routledge, 2005), 129–36.

101 Despite its absence from previous treaties, EU Supremacy had already been established, and contested, in case law. See the discussion in chapter 6 of this book.

102 Craig and de Burca, *EU Law*, 21.

103 Gerald Baier, "The EU's Constitutional Treaty: Federalism and Intergovernmental Relations – Lessons from Canada," *Regional & Federal Studies* 15, no. 2 (2005): 212.

104 Baier, "The EU's Constitutional Treaty," 211.

105 European Union, "Treaty Establishing a Constitution for Europe," *Official Journal of the European Union* C 310 (2004).

106 Church and Phinnemore, *European Constitution*, 134–6.

107 "Treaty Establishing a Constitution for Europe," Article 1–1.

108 "Treaty Establishing a Constitution for Europe," Title IV.

109 Craig and de Burca, *EU Law*, 35.

110 Church and Phinnemore, *European Constitution*, especially 136.

111 Nicolaïdis, "Demoi-cracy?," 77.

112 Nicolaïdis, "Demoi-cracy?," 80. Church and Phinnemore also discuss "dual legitimacy," *European Constitution*, 131.

113 Church and Phinnemore, *European Constitution*, 130.

114 Mark Franklin, Michael Marsh, and Lauren McLaren, "Uncorking the Bottle: Popular Opposition to European Unification in the Wake of Maastricht," *Journal of Common Market Studies* 32, no. 4 (1994): 468.

115 Protest votes against national governments accounted for 18 per cent of the "no" vote in France and 14 per cent in the Netherlands. Taggart, "Questions of Europe," 16–19. In both cases, reasons for opposing the constitution were highly heterogeneous, with opposition from the left and the right for an enormous variety of reasons. In this sense "the constitutional treaty appears to have become the vehicle for popular venting of any number of discreet grievances, most unconnected with the actual contents of the treaty." Robin Niblett, "Shock Therapy," *Euro-Focus* 11, no. 2 (2005); 1.

116 Donatella Della Porta and Alice Mattoni, "Cultures of Participation in Social Movements," in *The Participatory Cultures Handbook*, eds. Aaron Delwiche and Jennifer Jacobs Henderson (London: Routledge, 2012), 171.

117 Craig and de Burca, *EU Law*, 20.

118 For an extended discussion see John Fitzgibbon, "The Failure of Political Parties and the Triumph of Civil Society: Ireland's Two Lisbon Votes in Wider Perspective," paper presented at the *European Consortium for Political Research General Conference* (Porto, Portugal, 24 June 2010).

119 Hobbes, *Leviathan*, 83, 116–18.

6. Legal Practices

1 The Constitutional Treaty would later include such a provision, but it was never successfully ratified. The following Lisbon Treaty finally recognized the primacy of EU law, but did so in an ambiguous way that actually leaves the question of ultimate authority unclear. See Craig and de Burca, *EU Law*, 266.

2 *Van Gend en Loos v. Netherlands*, ECJ Case 26/62 [1963] ECR 1; *Costa v. ENEL*, ECJ Case 6/64 [1964] ECR 585.

3 See, for example, Eric Stein, "Lawyers, Judges and the Making of a Transnational Constitution," *American Journal of International Law* 75, no. 1 (1981).

4 *Van Gend en Loos v. Netherlands*, ECJ Case 26/62 [1963] ECR 1.

5 *Van Gend en Loos*, 23.

6 *Van Gend en Loos*, 12.

7 *Costa v. ENEL*, ECJ Case 6/64 [1964] ECR 585.

8 *Costa*, 593–4. The Court argues, "the law stemming from the Treaty, an independent source of law, could not, because of its special and original nature, be overridden by domestic legal provisions, however framed, without being deprived of its character as Community law and without the legal basis of the Community itself being called into question. The transfer by the States from their domestic legal system to the Community legal system of the rights and obligations arising under the Treaty carries with it a permanent limitation of their sovereign rights, against which a subsequent unilateral act incompatible with the concept of the Community cannot prevail."

9 See *Krzysztof Filipiak Case*, ECJ Case 314/08 [2009] ECR 1-11049.

10 *Internationale Handelsgesellschaft mbH v. Einfuhr- und Vorratsstelle für Getreide und Futtermittel*, ECJ Case 11/70 [1970] ECR 1125. The Court ruled that "a community measure or its effect within a member state cannot be affected by allegations that it runs counter to either fundamental rights as formulated by the constitution of that state or the principles of a national constitutional structure." See also *Commission v. Luxemburg*, ECJ Case C-573/93 [1996] ECR 1-3207. In *Ciola*, the Court clarified that supremacy applied not only to grand constitutional norms and legislation but to the most minute administrative decisions as well, *Ciola v. Land Vorarlberg*, ECJ Case C-224/97 [1999] ECR I-2517.

11 *Adminstrazione delle Finanze dello Stato v. Simmenthal SpA*, ECJ Case 106/77 [1978] ECR 629.

12 *Foto-Frost v. Hauptzollamt Lübeck-Ost*, ECJ Case 314/85 [1987] ECR 4199.

13 *Van Duyn v. Home Office*, ECJ Case 41/74 [1974] ERC 01337.

14 *Defrenne v. Sabena*, ECJ Case 43/75 [1976] ECR 455.

15 See, for example, Stein, "Transnational Constitution"; J.H.H. Weiler, "A Quiet Revolution: The European Court of Justice and Its Interlocutors,"

Comparative Political Studies 26, no. 4 (1994). Indeed, the functional, teleological nature of the Court's judgments in *Costa* and *Van Gend en Loos* strongly supports suspicions that the court was pursuing an integrationist agenda. See Craig and de Burca, *EU Law*, 258.

16 For discussion see Paul Craig, "The ECJ, National Courts and the Supremacy of Community Law," in *The European Constitution in the Making*, eds. Ingolf Pernice and Roberto Miccu (Bade-Baden, Germany: Nomos, 2004); Miguel Maduro, "Contrapuntal Law," in *Sovereignty in Transition*, ed. Neil Walker (Portland: Hart Publishing, 2003).

17 *Fromagerie Franco-Suisse Le Ski v. État Belge*, BCC Case 4750 [1972] CMLR 330 (Belgian Cour de Cassation).

18 *Orfinger v. Belgian State*, BCE Case 62/922 [1997] 116 JLT 256 (Belgian Conseil d'Etat).

19 To put the point another way, the decision of whether Belgium is a monist or a dualist legal system rests with national actors, such that even a monist stance is ultimately grounded in national rather than supranational authority claims.

20 André Alen and Willem Verrijdt, "The Rule of Law in the Case Law of the Belgian Constitutional Court: History and Challenges," paper presented to the *International Conference of the Constitutional Court of Slovenia – 25 Years* (Bled, June 2016).

21 Bruno de Witte, "Do Not Mention the Word: Sovereignty in Two Europhile Countries: Belgium and the Netherlands," in *Sovereignty in Transition*, ed. Neil Walker (Portland: Hart Publishing, 2003), 357–8.

22 *Constitutionality of the Accession Treaty*, PCT Case K 8/04 [2005] 86 PLG 744 (Polish Constitutional Tribunal); Craig and de Burca, *EU Law*, 293.

23 *Accession Treaty*, 14.

24 This issue came to a head when the Court found the European Arrest Warrant unconstitutional. See *European Arrest Warrant*, PCT Case P1/05, [2005] CMLR 1181 (Polish Constitutional Tribunal). Ultimately, the constitution was amended to remove the conflict.

25 *Constitutionality of the Lisbon Treaty*, PCT Case K32/09 [2010] 9 OTK-A 108 (Polish Constitutional Tribunal), 22, 40.

26 *Assessment of the Conformity to the Polish Constitution of Selected Provisions of the Treaty on European Union*, PCT Case K 3/021, [2021] unreported (Polish Constitutional Tribunal). Note, because this case was decided just days before the submission of this manuscript, it has not yet been reported in a law reporter. Hence the citation is incomplete.

27 For discussion see Robert Mezyk, "Member State's Lawlessness and European Law – the Case of Poland," *Journal of European Studies* 12, no. 1 (2020).

28 *Honeywell*, BVerfGÉ Case 2661/06 [2010] NJW 3422 (German Constitutional Court).

29 *Solange I*, BVerfGE Case 37/271 [1974] 14 CMLR 540 (German Constitutional Court).

30 *Solange II*, BVerfGE Case 73/339 [1987] 3 CMLR 225 (German Constitutional Court).

31 Mehrdad Payandeh, "The OMT Judgment of the German Federal Constitutional Court: Repositioning the Court within the European Constitutional Architecture," *European Law Review* 13, no. 1 (2017): 416.

32 *Maastricht Treaty*, BVerfGE Case 89/155 [1993] 33 ILM 388 (German Constitutional Court), 388, 422. In *Banana*, however, the Court clarified it would conduct ultra vires review only if the ECJ had already ruled on the question and the measure at issue was "highly significant." *Banana 2*, BVerfGE Case 1/97 [2000] 21 HRLJ 251 (German Constitutional Court), 60–1.

33 *Lisbon Treaty*, BVerfGE Case 2/08 [2010] 2 CMLR 712 (German Constitutional Court).

34 *Gauweiler and Others v. German Bundestag*, BVerfGE Case 134/366 [2014] 2 BvR 2728/13. (German Constitutional Court).

35 Giuseppe Martinico, "Is the European Convention Going to Be 'Supreme'? A Comparative-Constitutional Overview of ECHR and EU Law before National Courts," *European Journal of International Law* 23, no. 2 (2012): 420–2.

36 Martinico, "European Convention," 419.

37 *Marshall v. Southampton and South West Hampshire Area Health Authority* ECJ152/84 [1986] ECR 00723; Case C-441/14, *Dansk Industri v. Rasmussen* [2016], EU:C:2016:278; *Taricco and Others*, ECJ 42/17 [2017] ECLI:EU:C:2017:936.

38 *Minister for Justice and Equality v. LM.*, ECJ Case 216/18 [2018] ECR 0000.

39 Andrea Caligiuri and Nicola Napoletano, "The Application of the Echr in the Domestic Systems," *The Italian Yearbook of International Law* 20, no. 1 (2010): 126.

40 Caligiuri and Napoletano, "Application of the Echr," 128.

41 Caligiuri and Napoletano, "Application of the Echr," 146.

42 *Sanoma Uitgevers BV v. the Netherlands*, ECtHR Application no. 38224/03 [2010] ECHR 1284 at 59; *Petrovic v. Austria*, ECtHR Application no. 20458/92 [1998] ECHR 21 at 38.

43 Charles Sabel and Oliver Gerstenberg, "Constitutionalising an Overlapping Consensus: The ECJ and the Emergence of a Coordinate Constitutional Order," *European Law Journal* 16, no. 5 (2010): 524.

44 Martinico, "European Convention," 413–14.

45 For recaps of the following see Martinico, "European Convention," especially 404–22; Caligiuri and Napoletano, "Application of the Echr," especially 126–31. For an extended discussion see Hellen Keller and Alec

Stone Sweet, eds., *A Europe of Rights: The Impact of the ECHR on National Legal Systems* (Oxford: Oxford University Press, 2009).

46 Martinico, "European Convention," 404.

47 *Matthews v. U.K.*, ECtHR Application no. 24833/94 [*1999*] ECHR 12. In *Kokkelvisserij*, the ECtHR also found member states could be held liable for the rulings of the ECJ if their own courts had requested the reference. *Kokkelvisserij v. Netherlands*, ECtHR Application no. 13645/05 [2009] ECHR 286.

48 *Bosphorus v. Ireland*, ECtHR Application no. 45036/98 [2005] ECHR 440.

49 Sabel and Gerstenberg, "Coordinate Constitutional Order," 519.

50 *Yassin Abdullah Kadi and Al Barakaat International Foundation v. Council of the European Union and Commission of the European Communities*, ECJ Joined Cases C-402/05 P and C-415/05 P [2008] ECR 1-06351.

51 Piet Eeckhout, "Kadi and Al Barakaat: Luxembourg Is Not Texas – or Washington DC," *European Journal of International Law Blog*, 2 February 2009, accessed 10 November 2019, https://www.ejiltalk.org/kadi-and-al -barakaat-luxembourg-is-not-texas-or-washington-dc/#.

52 Satoshi Miura, "Heterarchy," *Encyclopedia Britannica* (2014). https://www .britannica.com/topic/heterarchy.

53 Maduro, "Contrapuntal Law," especially 520–2.

54 For discussion see Karen Alter, "The European Court's Political Power," *West European Politics* 19, no. 3 (1996), 466–70.

55 For discussion of judicialization see, for example, Martin Shapiro and Alec Stone Sweet, *On Law, Politics, and Judicialization* (Oxford: Oxford University Press, 2002); Alec Stone Sweet, "The European Court of Justice and the Judicialization of EU Governance," *Living Reviews in European Governance* 5, no. 2 (2010); Michael C. Tolley, "Judicialization of Politics in Europe: Keeping Pace with Strasbourg," *Journal of Human Rights* 11, no. 1 (2012); and Ran Hirschl, "The New Constitution and the Judicialization of Pure Politics Worldwide," *Fordham Law Review* 75, no. 2 (2006).

56 Craig and De Burca, *EU Law*, 366–72.

57 European Union, *Treaty on the Functioning of the European Union* Article 6(2).

58 *Nold v. Commission*, ECJ Case 4/73 [1974] ECR 491; Tommaso Pavone, "The Past and Future Relationship of the European Court of Justice and the European Court of Human Rights: A Functional Analysis," *SSRN* no. 2042867 (2012), 14.

59 Martinico, "European Convention," 420–2.

60 Anne-Marie Slaughter, "A Global Community of Courts," *Harvard International Law Journal* 44, no. 1 (2003).

61 Sabel and Gerstenberg, "Coordinate Constitutional Order," especially 545, 550.

62 Antje Wiener, *A Theory of Contestation* (New York: Springer, 2014), 10, 37, 45, 81.

63 For example, R. Daniel Kelemen, "On the Unsustainability of Constitutional Pluralism: European Supremacy and the Survival of the Eurozone," *Maastricht Journal of European and Comparative Law* 23, no. 1 (2016).

64 J.H.H. Weiler, "In Defense of the Status Quo: Europe's Constitutional Sonderweg," in *European Constitutionalism Beyond the State*, eds. J.H.H. Weiler and Marlene Wind (Cambridge: Cambridge University Press, 2003), 18.

65 J.H.H. Weiler, "The European Union Belongs to Its Citizens: Three Immodest Proposals," *European Law Review* 22, no. 2 (1997), 29.

66 For example, Miguel Maduro, "Three Claims of Constitutional Pluralism," in *Constitutional Pluralism in the European Union and Beyond*, eds. Matej Avbelj and Jan Komárek (Portland: Hart Publishing, 2012), 13–28; Mattias Kumm, "Who Is the Final Arbiter of Constitutionality in Europe?: Three Conceptions of the Relationship between the German Federal Constitutional Court and the European Court of Justice," *Common Market Law Review* 36, no. 2 (1999), 384–5.

67 Maduro, "Three Claims," 13.

68 Neil MacCormick, "Beyond the Sovereign State," *Modern Law Review* 56, no. 1 (1993), 1; Kumm, "Constitutional Conflict"; Kumm, "Final Arbiter." Maduro also makes this claim, see Maduro, "Three Claims."

69 Alec Stone Sweet, "Constitutional Dialogues in the European Community," in *The European Court and National Courts: Doctrine and Jurisprudence*, eds. Ann-Marie Slaughter, Alec Stone Sweet, and J.H.H. Weiler (Oxford: Hart Publishing, 1998), 319.

70 For a discussion of the functional division between community, convention, and national courts see Pavone, "Past and Future Relationship."

71 Pavone, "Past and Future Relationship," 17.

72 *Internationale Handelsgesellschaft*.

73 *Solange I*.

74 *Nold*.

75 Pavone, "Past and Future Relationship," 12.

76 Pavone, "Past and Future Relationship," 14.

77 Pavone, "Past and Future Relationship," 15.

78 *Solange II*.

79 Sabel and Gerstenberg, "Coordinate Constitutional Order," 529.

80 *Bosphorus*.

7. Economic Practices

1 In order to facilitate comparison, the structure of my inquiry into European pluralism has mirrored, in so far as possible, the structure of my

inquiry into Canadian pluralism. Attentive readers will notice, however, that this chapter does not focus on the nature of property ownership, as its Canadian counterpart did. Instead, this chapter focuses on this distribution and nature of fiscal and monetary powers. The reason for this is simple – in Europe, both state and Union actors share basic ontological assumptions about the nature of property and ownership, and these have been relatively stable over the course of the integration project. Fiscal and monetary powers, on the other hand, have been sites of significant change. Thus, the focus of this chapter is somewhat different than that of its Canadian counterpart simply because the focus of economic contestation is different as well.

2 Sauter, "Economic Constitution," 1.
3 Biebricher, "Neo-Liberalism," 2–5; Thomas Biebricher, "The Return of Ordoliberalism in Europe – Notes on a Research Agenda," *i-lex* 21, no. 1 (2014): 3–5.
4 Biebricher, "Neo-Liberalism," 5; Sauter, "Economic Constitution," 48.
5 Sauter, "Economic Constitution"; Mark Blyth, *Austerity – The History of a Dangerous Idea* (Oxford: Oxford University Press, 2013), 156–90.
6 Belgium, the Netherlands, and Luxemburg.
7 Sauter, "Economic Constitution," 49. For a discussion of Italian ordoliberalism in particular see Blyth, *Austerity*, 189–90.
8 David Parker, *Privatization in the European Union: Theory and Policy Perspectives* (London: Routledge, 1998), 10; Frank Vibert, *The Rise of the Unelected Democracy and the New Separation of Powers* (Cambridge: Cambridge University Press, 2007), 136.
9 Varoufakis, *The Weak Suffer*, 111; Isiksel, *Functional Constitution*, 13–14.
10 Sauter, "Economic Constitution," 51; Josef Hein, "The Ordoliberalism That Never Was," *Contemporary Political Theory* 12, no. 4 (2013): 252–4.
11 Hein, "Ordoliberalism That Never Was," especially 252–4.
12 Philip Cerny, "In the Shadow of Ordoliberalism: The Paradox of Neo-Liberalism in the 21st Century," *European Review of International Studies* 3, no. 1 (2016): 6.
13 Henrik Zobbe, "The Economic and Historical Foundation of the Common Agricultural Policy in Europe," paper presented at the *Fourth European Historical Economics Society Conference* (Oxford: University of Oxford, September 2001).
14 Barry Eichengreen, *The European Economy Since 1945 – Coordinated Capitalism and Beyond* (Princeton, NJ: Princeton University Press, 2008), 6; Parker, *Privatization*, 42.
15 Cerny, "Shadow of Ordoliberalism," 4.
16 In Cerny's words, the downturn "not only led to the delegitimation of what has been called 'embedded liberalism'—i.e., the coexistence and

interdependence of free trade and international capital flows alongside domestic Keynesian economic policies, an overarching 'international regime' that had dominated the international political economy from the late 1940s to the early 1970s, but also the growing dominance of neo-liberalism," "Shadow of Ordoliberalism," 4.

17 Michael Wilkinson, "Austerity, Grexit and the Battle for the Euro," *LSE Law & Policy Briefing Series* 10 (2014): 2.

18 Sauter, "Economic Constitution," 67; Hein, "Ordoliberalism that Never Was," 356.

19 European Union, "Integrated Financial Reporting Package Overview, Financial Year 2017" accessed 10 November 2019, https://europa.eu /!hK34QQ.

20 Philip Cerny, "Embedding Neo-Liberalism: The Evolution of a Hegemonic Paradigm," *The Journal of International Trade and Diplomacy* 2, no. 1 (2008): 30.

21 Parker, *Privatization*, 12–18.

22 Parker, *Privatization*, 19, 23, 39. Clifton, Comín, and Fuentes test the influence of the EU on privatization against a range of other possible explanations and conclude, "Pragmatic concerns connected to European integration requirements, particularly in sectors such as telecommunications, transport and utilities, were of the utmost importance in motivating governments to privatize from the 1990s. Europe is thus a powerful explanatory factor when considering ongoing EU privatization," Judith Clifton, Francisco Comín, and Daniel Díaz Fuentes, "Privatizing Public Enterprises in the European Union 1960–2002: Ideological, Pragmatic, Inevitable?" *Journal of European Public Policy* 13, no. 5 (2006), 736.

23 Parker, *Privatization*, 41.

24 David Cohen and Jeremy Richardson, *Lobbying the European Union: Institutions, Actors and Issues* (Oxford: Oxford University Press, 2009), 6. Indeed, Mahoney notes that business remains the dominant force in the Commission's consultations, making up approximately 72 per cent of the groups holding a committee position. Christine Mahoney, "The Power of Institutions: State and Interest Group Activity in the European Union," *European Union Politics* 5, no. 4 (2004): 455.

25 Sauter, "Economic Constitution," 51–7.

26 Blyth, *Austerity*, 19; see also chapter 4.

27 Biebricher, "Neo-Liberalism," 2.

28 Biebricher, "Neo-Liberalism"; Biebricher, "Return of Ordoliberalism," especially 7–9.

29 See Varoufakis, *The Weak Suffer*, generally and especially 151, 169–70.

30 Biebricher, "Neo-Liberalism," 1; Hein, "Ordoliberalism that Never Was," especially 356; Magnus Ryner, "Europe's Ordoliberal Iron Cage: Critical

Political Economy, the Euro Area Crisis and Its Management," *Journal of European Public Policy* 22, no. 2 (2015): especially 282.

31 Pastorella lists the following examples: Bajnai (Hungary 2009), Fischer (Czech Republic 2009), Monti (Italy 2011), Papademos (Greece 2011), Pikrammenos (Greece 2012), Raykov (Bulgaria 2013), Rusnok (Czech Republic 2013), and Bliznashki (Bulgaria 2014). Guilia Pastorella, "Technocratic Governments in Europe: Getting the Critique Right," *Political Studies* 64 no. 4 (2016): note 1. The case of Monti is probably the most widely accepted example.

32 Cerny, "Shadow of Ordoliberalism," 8. In another article, Cerny describes the mixture as "regulatory," "managed," or "social" neoliberalism. See Cerny, "Embedding Neo-Liberalism," 39.

33 At a formal level, the substantive content of the entrenched economic constitution is therefore reasonably compatible with a range of economic choices. The complex set of market pressures, monetary and fiscal constraints, and structural impediments, however, mean that it is significantly easier for governments to adopt ordoliberal policies than interventionist ones. See Sauter, "Economic Constitution," 67–8.

34 Fritz Scharpf, "The Asymmetry of European Integration or Why the EU Cannot Be a 'Social Market Economy'," *Kolleg-Forschergruppe* Working Paper No. 6 (2009), 211.

35 Isiksel, *Functional Constitution*, especially 99.

36 Vibert, *Rise of the Unelected*, generally but especially 2, 5, 15. Note that while I embrace much of Vibert's diagnosis, I do not share his conclusions. Vibert argues that the fourth branch actually enhances democracy by creating a more informed and engaged citizenship. This conclusion seems based on a "new division of powers" separating out the fact-gathering phase of politics from the judgment phase. I find this distinction both implausible in principle and counterfactual in reality.

37 Blyth, *Austerity*, 29.

38 Scharpf, "Asymmetry."

39 Scharpf, "Asymmetry," 217.

40 Scharpf, "Asymmetry," 214.

41 Scharpf, "Asymmetry," 222.

42 *Procureur du Roi v Benoît and Gustave Dassonville*, ECJ Case 8/74 [1974] ECR 837.

43 Scharpf, "Asymmetry," 217–19.

44 Agustín José Menéndez, "The European Crises and the Undoing of the Social and Democratic Rechtsstaat," in *The European Union in Crises or the European Union as Crises?*, eds. John Fossum and Agustín Menendez (Oslo: ARENA Reports, 2014), 420.

45 Menéndez, "The European Crises," 421.

46 In fact, the first proposals of monetary union came from de Gaulle's famously nationalist government and were rejected by the supranationalist Chancellor Erhard in accordance with their respective economic interests. Varoufakis, *The Weak Suffer*, 29.

47 Varoufakis, *The Weak Suffer*, especially 113–30.

48 Menéndez, "The European Crises," 418; Varoufakis, *The Weak Suffer*, 123.

49 Varoufakis, *The Weak Suffer*, 124.

50 See Wilkinson, "Battle for the Euro," 2. Although, as Lazzarato notes: "The 'Independence' of the Central Bank with regard to Treasury is, in reality, a mask for its dependence on the markets," Maurizio Lazzarato, *The Making of the Indebted Man: An Essay on the Neoliberal Condition* (Los Angeles: Semiotext(e), 2012), 97.

51 Varoufakis, *The Weak Suffer*, 142.

52 After the 2008 financial crisis, the ECB did lower interest rates and engage in massive quantitative easing in an effort to control the value of the euro and stimulate the failing economy. However, the Bank's decision to act in this way sparked enormous controversy, including an ECJ reference case and a German Constitutional Court case considering whether the bank had illegally exceeded its mandate. See *Gauweiler*. Furthermore, because of structural limits on public deficits, low interest rates did not translate to deficit spending by member governments. Instead, the extra euros the ECB printed went largely to recapitalizing failing private banks, and the lower interest rates were designed to stimulate private lending. Indeed, quantitative easing went hand in hand with a new round of privatization, deregulation, and austerity. See Varoufakis, *The Weak Suffer*, 191. Thus, even the ECB's rare interventions in European monetary policy are such that they impede, rather than facilitate, public control of the economy.

53 The European Semester is a cycle of six-month periods during which the Commission sets structural and fiscal objectives and member states work to integrate these into their economic policies under the SGP and the six-pack and two-pack regulations. See European Council, "European Semester," accessed 11 November 2019, consilium.europa.eu/en/policies/european-semester/.

54 European Commission, "The Stability and Growth Pact," accessed 11 November 2019, http://ec.europa.eu/economy_finance/economic_governance/sgp/index_en.htm.

55 European Parliament, "Review of the 'Six-Pack' and 'Two-Pack'" (2014) accessed 11 November 2019, http https://www.europarl.europa.eu/EPRS/EPRS-AaG-542182-Review-six-pack-two-pack-FINAL.pdf. McGiffen describes these developments as a "quantum leap of economic surveillance," McGiffen, "Bloodless Coup," 38.

56 Ton van den Brink and Jan van Rossem, "Sovereignty, Stability and Solidarity: Conflicting and Converging Principles and the Shaping of Economic Governance in the European Union," *UCD Working Papers in Law, Criminology & Socio-Legal Studies* Research Paper no. 04 (2014), 20–3.

57 Menéndez, "The European Crises," 456; John Fossum and Agustín José Menéndez, "Which Crises? Whose Crises?" in *The European Union in Crises or the European Union as Crises?*, eds. John Fossum and Agustín Menendez (Oslo: ARENA Reports, 2014), 17, 26.

58 Ugo Mattei, "Protecting the Commons: Water, Culture, and Nature: The Commons Movement in the Italian Struggle against Neo-liberal Governance," *South Atlantic Quarterly* 112, no. 2 (2013): 367.

59 For more on the bill see Tommasso Fattori, "Commonification of the Public Realm," *South Atlantic Quarterly* 112, no. 2 (2013).

60 Mattei, "Protecting the Commons," 368.

61 Saki Bailey and Ugo Mattei, "Social Movements as Constituent Power: The Italian Struggle for the Commons," *Indiana Journal of Global Legal Studies* 20, no. 2 (2013): 991.

62 Mattei, "Protecting the Commons," 367.

63 Mattei, "Protecting the Commons," 372.

64 Bailey and Mattei, "Social Movements as Constituent Power," 1000.

65 Andreas Bieler, "Mobilising for Change: The First Successful European Citizens' Initiative 'Water is a Human Right'," paper presented at the *ETUI Monthly Forum* (Brussels, 22 January 2015), 26–7.

66 Bailey and Mattei, "Social Movements as Constituent Power," 987.

67 Mattei, "Protecting the Commons," 374.

68 See, for example, Alexander Vasudevan, *The Autonomous City: A History of Urban Squatting* (Brooklyn: Verso, 2017); Squatting Europe Kollective, eds., *Squatting in Europe: Radical Spaces, Urban Struggles* (New York: Minor Compositions, 2012).

69 Miguel A. Martínez López and Ángela García Bernardos, "The Occupation of Squares and the Squatting of Buildings: Lessons from the Convergence of Two Social Movements," *ACME: An International E-Journal for Critical Geographies* 14, no. 1 (2015).

70 López and Bernardos, "The Occupation of Squares," 159.

71 Extinction Rebellion, "Act Now," accessed 11 November 2019, https://rebellion.earth/act-now/.

72 Extinction Rebellion, "Resources," accessed 11 November 2019, https://rebellion.earth/act-now/resources/citizens-assembly/.

73 Rachel Mar, "France's Yellow Vests Are Rebels without a Cause, French President Emmanuel Macron Is Trying to Figure Out What They Want," *The Atlantic*, 18 March 2019, accessed 11November 2019, https://www.theatlantic.com/international/archive/2019/03/france-yellow-vest-protesters-want/585160/.

74 Mattei, "Protecting the Commons," 997.
75 For example, Streeck argues, "it is now quite clear that the democratic states of the capitalist world have not one sovereign, but two: their people, below, and the international 'markets' above," Streeck, "Peoples and Markets," 64.
76 McGiffen, "Bloodless Coup," 41; Tanguay calls it "regime change," Liane Tanguay, "Governmentality in Crisis: Debt and the Illusion of Liberalism," *Symploke* 23, no. 1 (2015): 460, while Wilkinson refers to it as a "silent revolution," Wilkinson, "Austerity, Grexit," 3.
77 Indeed, a Google search for "fourth Reich European Union" will produce an alarming number of results, but a few examples include Simon Heffer, "Rise of the Fourth Reich, How Germany Is Using the Financial Crisis to Conquer Europe," *Daily Mail*, 17 August 2011, https://www.dailymail .co.uk/news/article-2026840/European-debt-summit-Germany-using -financial-crisis-conquer-Europe.html; Nikolaus Blome, Sven Böll, Katrin Kuntz, Dirk Kurbjuweit, Walter Mayr, Mathieu von Rohr, Christoph Scheuermann, and Christoph Schult, "'The Fourth Reich': What Some Europeans See When They Look at Germany," *Der Spiegel* 23 March 2015, accessed 11 November 2019, https://www.spiegel.de/international /germany/german-power-in-the-age-of-the-euro-crisis-a-1024714.html.
78 Grant Hollis, "The 'Sovereignty' Debt Crisis?" *North East Law Review* 10, no. 2 (2014): 10, 18.
79 Stephen Gill, "Globalisation, Market Civilisation, and Disciplinary Neo-Liberalism," *Millennium Journal of International Studies* 24, no. 3 (1995): 401.
80 Stephen Gill, "European Governance and New Constitutionalism: Economic and Monetary Union and Alternatives to Disciplinary Neo-Liberalism in Europe," *New Political Economy* 3, no. 1 (1998): especially 8–9.
81 Gill, "European Governance and New Constitutionalism," 8.
82 McGiffin describes "a considered and programmatic series of measures designed finally to remove any influence which parliamentary democracy may have afforded the peoples of the member states over their own economic governance," McGiffen, "Bloodless Coup," 37. Similarly, Hollis claims, "European citizens in the affected Member States are no longer able to influence microeconomic management through democratic input," Hollis, "'Sovereignty' Debt Crisis?," 18.
83 Gill, "European Governance and New Constitutionalism," 19; Sitrin and Azzellini make the same point drawing on interview work: "Since all governments respond increasingly to the dictates of economic actors, most parties in most countries agree on all fundamentals. Tariq Ali fittingly named this the 'extreme center.' Anestis, from Athens, tells us that the center-right and center-left parties of Greece, along with the fascists, are called the 'united party of the markets': Amador Fernandez Savater, a 15-M activist from Madrid, describes the common perception of party

politics in Spain as … 'market dictatorship,'" Dario Azzellini and Marina
Sitrin, *They Can't Represent Us!* (New York: Verso, 2014), 49.

84 Friedrich Hayek, "The Economic Conditions of Interstate Federalism," in
Individualism and Economic Order, ed. Friedrich Hayek (Chicago: University
of Chicago Press, 1939).

85 Hayek, "Interstate Federalism," section 2.

86 Hayek, "Interstate Federalism," section 3.

87 Hayek, "Interstate Federalism," 266.

88 Scharpf, "Asymmetry"; Claire Cutler, "Legal Pluralism as the 'Common
Sense' of Transnational Capitalism," *Oñati Socio-legal Series* 3, no. 4 (2013);
Wolfgang Streeck, "Peoples and Markets: Democratic Capitalism and
European Integration," *New Left Review* 73, no. 1 (2012). While maintaining
that the economic constitution is formally neutral, Sauter also concedes
that the overall structure of the system is biased towards liberalizing
outcomes. Sauter, "Economic Constitution," 64–6. Höpner and Schäfer also
forward a Hayekian interpretation of the EU. Martin Höpner and Armin
Schäfer, "Polanyi in Brussels? Embeddedness and the Three Dimensions
of European Economic Integration," *Max Planck Institute for the Study of
Societies Discussion Paper*, no. 10/8 (2010).

89 Compare Liesbet Hooghe and Gary Marks, "The Making of a Polity:
The Struggle Over European Integration," in *Continuity and Change
in Contemporary Capitalism*, eds. Herbert Kitschelt et al. (Cambridge:
Cambridge University Press, 1999), especially 75.

90 Polanyi's analysis stops short of the historical period normally associated
with neoliberalism and focuses primarily on the domestic national context,
but many authors extend his analysis to current economic trends in the
EU. See, for example, Eric Hake and Walter Neale, "Karl Polanyi's Great
Transformation and the Current Transformations in Central Europe," in
Economic Transition in Historical Perspective: Lessons from the History of Economies,
eds. Charles Andres Clark and Janina Rosicka (London: Ashgate, 2001);
James A. Caporaso and Sidney Tarrow, "Polanyi in Brussels: Supranational
Institutions and the Transnational Embedding of Markets," *International
Organization* 63, no. 4 (2009); Höpner and Schäfer, "Polanyi in Brussels?".
Caporaso and Tarrow argue that the dis-embedding of the market has
produced pushback – the so-called double movement in Polanyi's thought –
and that markets are becoming re-embedded as a result. Höpner and Schäfer
argue that re-embedding has not occurred and will not do so automatically.
My take is closer to the latter. It is noteworthy, however, that even Caporaso
and Tarrow (at 603) concede that political intervention is difficult, presenting
the ECJ and its rights jurisprudence as a technocratic vector of re-embedding.

91 Polanyi, *Great Transformation*, xxiv–xxviii.

92 Polanyi, *The Great Transformation*, especially 71–80.

93 It is important to clarify that the economy can never actually be dis-
embedded from the social or ecological. Rather, we can be convinced to
act as though it has been dis-embedded. See Fred Block, "Understanding
the Diverging Trajectories of the United States and Western Europe: A
Neo-Polanyian Analysis," *Politics and Society* 35, no. 1 (2007): 5–6.

94 See also Capra and Mattei, *Ecology of Law*, especially 17–19, 70.

95 Varoufakis, *The Weak Suffer*, 166.

96 Streeck, "Peoples and Markets," 65.

97 Varoufakis, *The Weak Suffer*, 173.

98 Isiksel, *Functional Constitution*, 32.

99 Varoufakis, *The Weak Suffer*, 151.

100 Varoufakis, *The Weak Suffer*, 169. Varoufakis compares the Troika's tactics
to waterboarding: "What does the term 'waterboarding' imply? You
take a subject, you engulf his head with water until he suffocates but,
at some point before death comes, you stop. You allow the subject to
take a few agonizing breaths and then you continue to engulf his head
in water again. You repeat until he confesses. Fiscal waterboarding is
obviously not physical, it's fiscal. But the idea is the same and it is exactly
what happened to successive Greek governments from 2010 onward.
Instead of air, Greek governments nursing unsustainable debts were
starved of liquidity while at once, they were banned from defaulting to
creditors. Facing payments to their creditors that they were forced to
make, they were denied liquidity until the very last moment, just before
formal bankruptcy. Instead of confessions, they were then forced to sign
new loan agreements … At that moment, the troika would provide just
enough liquidity in order to repay the members of the Troika (ECB, IMF):
Exactly like waterboarding, the liquidity provided was calculated to be
barely enough to keep the subject going without defaulting formally, but
never more than that. And so the torture continued with the effect that
the government was kept completely under the Troika's control."

101 See Varoufakis, *The Weak Suffer*, 254; McGiffen, "Bloodless Coup," 41;
Wilkinson, "Austerity, Grexit," 3.

102 Azzellini and Sitrin, *They Can't Represent Us!*; Argyrios Altiparmakis and
Jasmine Lorenzini, "Disclaiming National Representatives: Protest Waves
in Southern Europe during the Crisis," *Party Politics* 24, no. 1 (2018).

8. Pluralism and Sovereignty in Europe

1 Beth Dempster, "Sympoietic and Autopoietic Systems: A New Distinction
for Self-Organizing Systems," in *Proceedings of the World Congress of the
Systems Sciences and ISSS 2000*, eds. J.K. Allen and J. Wilby (Toronto:
International Society for Systems Studies, 2000).

2 See, for example, Niklas Luhmann, *Social Systems*, trans. John Bednarz Jr. (Stanford, CA: Stanford University Press, 1995); Niklas Luhmann, "The Autopoiesis of Social Systems," in *Essays on Self-Reference*, ed. Niklas Luhmann (New York: Columbia University Press, 1990). See also Dempster, "Sympoietic and Autopoietic Systems," 5.

3 Haraway, *Staying with the Trouble*, 58.

4 Dempster, "Sympoietic and Autopoietic Systems," 9.

5 For an overview of emergence in science and philosophy see, for example, Mark Bedau and Paul Humphreys, *Emergence: Contemporary Readings in Philosophy and Science* (Cambridge, MA: MIT Press, 2008).

6 Dempster, "Sympoietic and Autopoietic Systems," 14.

7 For Luhmann, autopoietic systems maintain their self-referential character by coding the world according to a binary. A legal system, for example, might code things as either legal or illegal. By translating everything into this binary – and by ignoring anything that does not fit the binary – the legal system is able to operate autonomously from other social systems. We might say that sovereign systems revolve around a sovereign/subject binary, in that each part of the system must be understood as either having total and exclusive authority or being subject to total and exclusive authority. On this account, order is a function of monism – it becomes possible to the extent that other influences can be excluded. David Seidl, "Luhmann's Theory of Autopoietic Social Systems," *Munich Business Research* 2 (2004): 14.

8 Indeed, it is frequently an issue for legal pluralists that non-state groups are counter-hegemonic vis-à-vis the state but hegemonic vis-à-vis their own membership. See, for example, Gad Barzilai, "Beyond Relativism: Where Is Political Power in Legal Pluralism?" *Theoretical Inquiries in Law* 9, no. 2 (2008): 407.

9. A Comparative Analysis of Pluralism in Europe and in Canada

1 Quoted in Walters, "Brightening the Covenant Chain."

2 The Ventotene Manifesto, quoted in Altiero Spinelli, "European Union in the Resistance," *Government and Opposition* 2, no. 3 (1967), 326.

3 See Kate Gunn and Bruce McIvor, "The Wet'suwet'en, Aboriginal Title, and the Rule of Law: An Explainer," *First Peoples Law Blog* (2020), accessed 1 November 2021, https://www.firstpeopleslaw.com/public-education /blog/the-wetsuweten-aboriginal-title-and-the-rule-of-law-an-explainer.

4 Leyland Cecco, "Wet'suwet'en Sign Historic Deal to Negotiate Land Rights," *The Guardian*, 15 May 2020, https://www.theguardian.com /world/2020/may/15/canada-wetsuweten-historic-deal-land-rights -pipeline.

5 Jessica McDiarmid, "Heavily Armed Mounties Dismantle Wet'suwet'en Blockade," *The National Observer*, 19 November 2021, https://www.nationalobserver.com/2021/11/19/news/heavily-armed-mounties-dismantle-wetsuweten-blockade; Jennifer Wickham, "Wet'suwet'en Water Protectors Evade RCMP as Police Mobilize for Raid," *Indigenous Environmental Network*, 4 January 2022, https://www.ienearth.org/for-immediate-release-wetsuweten-water-protectors-evade-rcmp-as-police-mobilize-for-raid/.

6 Matt Simmons, "Tracking What We Know – and Don't Know – About the Attack on a Coastal GasLink Worksite," *The Narwhal*, 23 February 2022, https://thenarwhal.ca/coastal-gaslink-attack-explainer/; Joseph Ruttle, "Four RCMP Vehicles and an Ambulance Torched in Smithers Hotel Parking Lot," *Vancouver Sun*, 26 October 2022, https://vancouversun.com/news/local-news/rcmp-vehicles-torched-smithers.

7 Havercroft, *Captives of Sovereignty*.

8 Lord and Magnette, "E Pluribus Unum," especially 184–8.

9 See, for example, Craig, "The ECJ, National Courts."

10 See, for example, Maduro, "Contrapuntal Law."

11 "All political institutions are manifestations and materializations of power; they petrify and decay as soon as the living power of the people ceases to uphold them. This is what Madison meant when he said 'all governments rest on opinion,' a word no less true for the various forms of monarchy than for democracies. ('To suppose that majority rule functions only in democracy is a fantastic illusion,' as Jouvenel points out: 'The king, who is but one solitary individual, stands far more in need of the general support of Society than any other form of government.'" Hannah Arendt, *On Violence* (London: HBJ Press, 1969), 41.

12 Mills lists three types of violence – violence towards persons, towards peoples, and towards world views. Mills, "Miinigowiziwin," 2–6.

13 This is not to say that the death toll, or death rate, necessarily increased from an initial low as sovereignization progressed. In fact, a significant proportion of deaths came early, mostly due to an initial wave of disease that was often passed without any direct contact with settlers at all. As sovereignization progressed, however, genocidal policies both drove depopulation in their own right and also made First Nations significantly more vulnerable to further disease, thus transforming an initial series of epidemics into a full-on genocide. For an overview see David Michael Smith, "Counting the Dead: Estimating the Loss of Life in the Indigenous Holocaust, 1492-Present," in *Proceedings of the Twelfth Native American Symposium*, ed. Mark Spencer (Durant: Native American Symposium, 2018); see also David Stannard, *American Holocaust: The Conquest of the New World* (New York: Oxford University Press, 1993); Laurelyn Whitt and

Alan Clarke, *North American Genocides* (Cambridge: Cambridge University Press, 2019). For Canada specifically see, for example, Andrew Woolford and Jeff Benvenuto, "Canada and Colonial Genocide," *Journal of Genocide Research* 17, no. 4 (2015); Pamela Palmater, "Genocide, Indian Policy, and Legislated Elimination of Indians in Canada," *Aboriginal Policy Studies* 3, no. 3 (2014); Alexander Laban Hinton, Andrew Woolford, and Jeff Benvenuto, eds., *Colonial Genocide in Indigenous North America* (Durham, NC: Duke University Press, 2014). Moreover, assimilative institutions which worked to destroy First Nations cultures, identities, and governance institutions extended the genocide without necessarily acting on population levels directly. See, for example, Truth and Reconciliation Commission of Canada, *Honouring the Truth, Reconciling for the Future: Summary of the Final Report of the Truth and Reconciliation Commission of Canada* (Kingston: McGill-Queen's University Press, 2015).

14 See, for example, Spinelli, "European Union."
15 Aimé Césaire argues cogently that European fascism is nothing but colonialism come home to roost, as the very techniques of rule and genocide that Europe developed abroad are finally applied domestically. Aime Cesaire, *Discourse on Colonialism* (New York: Monthly Review Press, 2001).
16 The logic of fascism relies, after all, on establishment of order through the elimination of plurality.
17 For a discussion of the EU as both an enabler and a constraint on authoritarian regimes see András Bozóki and Dániel Hegedüs, "The Rise of Authoritarianism in the European Union," in *The Condition of Democracy: Volume 2*, eds. Jürgen Mackert, Hannah Wolf, and Bryan Turner (London: Routledge, 2021).
18 Tully, "Lineages."
19 White, *Middle Ground*, 38–9.
20 White, *Middle Ground*, 179.
21 See, for example, Webber, "Relations of Force," 650–1.
22 See, for example, Grabowski, "French Criminal Justice"; Hermes, "'Justice Will Be Done Us.'"
23 "While Aboriginal self-government is a practical necessity for reserves, this ideal can reinforce the political segregation. The dominant issue now is how to create a true federalism," Henderson, "Treaty Federalism," 323.
24 Henderson, "Treaty Federalism," especially 258, 327.
25 Henderson, "Treaty Federalism," especially 310.
26 Henderson, "Treaty Federalism," especially 266.
27 Asch, for example, likens Treaty Federalism to consociationalism at 6–9 and to Indigenous forms of "linking-arms" at 9–12. Asch, "UNDRIP, Treaty Federalism."

28 Liebert, "Democracy beyond the State," 15.
29 Ryan Bowie, "Indigenous Self-Governance and the Deployment of Knowledge in Collaborative Environmental Management in Canada," *Journal of Canadian Studies* 47, no. 1 (2013): 95.
30 Murphy, *State of the Federation*, 135.
31 Murphy, *State of the Federation*, 137.
32 Smith, "Natural Resource Co-Management," 95.
33 Coulthard, *Red Skin*, especially chapter 1.
34 For extended discussions of 15M and its relationship to Podemos see Ouziel, *Vamos Lentos*; Ouziel, *Democracy Here and Now*. For attempts to draw elected representatives into assembly systems specifically see J. Vargas, "Partido X: 'Empecemos por lo más fácil: echémosles de ahí'," *Publico.es*, 10 August 2013; A. Riveiro, "El Movimiento por la Democracia Presenta su Hoja de Ruta para un Proceso Constituyente," *Eldiario.es*, 10 August 2013.
35 Ouziel, *Vamos Lentos*, 220.
36 See Pablo Ouziel, *Democracy Here and Now* (Toronto: University of Toronto Press, 2022), especially chapter 5.
37 For discussion see Craig and de Burca *EU Law*, 100–5.
38 European Commission, "The Stability and Growth Pact."
39 European Commission, "Six-pack? Two-pack?" For discussion see Streeck, "Peoples and Markets."
40 For discussion of the Greek bailout generally see Varoufakis, *The Weak Suffer*.
41 McGiffen, "Bloodless Coup," 41.
42 For an illuminating study of this dynamic as it relates to debt, see Lazzarato, *Indebted Man*, especially 33, 72.
43 See *Costa*.
44 *Internationale Handelsgesellschaft*.
45 For discussion see Craig, "The ECJ, National Courts"; Maduro, "Contrapuntal Law."
46 Sabel and Gerstenberg, *Coordinate Constitutional Order*, especially 545, 550.
47 Tsawwassen First Nation, British Columbia, Canada, *Tsawwassen Final Agreement*, chapter 1, sections 23–25. The following references take the Tsawwassen agreement as an illustrative example. For a broader range of modern treaties see chapter 1, section 2.1.
48 Tsawwassen First Nation, British Columbia, Canada, *Tsawwassen Final Agreement*, chapter 2, section 9.
49 Neu and Therrien, *Accounting for Genocide*, 125, 133, 140.
50 Trosper, *Resilience*, especially the summary at 14.
51 Trosper,*Resilience*, 22.
52 This logic is very different from a Rawlsian overlapping consensus, which requires each actor to bracket certain private commitments. Rather than

excluding fundamental differences from the political, conditional authority provides a way to manage their interaction over time. Compare John Rawls, "The Idea of an Overlapping Consensus," *Oxford Journal of Legal Studies* 7, no. 1 (1987).

53 Chantal Mouffe, *The Democratic Paradox* (London: Verso, 2000), 20–8.

54 For an excellent comparison of the two thinkers see Mark Wenman, "'Agonistic Pluralism' and Three Archetypal Forms of Politics," *Contemporary Political Theory* 2, no. 2 (2003). Wenman notes both share this conception of conflict as generative at 168.

55 For Wiener, the principle of contestedness is "both indicative of and required in order to establish and maintain legitimacy" Wiener, *Theory of Contestation*, 4.

56 Duncan Ivison, "Consent or Contestation," in *Between Consenting Peoples: Political Community and the Meaning of Consent*, eds. Jeremy Webber and Colin Macleod (Vancouver: University of British Columbia Press, 2010), generally and especially 189.

57 Ivison, "Consent or Contestation," 193.

58 Antje Wiener, "*A Theory of Contestation* – A Concise Summary of Its Argument and Concepts," *Polity* 49, no. 1 (2017): 113.

59 Wiener, "*Contestation*—A Concise Summary," 117.

60 Smith, "Co-management," 95.

61 Maduro "Contrapuntal Law," 524–5.

62 Connolly rejects entrenched limits on contestation. William Connolly, *Why I Am Not a Secularist* (Minneapolis: University of Minnesota Press, 1999), 92. Instead, he centres "agonistic respect" and a "generous ethos of engagement" as the keys to ensuring political conflict is productive and not destructive. See, for example, William Connolly, *The Ethos of Pluralization* (Minneapolis: University of Minnesota Press, 1995), xx; William Connolly, "Beyond Good and Evil: The Ethical Sensibility of Michel Foucault," *Political Theory* 21 no. 3 (1993): 368, 381. Likewise, Mouffe distinguishes between agonism and antagonism, arguing that the state must transform antagonism in productive political debate by fostering ethical respect between participants. See, for example, Chantal Mouffe, *The Return of the Political* (London: Verso, 1993), 2–3. Mouffe argues that citizens are "friendly enemies," Mouffe, *Democratic Paradox*, 13.

63 "Envisaged from the point of view of 'agonistic pluralism', the aim of democratic politics is to construct the 'them' in such a way that it is no longer perceived as an enemy to be destroyed, but an 'adversary', i.e. somebody whose ideas we combat but whose right to defend those ideas we do not put into question," Chantal Mouffe, "Deliberative Democracy or Agonistic Pluralism?" *Social Research* 66, no. 3 (1999): 760.

64 See Webber, "Relations of Force"; Jeremy Webber, "A Two-Level Justification of Religious Toleration," *Journal of Indian Law and Society* 4, no. 2 (2014), especially 11, 13.

65 As Shinko puts it, "democratic agonists paradoxically presume the existence of that which can only emerge from within the terms of the agonistic encounter. In an agonistic political encounter, respect and recognition are not the terms that precede the struggle as a precondition of its emergence, but are rather the hard-won fruits of a struggle," Rosemary Shinko, "Agonistic Peace: A Postmodern Reading," *Millennium: Journal of International Studies* 36, no. 3 (2008): 480.

66 Giandomenico Majone, *Dilemmas of European Integration: The Ambiguities and Pitfalls of Integration by Stealth* (Oxford: Oxford University Press, 2009).

67 White, *Middle Ground*, 34–5, 248.

68 For discussion see Webber, "Relations of Force," 638–41.

69 In those rare cases where Aboriginal title has been declared by the courts, and where the proposed project's impact on that title is severe, consent may indeed be required. Even then, however, governments can override First Nations' objections subject to a justificatory test. See *Tsilhqot'in*. To the degree that this justificatory test puts settler governments in need, they are not in need of their First Nations partners, they are in need of the approval of their own judges.

70 Michel Foucault, "Truth and Power," in *Power/Knowledge: Selected Interviews and Other Writings, 1972–1977*, ed. C. Gordon (New York: Random House, 1980), 122.

71 Michel Foucault, *"Society Must Be Defended": Lectures at the College de France, 1975–1976* (New York: Picador, 2003), 265–7. See also Andrew Neal, "Cutting Off the King's Head: Foucault's *Society Must Be Defended* and the Problem of Sovereignty," *Alternatives* 29, no. 4 (2004).

72 For example, Alfred, "Sovereignty"; Monture, "Sovereignty."

73 Alfred, *Peace Power Righteousness*, 56.

74 Max Weber, "Politics as a Vocation," in *Weber's Rationalism and Modern Society: New Translations on Politics, Bureaucracy, and Social Stratification*, ed. Tony Waters and Dagmar Waters (London: Palgrave Macmillan, 2015), especially 136.

75 Havercroft, *Captives of Sovereignty*.

76 Thomas Merrill, "Property and the Right to Exclude," *Nebraska Law Review* 77, no. 4 (1998).

77 For example, Rauna Kuokkanen, "From Indigenous Economies to Market-Based Self-Governance: A Feminist Political Economy Analysis," *Canadian Journal of Political Science* 44, no. 2 (2011), 283. See also Woolford, *Justice and Certainty*.

78 For discussion see Brian Thom, "Reframing Indigenous Territories: Private Property, Human Rights and Overlapping Claims," *American Indian Culture and Research Journal* 38, no. 4 (2014).

79 Woolford, "Transition and Transposition," 72. See discussion earlier in this book, page 30.

80 Stó:lō Nation, *Cultural Assessment*. See discussion earlier in this book, pages 29, 58.

81 Thom, "Reframing Indigenous Territories," 6.

82 Foucault, *History of Sexuality*, 8–10.

83 As James Tully puts it, "another world is actual," *Public Philosophy II*, 301.

Index